HOUSE*trap*!

Who Set It? And How to Escape From
America's Mortgage and Housing Crisis

Daniel R. Lee

iUniverse, Inc.
New York Bloomington

HouseTrap!
Who Set It? And How to Escape From
America's Mortgage and Housing Crisis

The information, ideas, and suggestions in this book are not intended to render professional advice. Before following any suggestions contained in this book, you should consult your personal accountant or other financial advisor. Neither the author nor the publisher shall be liable or responsible for any loss or damage allegedly arising as a consequence of your use or application of any information or suggestions in this book.

iUniverse books may be ordered through booksellers or by contacting:

iUniverse
1663 Liberty Drive
Bloomington, IN 47403
www.iuniverse.com
1-800-Authors (1-800-288-4677)

Because of the dynamic nature of the Internet, any Web addresses or links contained in this book may have changed since publication and may no longer be valid. The views expressed in this work are solely those of the author and do not necessarily reflect the views of the publisher, and the publisher hereby disclaims any responsibility for them.

ISBN: 978-0-595-53146-2 (pbk)
ISBN: 978-0-595-63208-4 (ebk)

Printed in the United States of America

<u>Dedicated to the American Homeowner</u>

And to my wife Veronica for all her support, patience and help in writing this book. To my good friend and colleague Kent, and to my trusted advisor Bob who both let me know that I was the right guy to write it. To my close friend Dave who made me understand what the book needed to be about if I wanted it to help people. To my kids - Nate, Meagan, Andrea and Truman who, one way or another, all reminded me that a person can do anything they set their mind to. I guess they really were listening.

And finally, to Ed. Thank you.

Contents

Forward: *Magic Wands and Silver Bullets*

"I'm a janitor. The math on this is simple. The smaller the mess the easier it is for me to clean up."
- George Clooney in "Michael Clayton"

I was talking with my father-in-law, Bob, the other day. He is in his mid-seventies and was born at the front end of the Great Depression. I don't know if he remembers it, but I know that it has influenced his entire life. From a family perspective, he may be the wealthiest person I've ever known. From a financial perspective, he is much better off than he is willing to admit openly or even to acknowledge privately. While he would disagree with me, I'm sure he could live comfortably if he never earned another dime. Yet, he still works full-time.

Bob loves our country, fought for it, and prays for it every day. He and my mother-in-law just celebrated their 50th wedding anniversary. They attend church every Sunday and donate generously to several charities. Bob is more physically fit and active than most people half his age. He is young at heart; yet, he is old-school. He's a throwback to the days when people could not rely on the government but could only depend on themselves. Our conversation made me realize how much things have changed since then.

We have come to depend on our government for a lot of things. And many of us take most of those things for granted. That's not a criticism; it's just normal. I suppose it's also normal that, over time, people come to expect more from their government for things like universal health care, public education, highways and roads, Social Security and so on. It makes sense that the role of the government grows along with the country it represents. But in that process, we should not forget the primary roles of government. I contend that the core responsibility of our government is to protect us from all enemies (foreign and domestic), to create and implement laws and to ensure a stable monetary system.

Intuitively, we all know this is true. Every four years, we elect a President based primarily on his (or someday, her) positions on war, the Supreme Court and the economy. This year looks to be no different. You will have to decide for yourself who the best candidate is, but I can tell you this: our government has fallen asleep at the wheel of the economy. Or worse yet, they may be wide-awake but confused and driving recklessly.

Our economy is at risk for several reasons including the price of oil, the value of the dollar, the trade deficit, our reliance on other countries and our involvement in wars on two different fronts. But the biggest issue, by far, driving the entire economy is the mortgage and housing crisis.

Millions of Americans are paying for it with their homes. There is tremendous activity all around the fringes, but no efforts taken to date will solve the crisis. Neither political party is to blame, yet both are responsible to some extent and complicit to a large extent. Don't get me wrong. The government should neither run the lending industry nor regulate it more aggressively. As Ronald Reagan once said:

> "The government's view of the economy could be summed up in a few short phrases. If it moves, tax it. If it keeps moving, regulate it. And if it stops moving, subsidize it."

Right now, our government is both subsidizing the industry *and* continuing to increase regulations against it. This has created a downward spiral that will soon eliminate any debate about whether or not we are in a recession. If we do not change course, we may blow right through that phase and place ourselves at the footsteps of the worst economic crash since the Great Depression.

The President recently submitted the largest budget in history to Congress. It was just over three *trillion* dollars! Meanwhile, one major investment bank, that has proven to be very accurate in the past, has put the impact of this crisis at two trillion dollars! That's hard to fathom, and it is uncharted territory to have a crisis so large it equals two thirds of the largest national budget in history.

We can easily get lulled into thinking that all this is being taken care of as banks go out of business and the government comes in with one bailout plan after another. But that is untrue, and it is very risky thinking. President Bush, Federal Reserve (the Fed) Chairman Bernanke and Treasury Secretary Paulson have been playing hopscotch over the housing crisis as if the economy can be bolstered without fixing the primary thing that drives it. At the very least, it suggests they are more concerned with the big picture than they are with all the individual ones that make it up.

For instance, in March 2007, Fed Chairman Ben Bernanke made this statement to Congress:

> **"Although the turmoil in the subprime mortgage market has created severe financial problems for many individuals and families, ... the impact on the broader economy and financial markets of the problems in the subprime market seems likely to be contained."**

Obviously, this turned out to be quite wrong as the problem continued getting worse, much worse. We know the numbers are staggering. Some analysts say we are facing eight thousand more foreclosures nationwide every day. Some say we should expect two million more foreclosures by the end of 2009, which is still about twenty-eight hundred foreclosures a day. Home sales and prices are way down, as is consumer spending, while unemployment is way up. The picture is not good. But the numbers are not the problem. The problem is all the people who are behind those numbers, the people who will lose their homes, their jobs, their net worth and, perhaps, their stability in life.

The most troubling aspect of Bernanke's statement is that it is indicative of a mindset and a strategy designed to address the *entire* economy while doing very little to help people keep their homes. Politicians rationalize this by telling us that there is no single solution, no magic wand and no silver bullet, and they need to approach the crisis from multiple directions. That last part is true, but some of those efforts should be directed solely to the benefit of the individual homeowners and not just at the overall economy.

I am not blaming the government, and I realize they are the janitor as much as they are the mess-maker. But what if I told you *there is a solution* that in one fell swoop would *significantly* re-open the mortgage market so that demand for housing would increase dramatically as more people will once again have access to capital? What if I told you this could be done *without* more financial subsidies or government bailouts and that it could be done without opening the market back up to the type of irresponsible lending and borrowing that got us here in the first place? Would you believe me? If not, would you bet your house on the likelihood that I'm wrong?

You should know that I am not a lender, a loan broker, or an investor on Wall Street. I've written this book for two reasons. **First, we need to implement solutions that will allow distressed borrowers to keep their homes. Second, we need to help companies stay in business so that people can keep their jobs and we can get the economy back on track.**

While these are lofty objectives, they are not beyond our reach. But **to solve our problem, we need to understand how we got here.** That objective is realized in this book through a balance of historical and current events along with candid, politically incorrect insight that reaches far beyond a collection of sequential press releases. The book is peppered with stories to keep the topic and the people behind it real. At the same time, it is intended to be educational so that you will come to understand exactly why we are in the midst of this crisis, what can and should be done to fix it and what will happen if we do not.

I obtained degrees in Economics and Psychology from the University of California at Davis in 1986 and have since acquired over twenty years of experience in the subprime lending industry. I started at the lowest level, pulling credit reports and making collection calls for a finance company. Eventually, I worked my way up and became Chief Credit Officer and Chief Operating Officer for a couple different companies. I was part of Ground Zero in Orange County California when the modern era of subprime lending was born in 1991.

My family and I moved around the country to pursue different career opportunities with major companies. Most recently, I spent quite a bit of time traveling back and forth to New York City and Washington, D.C. as a member of the group now known as the HopeNow Alliance. With that background, I greatly underestimated the difficulty of writing this, my first book. I thought I could just put everything I know about lending in writing, and that would be enough. But the project took on a life of its own as I learned more and more with every page I wrote.

For example, **I learned that this crisis did not have to happen, and unscrupulous, predatory lenders were *not* the primary cause of it.** Sure, they were out there and they participated and they ripped people off. Hopefully, those people will end up in jail. But the fact is, they did not exist in numbers large enough to drive an industry, let alone an entire economy! Healthy competition typically weeds out the majority of sleazy participants. While this may conflict with what you've been told or have come to believe, it is the truth. It also means that *something else caused the crisis.* That's important to know because we need to understand *the real causes* if we're going to come up with the right solutions.

Additionally, we need to hold our leaders accountable. Many of my colleagues and I saw this situation coming a year and a half before it actually hit us. Our alliance of lenders was meeting on a regular basis in order to create awareness in the highest levels of government. But the warning signs were ignored primarily due to the prejudices and preconceptions of certain leaders who had already made up their own minds.

To back up this strong, politically incorrect statement, you will see the text of a "Dear Colleague" letter written by Barney Frank (D-MA) and Chairman of the House Financial Services Committee. You will see for yourself that Mr. Frank played the race card before the end of the very first paragraph. Not only was his allegation untrue, I contend it was made opportunistically for the specific purpose of getting other congressional representatives to join his effort to restrict the lending industry.

Regardless of the reasons that the warning signs were ignored, our leaders chose not to be strategic and proactive when they needed to be. And now that the crisis is upon us, those in positions of power are launching a full-scale strategic campaign to prevent similar crises in the future (just like after the dot-com bubble burst). While that is definitely important, it cannot allow us to skip over the crisis at hand as if there were nothing we can do about it. This is not the time to be strategic. We lost that opportunity when we ignored the warning signs. This is the time to fix the problem.

* *Throughout the book, I often use bold font, italics or underlines for emphasis. Even when these are within the context of quotes, documents or other people's writings, the emphases are mine only. They are not meant to represent any intent on the part of the source.*

Chapter One: The Word of the Year

"Where the speechless unite
In a silent accord
Using words you will find are strange"
  - Pink Floyd, "On the Turning Away"

The American Dialect Society was founded back in 1889 and has been selecting the "word of the year" for the past twenty or so years. In January 2008, they announced the winner for 2007. The envelope please.…"subprime."

A spokesman for the organization went on to explain that the choice signifies the public's concern for a "deepening mortgage crisis" and explained why it is an odd word - at least as far as linguists are concerned. The prefix "sub" translates roughly to "below the standard," while "prime" means something close to "the best." Therefore, he said, the word really means "far below the best."

I'm not quite sure the word "subprime" deserves such a bad rap or so much notoriety, but the fact is that it beat out "green," even though the Nobel Peace Prize was just awarded to Al Gore and company in response to their efforts on global warming. And it beat out "waterboarding," despite its center-stage role in the war on terrorism. But more importantly, the selection of the word "subprime" and the rationale behind its selection suggests a significant misunderstanding of the subprime lending industry, as well as the mortgage industry as a whole.

Many in the media would have us believe that our economy is unstable and on the brink of a full-blown recession solely as a result of greed and corruption, specifically in the subprime lending industry. Media reports tend to blow in the prevailing wind. They generally blamed lenders when that was popular and then blamed former Federal Reserve (the Fed) Chairman Alan Greenspan when that became popular.

As of mid-2008, Greenspan led in the public opinion polls as the primary cause of this crisis. That's a far cry from a year earlier when the only apparent people to blame were the "unscrupulous," "greedy" and "irresponsible" lenders who knowingly made too many bad loans.

Even industry executives have something to say about the situation. Warren Buffet, generally recognized as one of the richest men in the world and most influential investors on the planet, made two contradictory statements in May 2008.

1

In early May 2008, Buffet delivered a lengthy message at his annual Berkshire Hathaway shareholders meeting. He castigated every industry participant from borrowers to brokers, lenders, investment banks, rating agencies, bond insurers and others for their role and responsibility in this crisis. Then, in an interview at the end of the same month, he said, "the banks exposed themselves too much; they took on too much risk .... It's their fault. There's no need to blame anyone else."

Blogs, while more insightful and comprehensive, are often quite technical to the extent that many people may not be able to make use of the analysis. Because this topic is so significant and timely, several books have recently been written about the subject. A chief economist on Wall Street wrote one of the books, a former Federal Reserve Governor wrote another and a couple investigative journalists wrote another. One was even written by a small lender who had something to confess.

Political leaders eventually chimed in with some interesting perspective. As mentioned in the Forward, in March 2007, Fed Chairman Bernanke said to Congress:

> **"Although the turmoil in the subprime mortgage market has created severe financial problems for many individuals and families,** the implications of these developments for the housing market as a whole are less clear. The ongoing tightening of lending standards, although an appropriate market response, will reduce somewhat the effective demand for housing, and foreclosed properties will add to the inventories of unsold homes. At this juncture, however, **the impact on the broader economy and financial markets of the problems in the subprime market seems likely to be contained."**

His statement turned out to be embarrassingly, egregiously and indisputably wrong. He corrected himself *over a year later* in May 2008, when he warned about a rising tide in foreclosures and said:

> "High rates of delinquency and foreclosure can have substantial spillover effects on the housing market, the financial markets and the broader economy. Therefore, doing what we can to avoid preventable foreclosures is not just in the interest of lenders and borrowers. It's in everybody's interest. Rising foreclosures add to the glut of unsold homes and that puts more downward pressure on prices, aggravating the housing slump. More rapid declines in house prices could have an 'adverse impact' on the broader economy and the stability of the financial system."

Amazingly, less than three weeks later (late May 2008), he went back *to* his earlier position when he said, "the danger that the economy has fallen into a 'substantial downturn' appears to have waned." This comment came despite the fact that foreclosures were up more than 50% in 2007 over 2006 and were continuing to increase at an even faster pace throughout 2008. Unemployment had shot up to the tune of about sixty thousand people per month for several months in a row, home sales and home sales prices plummeted and 800,000 homes had already been repossessed while another 300,000 were already in foreclosure. Moreover, the rate at which rising delinquencies are converting into foreclosures and then into repossessions is skyrocketing. Worst of all, thirteen million more loans have not even seen their first rate re-set; those will happen within the next couple years.

These inconsistencies are difficult, if not impossible, to reconcile. Bernanke was dead wrong in 2007. He got it right a year or so later, and then, in an apparent effort to calm nervous markets, he changed course only a few weeks later. At best, these inconsistencies continue to reinforce the lack of command that our leaders have over this predicament. Perhaps this explains why his most recent statement was made just days before the heads of the Fed (Federal Reserve) and the Treasury got together on a Sunday and agreed to shore up Fannie Mae / Freddie Mac if necessary. Apparently, our economic concerns had not "waned."

All of these people are entitled to their opinions. But it does not mean that they are right. And it does not necessarily mean that they are wrong. The situation is nothing less than complex and confusing. So what is the truth, and what are we to believe? Let's start with the basics. **As of mid-2008, we are less than halfway though the subprime crisis, and other markets (including other non-traditional products) will not even begin to collapse until about 2009 when those thirteen million loans start to re-set.**

If you want to know the truth about something, look for someone who understands it from the inside–out. I've spent twenty years in the subprime industry doing everything from pulling credit reports to building and running major companies. My career path included virtually every lending function in between, from processing, servicing, sales and operations to capital markets and loss mitigation.

With that experience, I might tell you things you don't want to hear, or things that contradict what others might have said, but you will get the full picture. We need to know the truth, or at the very least, have access to it. But most importantly, we need to be willing to see it. I have no interest in simply summarizing and regurgitating information, news, data and industry forensics that already exist through different sources. I want you to have the entire picture and to understand how all the pieces fit together. Only with this information can we understand the full scope of this predicament and, more importantly, be able to solve it.

I participated directly in the birth of the modern subprime era in 1991 and, subsequently, moved around the country seeking additional expertise and responsibility from different facets of the industry. Along the way, I was more than fortunate to have the opportunity to work directly with several industry pioneers and to learn from them. During that time, I maintained responsibility for branches, regions, divisions, companies, sales, operations, credit, secondary marketing, servicing and collections, retail (direct to the public), wholesale (originated through loan brokers) and correspondent (purchase loans that were already funded by other lenders) origination. In short, I saw and did it all.

Amongst other things, I ran the subprime division of one federally regulated lender and was the Chief Operating Officer and Chief Credit Officer for that same company. Later, I wrote the subprime business plan and the subprime credit policies that were adopted by GMAC/RFC, who happened to be the world's largest conduit (connects lenders to investors) of real estate loans at the time. That plan, once executed, catapulted them to a leader in the subprime arena. Later in my career, I ran the western region for all states west of the Mississippi for the publicly traded subprime lender, Saxon Mortgage.

I spent the last four years of my career at Option One Mortgage Co. (OOMC), which, over its twelve-year life span, was always in the top ten of subprime originators nationwide. My first two years were spent running sales and operations for a fifteen-state region for one of its key business channels. Then I was promoted to "corporate" where I landed the premium corner office on the executive floor. As a reflection of our CEO's natural and sincere humility, courtesy and respect for all associates, all the corporate offices were virtually identical in (minimal) size and decor.

But, a simple design quirk in the floor plan created something of a false hallway that separated my little corner of the world from the rest of the Capital Markets group on the 2nd floor. The fact is that I only got that office because no one else wanted it. It had become known as "the sauna" because it never cooled down. So, before my boxes were even unpacked, I had called the facilities department to have them check out the situation. It took them all of about ten minutes to determine that the ceiling vents were open but the A/C ducts themselves were never opened over that particular office.

This story would soon prove itself to be a microcosm of a company that took forever to do the simplest things. Except to die. That happened fast. Anyhow, the guys fixed the problem with the A/C ducts and from that point forward, people asked me how I had scored that office. That little quirk in the floor plan created a layout where I had glass on three sides of me but couldn't be seen easily by anyone. Yet, people knew where to find me if they needed me.

On May 17, 2007 my boss needed me. He walked into my office and told me that the next round of layoffs was going to cut to the company's bone and that "your [my] position would be affected by the layoffs." I don't know if it's a big company thing or if it was just us, but we used code words all the time in order to avoid saying anything really bad to one another. For example, we never talked about losing money. Instead we would usually talk about earning "negative profits." People just seemed happier that way.

So I knew immediately what my boss meant when he said that "your [my] position has been affected". The interesting part is that I had been promoted into that role only two years earlier in 2005 to lead one of the five key initiatives developed to move the company into the future. Conditions were ripe in 2005 for a perfect storm in the mortgage world. The market was over saturated with lenders all chasing the same customers. The value of the funded loans being delivered to the investment banks on Wall Street was diminishing, while the cost of operations for lenders was on the rise.

Most lenders were operationally inefficient and relatively expensive to run. However, because all industries become more efficient over time and never become less efficient, permanent changes started to happen. And those were only just the beginning. Meanwhile, the pressure for increased productivity and profitability was intense. Jobs across the industry and across the country were on the line.

Companies realized that credit standards could only be stretched so far. As an industry, we were dangerously close to offering 100% loan to value ratio loans (LTVs) to people with bad credit and no documented income. This is something of an exaggeration, but we were clearly going in that direction, and we were locked into a "vertical" approach to credit management. This meant that getting new business and increasing market share happened only by allowing weaker credit standards and offering lower rates. Neither of these tactics, however, supported the requirement to increase profitability.

So while production and market share (for some) were moving up, profitability was plummeting. It was not uncommon for lenders to have doubled their volume in 2006 compared to 2005 while earning only half the profit. This trend would continue to get worse, and we all knew that it could not be sustained. Even if the housing market remained relatively healthy, corporate Darwinism would kick in and only the strongest (i.e. wealthiest) lenders would survive.

Like most other lenders at the time, we knew that our future growth, profitability and even survival would depend on market differentiation.

That, in turn, would depend on our ability to go to market faster with new and innovative products. We were certainly not alone, as almost all lenders had turned to the same strategy. Product development would allow lenders to move across the product spectrum rather than down the credit scale. If implemented successfully, this would allow lenders to differentiate themselves in a market of same-ness, to maintain stricter credit and pricing standards and to increase market share and profitability. Easier said than done.

Even though product development had been established as one of our key initiatives at OOMC, it competed for the exact same internal resources, as did the other four key initiatives. This made the Herculean responsibility of simultaneously executing five key initiatives even more difficult. We spent more time perpetually shifting and reallocating resources than getting the job done. Many people in the company would say that we were good at strategy and bad at implementation. I argued that we were equally weak at both.

The most senior people in the company would campaign like politicians for interdepartmental support, and, as a result of their successful efforts, resources would shift or be reallocated. Ultimately, however, those resources would shift back once someone else was successful with their own campaign. It was as if we were running five different companies; one for each initiative. In our culture at OOMC, it was expected and assumed that we could all just do the right thing and work it out together. The problem was that we all had a different definition of what the "right thing" was. Unless this dynamic changed, we were doomed.

While other leaders were campaigning at the departmental level for resources, I turned to a different strategy. I conducted meetings with all the executives two at a time. I argued that we needed to be able to move across product lines and credit spectrums and get them integrated into our automated underwriting (AU) system. Otherwise, we would be locked into a de-facto strategy of subprime credit deterioration.

One executive, who shall remain nameless, told me in my meeting with him and another executive, "While your argument is persuasive, it is academic since nothing you are talking about has actually happened." I told him that it concerned me greatly that something that was a foregone conclusion to me and was something that was "when, not if" was only "academic" to him. I argued that if we followed his logic and maintained his prioritization, we would go out of business. Obviously, we know who won that debate.

In short, and like a number of other concerned people in the company, I spent the majority of my time over the last two years at OOMC waving the red flag. We were warning anyone who would listen, and even some who wouldn't, about the threat just over the horizon. When I wasn't doing that, I was traveling to New York and Washington, D.C. to participate with, and contribute to, the group called the HopeNow Alliance, which was recently introduced to the public by President Bush and Treasury Secretary Paulson. Those folks in HopeNow, who were from all corners of the industry, were well ahead of the curve as they (we) sought to hedge the impact of the pending mortgage and housing crisis.

We all saw how big the mortgage problem could become and how it would affect the rest of the housing market and the national economy. Yet, even with all that industry power and knowledge, we weren't able to get much done until the situation had left the conceptual world and had become full blown in the real world. Maybe it just says something about us as a culture that we're not ready to be preemptive, despite our knowledge, certainty and ability.

Over those last two years, it had become increasingly obvious that products were being legislated out of the market and investors were losing interest in buying any ones that remained. As a result, our profits were continuing to go even more negative, meaning that we were losing big money. Putting two and two together, it was obvious that OOMC would no longer need its only V.P. of Product Development. That was my job, until May 17, 2007, when it was gone.

The only thing that surprised me about that decision was that it took so long to happen. I had been thinking about future layoffs for the previous year and a half and was pretty sure that if we ever started having them, I'd be amongst the first to go. It turns out that I lasted well past the first couple thousand "affected positions." Nonetheless, I was ready in every possible way to step out of that role and out of my nice little corner office for the last time.

I was gone before most people heard the news, and I went home. My wife and I celebrated that night with a nice steak dinner followed by an aged and decanted bottle of pinot noir. We then capped off the evening sitting in the backyard while I enjoyed my favorite cigar. I couldn't have been any more at peace than I was that night.

Within seven months of my departure from the company, Option One Mortgage closed its doors to all origination channels, including retail, wholesale and correspondent customers. The company, which had been churning about $700M per year in profits for its parent H&R Block, and which originated about $200 million per day for customers around the country, was out of business.

Now this story is not about me, nor about Option One. The market was moving faster than any of us were able to move (for a variety of reasons). Most certainly OOMC was not the first to close its doors and nowhere near the last. This is a story about how obvious this whole situation was, or should have been, to those of us in the industry.

Since the market tanked in mid-2007, the retroactive prophets have emerged from the woodwork to all say the same thing. But I can tell you that right to the end, the pressure to continue chasing the market was intense, and no one was saying we needed to pull back. Nor would anyone have allowed it.

So, that night of May 17, 2007 I enjoyed my steak, wine and cigar. I was happy to have those two years in my rear view mirror. Then I started to wonder how my decades of comprehensive experience in this industry could be of the greatest value to the largest number of people. The answer came quickly after seeing and hearing the perpetual subprime bashing in the media. I felt a strong need to get the truth out to the public and to offer solutions at the personal, industry and national levels.

For the past several months now, I've had the opportunity to talk with many people about all this craziness in the housing and lending industries. These people were not hard to find. If I didn't seek them out, I overheard them talking with each other or they found me. I guess that happens when people know you've spent your career in an industry that's now under the microscope.

From those conversations, one and only one recurring theme was universal. Virtually every person believed that the main cause of this problem was the lenders who, in their quest for higher and higher profits, took advantage of borrowers or knowingly made loans to borrowers who would not be able to pay them back. Without more information, the situation was that simple. Occasionally, people would mention the responsibility borrowers had in the loan process, but, for the most part, borrowers were seen more as victims.

To be clear, I am not writing this book to defend lenders. Yet, this crisis was not caused just by lenders. If it were that simple, we could simply rely on Congress to legislate these unscrupulous lenders out of business. The situation is, in fact, significantly more complex than that.

Likewise, **this is not just a subprime issue. Many people in high, public positions use the subprime industry as a scapegoat to mask the bigger picture.** While subprime needs to be discussed in depth, its collapse is not the trigger event that has put our economy on the brink of a serious recession. Rather, it was the first industry to take a bullet. The subprime industry went down first because it was most vulnerable to the same legislative, regulatory and financial actions that will bring down several other related industries in the near future, unless we stop them.

Exactly what is the whole picture, and is it really a crisis? The first part of the question will be answered throughout this book. The answer to the second part is "it depends." It's possible that today's mortgage and housing industries may be seen as a problem, a crisis or a market in correction. Whatever label you place on it may very well depend on how it affects you personally. It may be a problem if you want to sell your home while property values are declining and potential buyers can't obtain the financing they need. It may be a problem if you face that same restriction as the potential buyer for another home. It may feel like a problem if you are in a mortgage and housing-related, or dependant, industry including builders, realtors, car sales, home improvement contractors and retail sales, to name but a few.

But **it is definitely a crisis if your home is in, or is headed towards, foreclosure and you don't have a solution.**

You might believe that the market has already begun to correct. Lenders from the reputable to the unscrupulous (as many in Congress and the media like to call them) have gone out of business by the boatload. The stock market has fallen well over 10% from its all time high, which exceeds the official requirement of a "market correction." Additionally, the Fed has lowered short-term rates down to 2% over the past several months and new lending standards have been legislated by political forces at the Federal level and in various states.

Whether or not the market has already begun to correct, we know that, left to its own forces, eventually it will correct. Markets always do. The question is, how long will it take and how much damage will be done before it does? Just waiting for it to correct itself is likely to be slow, painful and expensive for all of us. Without a doubt, housing and mortgage are cyclical industries, but there are important drivers behind the unprecedented boom that recently ended. And more importantly, there are equally powerful drivers behind the current correction efforts.

Some of these efforts are well-intended and pointed in the right direction. Others may be tactics implemented by opportunistic politicians using this disaster as a platform from which to advance their own political and philosophical agendas. However, these often contradict good old-fashioned American capitalism.

These misguided and opportunistic efforts may interfere with the normal market forces that would eventually correct the situation. Make no mistake, this crisis can get worse. And not just in a "things get worse before they get better" kind of way. To the contrary, it is possible that they get worse and then stay that way. I'm not sure this would be, by definition, a "correction," but to those who are driving these changes, that may not matter. To be clear, I am not suggesting that we sit back and watch the downs of this market as we previously enjoyed the ups, all the while waiting passively for the market to correct itself. Remember, the fundamental premise is that we are in a crisis.

Rarely is the best course of action in a crisis to sit back and do nothing. On the other hand, doing the wrong things may make the situation even worse in both magnitude and duration.

While some influential people are fully engaged in aggressive action, right, wrong or indifferent, others have been saying that the problem has been addressed and is "contained." If they're not saying it now, they were saying it quite recently. Meanwhile, the Fed continues to lower rates while also making cash available to investment banks at auction prices, FHA has been enacted to refinance specified subprime loans, and several HopeNow participating lenders have agreed to freeze rates for other specific subprime borrowers. Doesn't that all seem like a lot of action for a problem that is "contained"? Ironically, these efforts have helped relatively few homeowners facing foreclosure and the number of new foreclosures has continued to rise at an unprecedented pace. Unfortunately, it has been a lose-lose-lose proposition for all parties involved.

Because **this book is about truth, information, knowledge and power**, let's start with a couple facts. First, this crisis is not behind us. To the contrary, it is as squarely in front of us as is the screen on which I am writing. To be equally clear, this disaster is not, and will not, be limited to the subprime market. Consider that Countrywide, generally recognized as the best and largest lender in America, has seen its stock price drop from almost $45.00/share to just about $4.00/share within the past year.

Countrywide has only survived based on an enormous capital injection from Bank of America who subsequently agreed to purchase Countrywide outright. For sure, they were a part of the subprime industry, but their subprime origination volume paled in comparison to the volume they originated within their higher grade and conforming channels. And consider that Stan O'Neal, CEO of Merrill Lynch, and Chuck Prince, CEO of Citicorp, both resigned from their lucrative posts within a few days of each other in November 2007. Are Countrywide, Merrill Lynch and Citicorp the "unscrupulous" lenders that come to your mind when you think about the subprime market?

What about Fannie Mae / Freddie Mac? Their stocks have plummeted by more than 80% and the government has agreed to shore them up if necessary. Are they the unscrupulous lenders that come to your mind?

It may be helpful for you to know that lending, like most industries, has a language all its own. It's second nature for us to talk about things like IO strips, credit swaps, derivatives, and a very long list of additional potential "etc."s. But understanding all this stuff is about as relevant as knowing the growing, roasting and purchasing technicalities at Starbucks when all you want is a good-tasting cup of coffee.

So, as best as possible, I will leave out any confusing lingo and unnecessary details. While I'm sure there are other things I could address in this book and there are things I could learn about this industry, in general, any omissions of structures, functions, terms and lingo, are on purpose. I'm not writing this book just to my lending colleagues, nor am I writing it in a way that captures Wall Street but loses everyone else.

I have two objectives. **First, we need to help Americans keep their homes. Second, we need to help lenders and other companies stay in business so that hundreds of thousands of employees across numerous industries can keep their jobs.** These hefty goals start with a fundamental understanding of several key issues:

First, the crisis is not behind us.

Second, it is not limited to the subprime market.

Third, there is reason why the situation really exists.

Fourth, we need to understand how widespread the situation is.

Fifth, we need to know why we are at risk of it becoming even worse.

Sixth, we must understand why the efforts taken to date will not solve the problem.

Finally, with that information I want to help you get involved with the process of creating true solutions that will get us all back on track.

If, on the other hand, we just sit back and allow the problem to be marginalized by subprime publicity, we are at great risk of being caught off guard by the big picture and of having to pay an enormous price for many years to come.

Chapter Two: Subprime Stories, Myths and Facts

"Armchair warriors often fail
And we've been poisoned by these fairy tales"
 - Don Henley, "End of the Innocence"

The Lawsuit:

The attorney's questions were clear, concise and purposeful. He had taken the case pro bono on behalf of his client for whom my company (before I was even employed there) had made a home loan. For the first time in my career, I was being deposed for a pending trial.

We were in a large conference room somewhere within the corridors of an innocuous mid-rise office building in downtown Seattle. It was the summer of 1998; the weather was perfect, but the view was the only comfortable aspect of that meeting. The stenographer sat to my left. She never said a single word. She simply stared forward and up slightly, as if something on the wall had her full attention. She captured the entire conversation by pecking away at some keyboard that appeared to have symbols, which presumably represented the English language. As she tapped on the keys, the machine spewed a narrow strand of paper from its top, as if it were a circa 1900 adding machine. I found it difficult not to get distracted by the weirdness of it all.

I remember that the attorney was well dressed and cordial. But, much like the traffic on the street below us, the information was flowing one way, and one way, only. While I'm a visual person, I can't at all remember what the stenographer looked like. The same goes for the attorney. To his right, however, was a man I will never forget.

He was quite elderly; his skin was very dark, pocked, wrinkled and weathered. He had walked in with a heavy limp, and he held a cane for support. He sat down and remained motionless while he stared at me for the entire meeting. Between the old man and the stenographer, I had never been around so much stillness. So, one person was tapping keys, another was staring at me and the other was asking quite pointed questions. To make an uncomfortable situation a little worse, I wasn't even able to make eye contact with the elderly man because his glasses were too thick and opaque. I assumed he could see me, but I certainly couldn't see him, at least not his eyes.

Sometime during the deposition, the attorney introduced his client to me. He told me that his client was legally blind and that his only sources of income were Social Security and various forms of public assistance. It turns out that my company had made him a loan that he could not afford to pay. His loan was in foreclosure, and he was about to lose the home where he had spent his entire life. Suddenly, the whole situation became very personal, and it was not the scenario that any of us wanted for this elderly borrower.

At the time, I was one of four executives with a company called Investors Mortgage. We had a national footprint and originated loans through three different channels. One channel was retail, where we marketed directly to the public and processed the loans ourselves. The second channel was correspondent where we purchased loans that other smaller lenders had already funded. The third channel was called wholesale, whereby we received loan applications from loan brokers. We did some processing on these loans, but, for a variety of legal and licensing reasons, the broker maintained all contact with the borrower. In fact, as the actual lender, we never spoke directly with borrowers. Even the document signings were conducted by the broker or by contracted third party signing services. This particular borrower had come to us through our wholesale channel by one of our wholesale brokers.

As with all wholesale-originated loans, our customer was the broker, and our contact was only with him. Nonetheless, during that meeting, the attorney and I both learned that my company had funded the loan based on fraudulent information provided to us by our customer, the loan broker.

Like all other mid-size mortgage banks, we sold all the loans that we funded. The buyers were larger mortgage companies that purchased pools of closed loans from smaller lenders like us. In our case, as with most small lenders, the responsibility for servicing and collecting on the loans was transferred to the buyer. Therefore, once the loans were sold to the buyer, we were virtually out of the deal. The only time we might become re-involved was if the buyer conducted an audit of the loan and determined that there was fraud. In that case, the buyer could require us to repurchase the loan from them. Since that did not happen in this particular case, neither my company nor I were aware of the fraud.

The deposition went on for a few hours, after which the attorney informed me that he originally intended to include my company as part of the defense in the pending lawsuit and to sue the broker and us. However, based on the information provided at this deposition, he had changed his mind and asked me to testify on behalf of the plaintiff and against the broker-defendant. While not a complete 180° turn, it was at least 175° and I wasn't even aware anything was turning at all. I was simply answering his questions truthfully. Ultimately, I was able to testify in court.

Weeks later, the attorney called me to let me know that they had won their lawsuit against the broker and that his client would not lose his home. He thanked me and my company for our support of his efforts.

So what's the point of this true story? Certainly it is not an indictment of all, or even most, brokers. I have worked with brokers for the past twenty years, and I can tell you that the vast majority of them are honest people who would not knowingly put a homeowner in a bad situation. Nor is this story a vindication of all lenders. While my company did not intend to harm this man, some lenders have knowingly made loans that put borrowers in bad situations. This story does not suggest that all borrowers who are in foreclosure are victims. Some borrowers have intentionally provided false information in order to obtain a loan that they could not afford to pay each month. Why they might have done this is another story.

The point of this story is really about the attorney. He was willing to hear information that challenged his preconceptions about the situation. With that information, he was better able to build a case so that his client was able to keep his home.

I'm not suggesting that every reader retains an attorney and goes after their lender or their mortgage broker. The picture is bigger than that. The picture is about the connection between perspective, knowledge and potential solutions. I hope this book helps you obtain all three.

Let's start by dispelling a number of pervasive myths about the subprime lending industry.

Myths- Debunked:
Myth # One – Lenders Want to Foreclose on Borrowers:

While admittedly difficult for most people outside of housing, lending and loan servicing to understand, foreclosure costs tend to run about 50% of the property's original appraised value. It's amazing, all other things equal, how much less a property will appraise for when the purpose is for a pending foreclosure as compared to the value it gets when the purpose is to obtain a new loan. They are never the same and are rarely even close. Then there is the people factor.

People who are losing their homes in foreclosure have been known to do some interesting things like selling the windows and shudders, built in appliances and cabinets, plants and trees, bathroom and kitchen fixtures and even garage doors. They sell anything that can fetch them a dollar. And if they're angry, they might even do some damage like tearing out the drywall, breaking tile on the floor or on the roof, removing insulation, breaking the plumbing, cutting electrical wiring and even cutting sections out of the internal framing. Angry people can be very creative, indeed.

Total foreclosure costs are certainly influenced by the foreclosure laws of the state in which the property is located. Some states allow for judicial foreclosures and some require non-judicial foreclosures. The differences are significant but not that important, except to the extent that they do create different costs to the foreclosing lender/ servicer. Regulated lenders may be required to hold cash reserves to cover the anticipated losses of the defaulted loans. At best, this ties up their capital and prevents the lender from earning money on it. At worst, it requires the lender to borrow the funds necessary to cover the reserves.

Taking all of these factors into account, lenders lose an average of 40%-50% on any loans they foreclose on. Suffice it to say, the last thing a lender wants to do is foreclose because there is literally no upside for them in the foreclosure activity. This is a key piece of information and one that should put a convenient, but inaccurate, myth to bed. The fact is that institutional lenders never want to foreclose and they never originate loans hoping they will have to foreclose.

Myth # Two – Subprime Lenders are Predatory Lenders:

Subprime lenders have a higher denial rate than even conforming lenders and ultimately fund only about 50% of the loans that are submitted. Conversely, predatory lenders are alleged to seek out the highest-risk borrowers possible.

Similarly, predatory lenders are alleged to concentrate their operations either exclusively or largely among racial and minority communities. Meanwhile, subprime lenders make loans to borrowers closely matching the racial and ethnic composition of the United States. No more than 70% of subprime loans were made to white borrowers.

These statements can be verified by looking into any Federal HMDA report from any year.

Myth # Three – Lenders Control the Process and Have All the Power:

Personal experience has proven to me that no one in the lending industry has all the power or calls all the shots. The industry is highly segmented and interdependent. I've been a borrower, a loan broker, a lender (small, medium and very large) and an issuer of loan securities (more on this later) directly into Wall Street. I've worked with the rating agencies and bond insurers who validate and support the securities. I've run servicing departments that collect on the loans.

The fact is that all of these parties have power. Lenders typically rely on information provided by third parties, like loan brokers, and then sell the loan to investors. Lenders only make money if they fund "investment quality" loans that investment banks are willing to buy at a premium. The lenders typically transfer servicing rights and responsibilities to investors along with the sale of the loans and are removed from the communication loop. Unless lenders retain servicing (do it themselves), they generally have no idea how the loans they originated are performing.

Competition, technology and shareholder expectations all have enormous power. They exert pressure and force lenders to stretch the limits beyond their own comfort level. Lenders are the most visible party in the lending industry, but they do not have all the power or operate in a vacuum. Many other parties and forces are directly and actively involved in the lending process.

Myth # Four – Subprime Lenders Only Make Loans to People With Weak or Poor Credit:

Loan approvals are dependent on many various components, not just credit. So, even people with good or excellent to perfect credit histories may not qualify for conforming or "prime" loans. Common reasons for conforming loan denials include low property values, high debt to income ratios, short time on job, insufficient income documentation, reliance on an unusually high number of different income sources and reliance on income that tends to vary, like tips and bonuses.

Additionally, subprime lenders would often make very large loans that were not generally available through other channels. These loans would only be made to very strong borrowers with excellent income and credit profiles. Subprime lenders were generally much more tolerant regarding the amount of equity, or cash-out, the borrowers could receive at funding. Sometimes, subprime lenders offered rates comparable to conforming or prime loans, but required fewer conditions and provided faster processing. This list is not exhaustive but illustrates the point that the subprime industry supported many types of borrowers other than those who had weak credit and income.

In fact, the mortgage industry is generally divided into three categories. Conforming, also known as "traditional" or "prime," loans meet government standards. They are Fannie Mae / Freddie Mac eligible and approved. Non-traditional or non-conforming loans, the second type, often share the credit characteristics of conforming loans but provide for more flexible documentation and offer more creative or "exotic" loan features. Subprime, or non-prime, loans often involve spottier income and credit histories but, as described above, also support a wide array of borrower profiles. While there is no strict dividing line between non-traditional and subprime loans, the industry recognizes that they are two different things.

FOR CONSISTENCY AND SIMPLICITY, THE THREE LOAN TYPES WILL BE REFERRED TO AS "CONFORMING," "NON-TRADITONAL" AND "SUBPRIME" THROUGHOUT THE BOOK!

Myth # Five – Subprime Lenders Charge Unusually High or Usurious Rates:

In years past, the difference between conforming loans and subprime loans was about 400 basis points (bps.) or 4%. That's a wide spread but difficult to compare because the borrowers and the total risk associated with them were so very different. What is for certain is that that gap had narrowed down to about 250 bps. or 2.5% by the year 2000 and down to about 100 bps. or 1% before the market started to decline in 2006.

These spreads decreased over the years for a variety of reasons, but mostly because the credit quality of subprime borrowers steadily improved such that the line between conforming, non-traditional and subprime borrowers became blurrier and blurrier. You may be surprised to learn that a few years ago I personally obtained a 30-year fixed-rate at 5.25% and no points through a subprime lender even though I qualified for a "prime" loan. Why? Because that particular subprime lender offered lower rates than any conforming lenders offered at the time. While that's not typical, it shows how close rates can be between prime and subprime lenders and borrowers. For the record, I locked that loan through a broker whom I did not know and with a lender who did not know me. In other words, my position in the industry had nothing to do with the terms of the approval.

Additionally, over the past couple years, major conforming lenders directly entered the subprime marketplace in order to access the relatively higher profit margins and profits. In 2006, the top two subprime lenders were Countrywide and Wells Fargo. These companies are used to operating on spreads of less than 50 bps. or ½% because their infrastructures are so large and they can greatly leverage their economies of scale. As a result, they were able to charge lower rates (which helps explain their market dominance), but other lenders needed to follow suit if they expected to stay in business themselves. This is true even though the other lenders had a higher cost of production associated with smaller operational platforms.

Most subprime lending is generated Wholesale through mortgage brokers. Brokers competed against each other to earn borrowers' business, and this made brokers hypersensitive to the rates charged by the lenders. It was commonplace for brokers to submit loan applications to six or seven subprime lenders at the same time. The winner was usually the lender that came back with the highest loan amount, the lowest rate and the fewest conditions in the least amount of time. While this might not have been smart in the long run for lenders, it was anything but predatory and was hardly a dynamic in which lenders could charge above-market rates.

Yet, subprime lenders were not saints. They were in business to make money, and they faced tremendous competitive pressures that could, and often did, fuel unprofessional behavior. It certainly drove some people to compromise their ethical standards. Cultures varied widely from company to company, and, frankly, there were some companies that many people, myself included, would have nothing to do with. Having said that, neither the lenders nor the industry as a whole are the villains they are made out to be by the media and by many in the government.

With these key myths now de-bunked, you might be wondering what the industry is *really* about. To answer that, we need to go back to the days of consumer finance.

Consumer Finance:

The consumer finance industry was a good place to be… from. I had joined it in 1987 but could not understand how and why I had just spent five years at the University of California, earning degrees in Economics and Psychology just to end up pulling credit reports for ITT Financial in Sacramento. It wouldn't have mattered, but I could have been at any finance company and the story would have been the same. At the time, the American landscape was dotted with ITT's, Beneficials, HFCs, and Dime Financials, to name a few.

In my particular office, cigarette smoke hung in the air as if it were a permanent fixture suspended from the nicotine stained ceiling. The laws in California that prohibited smoking inside public office spaces had just changed, but at least eight people in my particular office apparently hadn't heard yet. This included my boss, Jim, who sat one desk behind me to make sure I was properly indoctrinated into the world of consumer finance. And for me, that was the reward for being the new guy.

Jim was a wizard with the cigarette. Nothing got in his way of smoking. Making loans, collecting on them, counseling employees, training new ones (like me), reporting in by phone to his regional and district managers, handing out paychecks or whatever else branch managers had to do were simply things that he did while he perfected his true mastery. While sickening to me (literally), in a weird way, it was still quite impressive. Others in the office were talented themselves, but Jim was in a whole different league.

While that was the scene inside, the one outside was not much better. We were only one shoebox of space within a large chain of storefronts in that particular strip center. Large strip centers need large parking lots. And large parking lots are usually a good place to find shopping baskets. Many of the baskets in this particular lot were used as arsenal by some of the local teenagers who had become quite good at striking cars (for no apparent reason, mine seemed to be a favorite) from a distance before they would run away to avoid being caught. I didn't understand this "sport" since my mundane athletic experience was limited to baseball, football and basketball.

There were two good things about the consumer finance industry. The first was that it was easy to move up. All you had to do was be more aggressive, tenacious and productive than everyone else around you. A college degree gave you no advantage while lacking one created no limitation. The business was about performance. The other good thing was that I didn't personally need to borrow money from it.

So who did? Lots of people; otherwise, the industry would not have been so prolific. For sure, most of the loans we made were either unsecured (signature) loans or they were collateralized by merchandise we financed for one of our vendor-clients, like furniture stores and pet shops. Technically, these loans were secured by something, but practically speaking the collateral made no difference. On one collection call, I reminded a borrower that we had security on his loan and that he risked losing it if he didn't make his monthly payment. He reminded me that my company had financed the purchase of a puppy which was now a full grown German Shepherd that crapped (he used a different word) all over his rug. He invited me to come pick it up. I didn't know if he was referring to the dog or to the crap.

We also made home loans to less than credit-worthy borrowers. The term "subprime" had not yet been invented so these people were simply referred to as "consumer finance customers." High interest rate loans were made to borrowers with credit problems, blemished credit histories, insufficient proven income, inability to document income or people who had high debt ratios (percentage of debt compared to gross income), or who, in general, could not obtain home loans through more traditional channels including banks and S&Ls (Thrifts).

Doesn't this sound strikingly familiar to the subprime borrowers we talk about today? Because these borrowers typically did not have much in the way of cash reserves, home loans made to these folks were usually cash-out refinances while loans made for the purpose of purchasing homes (purchase money loans) were a rarity. Either way, the consumer finance companies (CFCs) held on to the loans they funded, which were therefore called "portfolio" loans. The CFCs then collected on these loans and enjoyed the high interest rate paid by these riskier borrowers.

The CFCs had some interesting, if not questionable and deceptive, lending strategies. For example, they would aggressively sell credit life and disability (L&D) insurance as part of the loans. Then they would sell another policy when the loan refinanced (they always did) and after the original L&D policy was rolled up into the new principal balance. In effect, they were selling credit L&D on top of credit L&D policies. Since these policies were financed by the loans themselves, the borrowers were, of course, charged the same high interest on those policies. Therefore, the CFCs were selling insurance on top of insurance and charging interest on top of interest.

Another strategic practice was to allow borrowers to go delinquent, often with little or no collection activity and then to charge late fees. These were often the most profitable loans on the books – the ones that went delinquent and then paid regularly from that point forward. We gave it a cute name, "rolling 30s" (days delinquent), but each month the CFCs earned late fees because those loans always remained delinquent. At the same time, little to no principal was paid down because payments were going to current interest due, past due interest and to late fees. Many, if not most, homeowners who financed through the CFCs were surprised to learn that after late fees, interest on interest payments, deferments, loan modifications, credit life insurance financed on top of the principal, etc., that their balances went UP over the typical lives of their loans.

The industry was non-regulated, arrogant and greedy. It was common throughout the industry for CFCs to call their home loans by one of two despicable names. They were either called "Hugh Downs loans" as Hugh was the first host of the TV news show "20/20" or they were called "perfect vision loans" because they often charged 20% interest and 20% in fees.

As abusive, predatory and opportunistic as these lending practices were, the fact is that the CFCs were the only "legitimate" companies who had been willing to provide loans to people with credit, income, and /or debt ratio problems. This was so obvious to the consumer finance industry that if potential borrowers balked at the terms of their approval, they would often, albeit politely, be told that they could always find some guy with white shoes and a white belt who would be willing to lend his money on even less favorable terms.

The good news was that, while many people needed the CFCs, most people were able to get their borrowing needs met by the government regulated Thrift industry, which included banks and Savings & Loans. Unfortunately, the Thrifts were not immune to financial upheaval either –at least, not to the extent that was created during the Carter years of 1976 – 1980.

In October 1979, the Fed began raising rates dramatically to offset runaway inflation. At the time, government-regulated Thrifts (Savings & Loan Companies) had a collective trillion dollars in loans on their balance sheets. The income stream the Thrifts were receiving on their outstanding, long-term, fixed-rate loans were, by definition, constant. Their cost of borrowing money, however, was skyrocketing as the Fed continued raising rates. There was no end in sight for all the red ink that was pouring from the Thrifts.

To the rescue: on September 30, 1981 Congress passed a massive tax break for Thrifts. In order to take advantage of it, the Thrifts had to sell their loan portfolios. Due to a series of interesting events, the Wall Street investment bank, Salomon Brothers (SB), had recently set up a mortgage-trading desk; it was under the direction of Lewis Ranieri. More importantly, SB was the only investment bank on Wall Street to have such a facility. So the Congressional tax break for the Thrifts became a windfall for SB.

Mortgage Securitization:

Salomon Brothers' objective was to transfer the mortgages into bonds that would be stamped by the U.S. Government. Then, they would sell the mortgages as relatively "riskless" government bonds. Salomon Brothers was able to obtain approval to use the Federal Home Loan Mortgage Corporation (Freddie Mac) and the Federal National Mortgage Association (Fannie Mae) to stamp these bonds with the government's seal of approval. Together, Fannie Mae & Freddie Mac guaranteed the mortgages that did not qualify for the previous government stamp for mortgages called Ginnie Mae.

But that structure was short–lived. In 1983, the collateralized mortgage obligation (CMO) was invented. While the details are not important for the purpose of this book, it is useful to understand that CMOs involved large ($100M ±) pools of loans. Within three years, CMOs dominated the marketplace and the Fannie Mae / Freddie Mac-backed bonds became obsolete. This new facility gave institutional investors a new place and way to invest in mortgages. These would be expected to perform better than other types of assets. Trillions of dollars were now in play.

The CMOs that made Ranieri's mortgage bonds obsolete within a few short years are now more commonly known as securities or securitizations. Keep in mind that entire companies and bureaucracies exist to run, sell, invest, service and regulate securitizations. Lengthy books can be, and have been, written on the securitization mechanism. Suffice it to say that securities are complex, but they are critical to the growth of the lending industry as we know it.

Some critical benefits resulted from the creation of mortgage securitizations. And it was these benefits that launched the conforming loan industry into the stratosphere. Lenders /originators were able to get their principle back almost immediately upon funding loans to borrowers. Additionally, they immediately received some premium (their profit) on those loans based on the anticipated future cash flow and performance of those loans as predicted by the investor.

This mechanism prevented lenders from having to hold their loans in portfolio and, therefore, dramatically decreased their own cost of borrowing money for lending and operating capital. It also protected them from future interest rate fluctuation since they would not be holding the loans if and when rates increased. Together, these features could drive down the interest rate charged to borrowers or increase lender profits. The reality is that it did some of both.

Securitization was an immediate win-win-win for borrowers, lenders and investors. Borrowers obtained lower rates. Lenders were able to generate greater volume (because they could offer lower rates) and higher profit margins. These two factors together helped create higher real profits. Investors were able to put their money in a new investment vehicle and the returns were attractive.

By 1986, securitization had become the dominant investment mechanism on Wall Street for Fannie Mae or Freddie Mac qualified mortgages. As fate would have it, the timing of that dominance was perfectly in synch with another boost from Congress. In that very same year, Congress passed the Tax Reform Act of 1986, which, amongst other things, eliminated eligible deductions for interest paid on all loans except real estate secured mortgages. This meant that people could no longer deduct the interest they paid on credit cards, unsecured consumer loans or credit lines and even their car loans. This created an immediate incentive for homeowners to consolidate as much consumer debt as possible into their tax-deductible mortgages. This same incentive is alive and well today.

At about the same time, the consumer finance industry was coming under intense and increasing legislative pressure due to their consumer un-friendly practices as described earlier in this chapter. One by one, the CFCs began to fall by the wayside. The few who remained by 1988 had changed their lending practices and their business strategies to conform to the legislative expectations.

Again, **mortgage securitization had driven lender costs down, which allowed for relatively lower rates and higher profits – at the same time. As a result, the real estate market was booming nationwide,** new mortgage companies were popping up everywhere and existing mortgage companies were growing exponentially.

New Lenders & New Challenges:

One of these companies was Long Beach Bank (LBB), headquartered in Southern California. It was owned and operated by Roland Arnall who went on to become one of the richest men in America and the US ambassador to the Netherlands. Roland retired in February 2008 and, unfortunately, died less than one month later and within a few weeks of his 69th birthday.

Back in the old days (prior to 1990), LBB's strategy was to originate Fannie Mae / Freddie Mac eligible loans and then sell them "whole" or securitize them through their relationships on Wall Street. Again, this was a typical practice throughout the mortgage industry and there was nothing wrong with it. In theory, the better execution the lender received, the better able they were to offer more favorable terms to their borrowers. The decision about whether to sell loans "whole" or to securitize them was driven by many factors, but suffice it to say that the lenders' objective was to maximize their profits.

Over time, LBB originated many millions of dollars in loans that did not meet Fannie Mae / Freddie Mac guidelines and were, therefore, kicked out of sales and securitizations. Because there was no other established outlet for these loans, LBB held them in their portfolio. The vast majority of these loans paid as agreed right from the beginning. Yet, the interest rate LBB charged was too low for them to justify holding the loans in portfolio and tying up their capital for up to thirty years.

At the time, Mark Schuerman was the President of the Mortgage Division at LBB. Mark is an idea guy, a visionary and a leader. He is humble, almost shy, very caring, passionately dedicated to customers and equally committed to the service he provided to them. Tim Hayes was the head of secondary marketing, and his job was to get their loans sold or securitized and to clear their credit lines. But they were stuck with these loans.

While I would not meet Mark or Tim until a couple years later, I can tell you that Tim is one of the most tenacious people I've ever known. He, like Mark, always appeared calm regardless of what was churning underneath. I'm not sure if Tim played poker, but to this day, he is the one who comes to my mind when I hear the phrase "poker-face." Tim rarely, if ever, got openly flustered, or acted with any obvious sense of urgency or nervousness and he never took "no" for an answer. We called him "the bulldog." He and Mark had a solution in mind.

Their vision was to convince an investment bank on Wall Street to put these non-Fannie Mae / Freddie Mac eligible loans into a security. This was no easy sell as securitization, while having matured into the dominant mortgage mechanism on Wall Street, was limited only to Fannie / Freddie conforming loans. But, in time, Mark and the bulldog came through. They entered into an agreement with Greenwich Capital to securitize these loans, and LBB's problem was solved.

At about the same time, and on the other side of town, Quality Mortgage (QM) developed the same challenge that faced Mark and Tim at LBB. In its previous life, Quality Mortgage was known as Guardian Savings, which had been owned by Russ Jedenik and his wife Beckey. Guardian had come under some intense regulatory and financial scrutiny which it successfully sidestepped by closing down, dropping the "savings" part of their name and their business function and then re-opening under the name Quality Mortgage.

Quality Mortgage solved their problem the same way as LBB, but used a different Investment Bank on Wall Street. Suddenly, there were two non-conforming securities on Wall Street. Meanwhile, LBB and Quality Mortgage went back to the prolific and profitable business of originating Fannie Mae / Freddie Mac conforming loans.

Then, something unexpected happened. Several months after securitizing the deal for LBB, Greenwich called Tim and let him know that the loan pool was performing better than they had expected (which also means better than they priced for). **Then they asked the question that would change the industry forever...... "Can you get us more?"**

This was relatively easy to do. Remember that the consumer finance industry had essentially gone away and only two company's (LBB and QM) had issued any non-conforming securities on Wall Street. Within a very short period of time, LBB opened a mortgage banking operation in Orange, CA that was devoted exclusively to the wholesale origination of subprime mortgages. Quality Mortgage continued making conforming loans out of their Huntington Beach location but also started to intentionally originate subprime loans for securitization.

Soon, LBB was out of the conforming business altogether. But its mortgage banking division was loaded with leaders who were the first and the few to have this subprime securitization experience. Mark Schuerman was still the President while Pat Rank and Bob Dubrish rotated responsibility running Sales and Operations. All of them, however, were under the shadow of the company's owner, Roland Arnall. They saw an industry developing and wanted more freedom to help build it. They wanted out.

In 1991, Mark left LBB and stepped in as President of Royal Thrift & Loan, which was located about 60 miles north in West L.A. Royal had several different lending divisions and it was one of the few remaining Thrifts left standing in California after the collapse of the Thrift & Loan industry in 1990-1991. Royal was FDIC (Federal Deposit Insurance Corporation) insured and was therefore under the purview of the FDIC and the DOC (Department of Corporations). While Royal Thrift & Loan was never a consumer finance company, it suffered from the same legislative pressure that had compressed the consumer finance and Thrift & Loan industries. Royal needed a person at the helm who had the credibility to work with the regulators, turn around their company and grow it. No one fit the mold better than Mark Schuerman.

Mark accepted the role of President under the agreement with its owners, John Tonoyan and Stanley Zimmerman, that he would be able to build a stand-alone, subprime mortgage banking division. By then it was about mid-1992, and I was hired by Mark to build and run Royal's subprime division. Pat Rank had departed from LBB and went to Quality Mortgage to run it's subprime business. That was a short stint as Pat, who fit very well with Mark and Bob at LBB, did not fit well within the culture at Quality Mortgage. Pat re-connected with Bob and together they set up a subprime origination company called Option One. It was owned by Plaza Savings - one of the leading conforming lenders in the country. Option One was, therefore, the first stand-alone subprime company wholly owned by a major conforming lender.

With the departure of Mark, Pat and Bob from LBB, Roland had some positions to fill. This started somewhat of a revolving door of executives at LBB, where people like Steve Holder and then Jack Mayesh took the helm before moving on to run other large mortgage banks like New Century, Encore and ResMae. Eventually, LBB settled down when Kirk Langs became the new President. Kirk and I had worked together in the past and had spent some time on the slopes in Tahoe and at the racetracks. He is smart, direct, energetic and accomplished. He was the right guy to continue building LBB into a *major* subprime lender.

After Pat's quick departure from Quality Mortgage, Russ Jedenik split off a dedicated subprime origination company called "First Security Mortgage (FSM)." This venture was short-lived due to its tremendous redundancy in operation and in costs. FSM shut down and Quality Mortgage converted its business plan to the dedicated origination of subprime loans.

So almost overnight, the subprime industry went from an abusive market supported by the consumer finance companies, to a mistake made by conforming lenders, to an experiment on Wall Street, to a purposeful business platform shared by four companies all within a stone's throw of each other. They were Long Beach Bank, Option One, Quality Mortgage (collectively known as the "Big Three") and Royal Thrift.

Chapter Three: Subprime: Rise. Fall. Then Repeat.

"If at first you don't succeed, try, try again."
   - Thomas H. Palmer, "Teacher's Manual of 1840"

By 1992, Wall Street had developed a healthy appetite for subprime mortgage securities, which was mostly being fulfilled by the Big Three. By now, the consumer finance companies were essentially gone from the marketplace. Congress could not have been more pleased, as it had spent significant effort in the 1980s putting pressure on the consumer finance companies until they were out of business. Lenders who were enabled by the creation of subprime mortgage securitization were now filling the resulting subprime vacuum. **As a result, credit-challenged people had much more access to competitively priced money.**

Without a doubt, subprime lenders (like all lenders) were in business to make a profit. They achieved that objective by serving the customers who were abandoned by the collapse of the consumer finance industry. Consider that, by 1992, these same borrowers were paying 9-10% rates with 2-3 points in fees instead of the 20%+ rates and 20 points in fees they had been paying to the consumer finance companies. But without the profits, the new industry would not even exist to serve these borrowers.

Although the consumer finance industry had basically vanished, Congress did not want the *customer* finance customer to be abandoned by the demise of the industry. At the same time, they did not want to see some old habits re-emerge in the subprime mortgage banking industry. The Regulatory Agencies became very active in the monitoring of this new breed of lender. Their intentions were probably good, but the legislators seemed to lack a fundamental understanding of credit risk. Either that or they didn't think that lenders and investors should be paid for taking on the higher risk associated with credit-challenged borrowers. Either way, their efforts applied even greater pressure on the fledgling subprime industry.

It was as if some in Congress thought the purpose of the new industry was to be a non-profit branch of the government making identical looking loans to all borrowers regardless of the risk those borrowers brought to the table. Congress was Democratically controlled, industry competition was not recognized as a viable force by which reasonably priced loans would be provided to low income borrowers in poor neighborhoods, so the legislative, full-court press was on. The debate over whether best business practices should be legislated or, alternatively, driven by competitive forces is as old as dirt (or at least as old as the Democratic and Republican parties). This is more than just a philosophical-political talking point. It's a critical point and a recurring theme throughout the evolution of this industry.

The four subprime lenders, all located within a few miles of each other in Southern California, were suffering from some serious growing pains and had some very significant challenges to address. In order to generate the win-win-win benefits associated with mortgage securitization, each of the lenders needed to achieve critical mass on a monthly basis. Generally speaking, this proved to be about $100M each per month.

In order to originate $100M per month in subprime volume each, the Big Three needed some new strategies. They had always *wanted* to originate more volume in order to generate more profits. But now, they *needed* to originate more volume in order to realize the benefits of securitization and to execute their business plans. Reaching down and out to higher risk borrowers was one logical and legitimate way (so long as they were paid for that risk) to achieve that critical mass.

In fact, the subprime lenders *needed* these borrowers. For this reason, Congress did not need to pressure lenders who failed to reach out to under-served communities. But they did.

Achieving critical mass could be achieved through other strategies as well. The Big Three expanded nationally and very quickly. Meanwhile, Royal Thrift was on the financial bubble, as it did not have the resources to achieve critical mass. Enter John Dewey.

Few, if any, people in this industry are smarter than John. He recognized that Royal was not alone. John knew that there were several other small lenders who wanted to join the subprime arena and enjoy the competitive benefits of securitization. But they too would have the same key challenge; how could they possibly achieve critical mass? John had the answer: put them all together. This sounds easy, but it took an already sophisticated process of issuing securities to an even higher level of difficulty. It took someone who knew how to navigate around the investors, rating agencies and bond insurers required to make securities work. John became the Transaction Coordinator for a new mechanism called the Co-Originated Securitization.

John rallied several small banks and mortgage companies together to combine their volume with Royal's and to issue securities. There were many bumps along the way. Some lenders dropped out, others came in, some investment banks could not let go of their conforming mentality, and others lost the stomach for the business. But John, Mark Schuerman and Tim Hayes (the bulldog) always had a plan B on the back burner. If needed, we could always sell our loans "whole" to one of the Big Three. In this event, we typically used Option One as it was run by Pat and Bob, both of whom had worked for Mark at LBB. They had a good relationship, and we leveraged it.

These were by no means, easy times. The junk-bond market had just tanked, Orange County, CA had filed for bankruptcy protection, and military bases were being shut down in record numbers and in record speed. As a result, the aerospace industry fell in on itself. Home values dropped dramatically in California. Other states were affected, but to a far lesser extent. Fortunately for the Big Three, they had already expanded nationally as part of their strategy to fulfill the volume demand of Wall Street. This took significant pressure off them to originate more loans in California, where property values were plummeting.

Fortunately, hard times were expected and endured. In part, this was due to one amazing truth. While the lenders were doing their best to meet their challenges, including critical mass, home de-valuation, Congressional pressure and low availability of talent (industry growth had out-paced supply of a knowledgeable work force), the loans they were originating were continuing to perform quite well within the securities in which they resided.

Investors conceptually understood the inherent risk-reward nature of the subprime industry, but, to this point, they had only experienced the reward side. Their collective appetite intensified until just about every investment bank on Wall Street was issuing subprime securities. Not only were they issuing them, they were demanding them. Wall Street had solved the problem experienced by a couple conforming lenders a few years earlier. It acquired the taste for the product. Then, it couldn't get enough. The needle was deep into Wall Street's vein, and they needed their fix. The responsibility of the lenders was to continue pumping the drug and to keep the syringe full. Over time, the quality and purity of the drug became less and less important.

It was these events of 1992 that ushered us into the modern era of subprime lending. Large companies were expanding nationally and some small companies were combining their volume into co-originated securitizations. Even companies that didn't participate in this structure had become able to sell individual funded (closed) loans to larger lenders who would subsequently re-sell or securitize them.

Yet, despite all the other dynamics that were developing about the same time, Wall Street had more demand than they were receiving supply. Meanwhile, lenders were struggling with generating necessary volume because there were so many other lenders going after the same borrowers on a national level. There was only one solution to the problem: the subprime pie needed to be made much larger and not just cut into thinner slices as more lenders entered the market.

This is when new products and program variations started to show up on the scene. Until that point in 1992, the subprime menu looked basic. The industry was kind of like In-N-Out Burger for loans. Consumers liked the products, but there were only a few items on the menu. The process of preparing them was well designed and standardized as more and more people developed an appetite for the product. But quickly, that would not be enough.

The choices needed to grow beyond the 30-year fixed-rate loans and 6-month ARMs that were the mainstay of subprime to that point. Out came 5/25s, where the first five years were fixed and the next twenty-five years could adjust every six months thereafter. Out came the 3/27s, where the first three years were fixed followed by twenty-seven years of six month ARMs.

Wall Street was comfortable with these developments because they wanted more volume and they had become more comfortable with the subprime industry and products. Up to that point, subprime origination had continued to perform better than expected and was generating healthy profits for investors. So, Wall Street was ready, willing and able to chart new product territory.

Unlike the conforming market, subprime loans typically carried pre-payment penalties that would discourage borrowers from paying off their loans for certain periods of time. Usually, the pre-payment periods matched the fixed-rate portion of their loan. So, for example, a 5/25 (and other long-term fixed-rate loans) would have a 5-year prepayment penalty and a 3/27 (as well as 6-month ARMs) would have 3-year penalties. There were variations on the penalties: some might be longer up to the maximum allowed by law, others had "windows" where the penalty was inactive with a certain amount of days before and after any scheduled adjustments. But, for the most part, anyone who paid off with an active penalty in place would have to forfeit an amount approximately the same as the total of four and a half payments.

This was usually sufficient to influence borrower behavior and was, therefore, quite valuable to Wall Street because they could determine two very important things that drove some critical uncertainty out of their deals. First, they could determine the projected yield because it was shown on the rates and the loan terms were known. Second, it allowed them to more accurately forecast the duration of that yield over time because of the prepayment penalties and their consequences. In time, other products or features developed as the subprime menu expanded. For example, prepayment penalties could be bought out. People could buy their rates down by paying points or they could buy their points down by paying more rate. Subprime was starting to look more like a Soup-N-Salad buffet than an In-N-Out Burger.

Through all this expansion, Wall Street was getting more comfortable with subprime lending. Yet, they were somewhat guarded. They anticipated that, compared to conforming borrowers, subprime borrowers would be pre-disposed to not paying on time. And if this were true, higher rates would not help the investors. However, lower LTVs (loan to value ratios), which represented the loan amount relative to the fair market value of the property on which the loan was secured, and higher equity would protect them from actual losses. As a result, investors paid lenders a comparatively higher premium (more money) for lower LTVs (more equity) than for higher rates. This is why loans were priced for risk but collateralized (LTV) for lender and investor protection.

This dynamic kept significant downward pressure on LTVs such that the average hovered around 72%. This meant that if a lender needed to foreclose, they would have about 28% of the property's value to cover all foreclosure costs, including past due interest, realtor fees, repairs, etc. As described in Chapter One, this amount was insufficient to cover the typical costs associated with foreclosing. But this was offset by the fact that very few loans would need to be foreclosed upon.

Even though all other industry growth mechanisms were already in place, the growing demand of Wall Street could not be met. So, the last line of subprime defense was knocked down and the slippery slope of LTVs was opened to all takers. Within a few years of becoming mainstream, the highest-end subprime borrowers could obtain 80% LTV loans. In lending, everyone gets a name, and we called these people at the higher end of the subprime spectrum the "cream of the crap." 80% LTV quickly became obsolete and it didn't take long for most sales people to master the expression "we're only at 80." Yet, despite these higher potential LTVs, the industry average hovered in the low to mid 70% range, although it was creeping upward.

Unlike conforming borrowers who would refinance for the sole purpose of getting a lower rate, subprime borrowers typically were not driven primarily by rate or by the desire to get a lower one. Like everyone, they wanted the lowest possible rate they could get, but what they wanted even more was the maximum amount of cash out they could get. The combination of downward pressure on LTVs and the borrowers' motivation to obtain maximum possible cash out created a problem. Brokers wanted to be paid more for the greater complexity of processing subprime loans, while borrowers wanted to sacrifice as minimal proceeds as possible, whether for fees or otherwise.

It is universal amongst lenders to offer lower rates to borrowers generated through wholesale channels (by loan brokers) than they would offer to the same borrowers if the loans were originated retail. The reasons for this are fairly obvious. On wholesale loans, lenders don't have the marketing cost associated with obtaining every single loan directly from a consumer. Rather, they leverage broker relationships, which means the broker finds the borrowers. Additionally, loan brokers are required by law to provide a bundle of certain functions, which one way or another included a significant amount of loan processing. This is loan processing that the lender doesn't need to do. These two things drive down lender costs but also justify the fees brokers obtain for their services.

A problem developed as three great forces started to work against each other. Investors wanted to keep LTVs down. Borrowers wanted the maximum cash out possible. Lenders wanted to originate their volume wholesale.

The solution came mainly in the form of yield spread pricing (YSPs), or rebates, as they were called at the time. YSPs shot straight to the heart of subprime lending. It allowed brokers to earn rebates (money) from lenders by getting borrowers to accept a higher rate than the lender had required based on that borrower's assessed risk. The purpose of this structure was very well-intended. In concept, borrowers who didn't have enough equity in their property to pay their broker out of loan proceeds could instead pay a higher rate, and the broker would be paid some of their fees in the form of rebate from the lender. The lender in turn would receive a higher market price on these loans when they either sold or securitized them. From that perspective, all that mattered was the rate, not how it got there.

At any rate, pun intended, rebates were initially limited to about 1%. But, in typical fashion, as soon as all market participants became comfortable with them, rebates jumped in quantum leaps. Within a year, the major subprime lenders were racing to out-do each other by offering two, then three and then four YSPs. While the "buy-ups" (paying more rate and less fees) varied from lender to lender and adjusted over time, borrowers would typically pay about .40% in rate for 1 YSP to the broker.

As well intended as rebate pricing may have been, it was riddled with problems. For instance, borrowers never knew what rate they were approved for or how much extra they were paying in rate in order for the broker to earn their fees. And until some disclosure laws were changed, brokers and lenders did not even need to clearly disclose how much the broker was receiving in fees. Additionally, brokers could charge both fees and higher rebate pricing. For these reasons and others, rebates or yield spread pricing became the single hottest regulatory and legislative issue hovering above subprime lending for several years.

For sure, though, it did achieve the objective of the structure, which was to allow lenders to generate more loans than they otherwise would have been able to originate. And it allowed lenders and investors to keep LTVs low. This was the ultimate protection against foreclosure. Wall Street couldn't have cared less how much the lenders were paying to the brokers in rebates. What mattered to them was that they would generate a higher yield, based on the higher note rates, for the duration that the loans stayed on the books. This drove Wall Street's appetite even higher.

At the same time, there was an inherent problem with the product offerings of the subprime industry. 6-month ARMS offered the lowest rates, but they had too much rate risk and volatility associated with them. Fixed-rate loans, and ARMS with longer fixed-rate periods like the 5/25s and 3/27s were too restrictive for subprime borrowers. These borrowers had a strong tendency and desire to refinance every couple years in order to access any accumulated equity, as if it were part of their annual income. The higher rates and longer prepayment penalties on these longer, fixed term loans did not allow them the flexibility to refinance as often as they wanted.

Their desire to refinance more often was further reinforced by loan brokers who religiously sold borrowers the idea that if they paid as agreed for two years, then their credit would improve and they would become conforming borrowers and would get a conforming loan. In my career, I don't know that I ever saw that happen, but that was the brokers' pitch. And it resonated with borrowers.

So the market responded to these challenges by creating the big kahuna of subprime products, the 2/28. In reality, it was not a different product as it was simply a different amortization and term structure. Like its 1st cousins the 3/27 and 5/25, the 2/28 was fixed for the first two years, at which point the prepayment penalty would expire and the remaining 28 years could adjust every 6-months depending on prevailing market rates.

Everyone in the industry loved these loans. In the world of fairy tales, it was the porridge that was just right. This structure met the needs of the borrowers who wanted a product that more effectively balanced payments with rate protection and flexibility. Now, borrowers could obtain loans with relatively low start rates. They were somewhat higher than the rates of the 6-month ARMS, but significantly lower than rates on the longer fixed term loans. Additionally, the borrowers had interest rate protection, knowing that their rate wouldn't change for two years. At the same time, they would not be locked down for too long if rates started to drop over the next couple years. The timing fit perfectly with their broker's guidance that if they paid as agreed for two years they would become conforming borrowers and could get an even lower rate.

So the cycle began. Wall Street loved the 2/28s because they could still measure, and price for, the two things most important to them, yield and duration. Lenders liked them because they allowed the lenders to generate more business. Brokers loved them because they allowed the brokers to work a "rolodex" of repeat customers. Borrowers liked the product because the rates and payments were far lower than those offered by the longer fixed term loans and because they had payment certainty for the first two years. With this product love-fest happening, the lenders' role solidified as an effective and valuable conduit between their front-end customers - the brokers and borrowers, and their back end customer - investors on Wall Street.

Today, these loans are often called "exploding ARMs." It's a catchy term that helps politicians and the media draw attention to a problem. Why they started to "explode" will be discussed a little bit later. But for now, suffice it to say that this structure became the mainstay of subprime to the point that it accounted for about 85% of all subprime volume.

As the fledgling subprime industry became increasingly mainstream, more and more conforming lenders and mortgage conduits (companies that purchased closed loans from a wide array of smaller lenders and connected them indirectly to investors on Wall Street) were adding subprime loans to their menu of products and services.

Perhaps the best example of this was demonstrated by GMAC/RFC. Originally, RFC (Residential Funding Corp.) had been established by a group of people including Lewis Ranieri, who was the guy at Salomon Brothers who had originally set up the only mortgage-trading desk on Wall Street. RFC specialized in the origination of adjustable rate (ARMs) home loans and was quickly acquired by GMAC (General Motors Acceptance Corp.), the finance arm of GM. GMAC, with it's foothold in auto financing and conforming mortgages, was the largest consumer lender in the world.

Shortly after the acquisition, the leadership at RFC turned over to Bruce Paradis who became the President and CEO of GMAC/RFC. Bruce immediately implemented a strategic shift at RFC, driven by his visions around the future impact of technology on lending, the need to support customers geographically rather than around products and his commitment to make markets (internationally) and to manage risk. Bruce was well ahead of his time.

RFC became a mortgage conduit that purchased a variety of different loan types from other lenders and then issued them into securities on Wall Street. While it did not have a subprime division, that did not stop them from setting their sights on becoming a top issuer of subprime securities. They knew what they wanted; they just didn't know how to get there. The subprime talent pool had not yet made its way to Bloomington, MN where RFC was headquartered.

In 1994, I was retained as a consultant by RFC to help them build a subprime division. After a couple months studying RFC, I put forth a subprime business platform to the executive group. There was much candid conversation and debate, but, ultimately, the plan was adopted.

To Bruce's credit, he accepted a plan that, in a significant way, conflicted with the re-organization of the company he had just implemented. My plan was not organized around geographically centered lender-customers, but around products-specifically, the subprime product. The rationale was that subprime lender-customers were isolated from all other types of lenders. So, to some extent, we were organizing resources around customers and not just around products. At least, that's the argument I made to Bruce.

With that move, we became a stand-alone division within RFC and maintained responsibility for our own credit policies, pricing, sales, trading etc. Bruce was a "better mouse trap" kind of guy, so he openly encouraged the pursuit of different strategies towards the same objective. Eventually, he thought, one would prove out better than the rest. And if not, he knew that we would capture more market share by pursuing it from various angles simultaneously.

Immediately upon the executive group's acceptance of my proposal, Bruce, who sat to my immediate right, leaned in front of and across me to get the attention of George Westfall, who sat to my immediate left. George ran all of Capital Markets. Bruce acknowledged the acceptance of my plan and then requested that George go buy a company and build it more according to Bruce's vision. Within a few weeks, RFC had acquired Mortgage Service America and changed its name to Homecomings Financial Services. Homecomings quickly became a leader in the mortgage industry but ended up gravitating towards slightly better credit caliber borrowers (Alt-A), while my business unit remained focused on the subprime sector. They both became big successes, and it all started as an experiment in better business strategies.

As RFC was a relatively new entrant to the subprime market, they relied on some typical conforming loan practices such as Reps and Warrants against fraud. This meant that if any loans they purchased were subsequently determined to involve fraud of any kind, they could require or force the lender to repurchase the loan. This included misrepresentation of value such that when a loan went delinquent, they could re-appraise the property. If the value came in substantially lower, they could claim appraisal fraud and require the repurchase. Easier said than done.

On New Years Day, 1996, I sat at a conference table face to face with Pat Rank, the President and CEO of Option One Mortgage. Our two companies had been haggling for some time over the repurchase request on a rather small bundle of loans. Pat was in town for the holidays, so he and I met to discuss the loans. The biggest challenge for me was that these loans were purchased by RFC before I worked there, and, more importantly, I agreed with Option One. But I worked for RFC.

The issue at hand was a number of loans that had been originated months or years before RFC had purchased them (a clear signal that the loans were not good enough to have been sold earlier to some other investor) and had passed through RFC's underwriting process before the loans were purchased. From Pat's point of view, RFC knew what they were buying and therefore, owned the risk. RFC, on the other hand, contended that their due diligence was low as they would ultimately rely on reps and warrants if necessary and that these loans represented one type of fraud or another.

After some rather vocal expressions of opinion, Pat and I reached an agreement and executed it in writing. What a way to start the year. Unfortunately, I was subsequently told by an executive at RFC that I may have moved too soon as the company was potentially willing to raise this to a level of litigation between the parent companies, GM (RFC) and Fleet (Option One Mortgage). I responded that it was for that very reason that the compromise between Pat and me was a good one. One thing I can say for sure is that, while RFC and Option One may have disagreed on the credit tolerances on those deals, there was no intentional fraud on the part of Option One. But that didn't matter to RFC, who had become accustomed to reps and warrants on any misrepresentation, whether intentional or otherwise.

So RFC learned that while reps and warrants were commonplace in the conforming business, the subprime business was a different animal. As a result, subprime underwriting due diligence needed to be enhanced substantially in order to monitor and ensure loan quality prior to purchase.

In time, RFC realized its vision to be one of the top ten originators and issuers of subprime securities in the nation. Our success along with success of other similar companies, who could both purchase and directly securitize closed loans, removed any remaining barriers to entry that may have kept small lenders from getting in on the subprime action. By 1996, everybody who wanted to be in the subprime game was in. New companies began appearing out of nowhere like lightning strikes from a clear, blue sky.

Even so, Wall Street's appetite for subprime loans continued to grow. For sure, there were now exponentially more lenders and mortgage banks originating subprime loans. But they all seemed to be eating from the same pie. This was for two reasons. First, most loans were originated wholesale through loan brokers. Second, most loan brokers identified themselves as either conforming or subprime, but not both. This meant that supply of subprime loans was generally determined by a fixed number of loan brokers. The only question was where the loans would go. In order to increase the amount of subprime volume available to lenders, the lenders would need to get more loan brokers originating more subprime business.

Subprime companies nationwide launched training campaigns to teach self-identified "conforming brokers" to originate subprime loans. Most of these campaigns were well thought out and comprehensive. But stripped down to the basics, all they were meant to do was get more mortgage brokers comfortable with the subprime market and to convince them not to throw away their conforming turndowns, but instead to submit any such loan packages to these subprime lenders. That helped create a bigger pie for Wall Street and bigger slices for the lenders themselves. It was a classic win-win-win for the brokers, lenders and investment banks.

That was when the light went on for me. I had previously learned and always believed that a balanced market exists when supply equals demand. The problem is that I had the supply and demand ends of the economic equation backwards. Homeowners were not demanding these subprime loans (at least not on the scale that Wall Street wanted them). Similarly, Wall Street (by way of all the lenders feeding it) was not the one meeting the supply end of the equation. For sure, they were providing the money so that they could make more money themselves and so that lenders could get their own money back faster and continue to grow their businesses- the volume of which would then feed back into Wall Street. But they were only providing supply to the extent that their own needs and objectives created market demand.

In very simple terms: Wall Street wanted (i.e. demanded) more and more subprime loans for investment. It was the responsibility of any lenders and brokers who wanted to participate in the business and to enjoy its profits to create a supply of interested, qualified borrowers. If this sounds backwards to you, just think about all the advertisements you received in the mail, saw on TV or heard on the radio. Isn't it easy to tell who was pursuing whom?

This is a key point, maybe the most important point, to understand. <u>Wall Street was, and is, the demand side of lending. If they want more loans, lenders find borrowers. If they don't want them, lenders go out of business and borrowers find it very difficult to obtain loans.</u> For the most part, the lenders are simply the vehicle by which Wall Street gets its supply of borrowers.

By this time, the proliferation of new products and loan structures had some time to mature and perform for the investment banks. They and their underlying investors were quite pleased. And once any new product works, an increased appetite and increased tolerance to risk develops for all potential new products and loan features. This triggered the development and expansion of more "non-traditional" mortgages, which generally fell somewhere between conforming and subprime loans.

For example, the Alt-A (alternative to conforming "A" business) industry launched to support higher credit–worthy borrowers with loans priced and structured somewhere between typical conforming loans and typical subprime loans. That industry was designed to fill the credit gap between conforming and subprime lending or to support "hybrid" borrowers who were, in some ways, both conforming and subprime. The 125 % LTV product and market sector also came on the scene about the same time. The 125 market, as it was known, made loans to higher credit caliber customers at loan amounts exceeding the values of their properties, up to a maximum of 125% of market value.

Between 1994 and 1998, the 125 market was growing faster than any other sector in lending even though the investment community did not quite know what to make of these loans. Were they real estate secured or not? They were secured by real estate, but not necessarily all the way up to the loan amount. So, not only was there low equity for lender protection, the loans could likely be "upside down," with the loan amount exceeding the value of the property on which the loan was secured. Yet, even that could change over time if property values appreciated, thus increasing the value and effectively reducing the LTV. Were they prime loans because of the higher credit quality of the borrowers or were they subprime because they involved higher risk associated with having less security/ equity? In some ways, they were all these things, and, in some ways, they were none of them. 125s were a true enigma in the marketplace. But whatever they were, they were popular.

The biggest of these 125 lenders was First Plus. You might recall being inundated by all their commercials with Dan Marino as their celebrity spokesperson. First Plus had a lot of "Dan"s. In addition to Dan Marino, they had Director Dan Jesse, Chairman Dan Phillips and Board Member, former VP of the United States, Dan Quayle. Like most other lenders, First Plus started as something else. Originally, it was known as RAC (Remodelers Acceptance Corp). Later, they entered into a capital financing structure with Bank One and changed their name and their business strategy to create and grow a new market.

They were the talk of the industry. Nothing could be discussed or evaluated without First Plus being thrown into the equation for comparison. It was often like the "if we can put a man on the moon, why can't we...fill in the blank" thing. They were the big s---.

Most of these developments within the subprime and non-traditional industries, including national expansion, changed business strategies, new market entrants, higher LTVs, higher debt ratios, easier qualifying standards, YSPs, new products and program variations, etc., were happening with some fair amount of overlap. But, collectively they fueled the uninterrupted expansion of the subprime and non-traditional mortgage industries for the next several years through the middle of 1998.

In August 1998, Russia was ten years out of communism and only ten years into its life as a capitalist democracy. Like most ten year olds, they weren't yet very good at higher math, banking or money management. Then, during the second week of August, Russia's financial markets froze up. Its banks closed shop, the market stopped trading and the government issued a debt moratorium, which prevented the payment of moneys due to western bondholders. The devaluation of the Russian ruble and the financial default of a nuclear power sent shockwaves around the world.

Nervous American investors immediately pulled their money from anything and everything with risk associated with it and transferred their money into the safest known investments – 30-year US Treasuries. This sequence of events resulted in what the capital markets call a liquidity crisis. Money just dried up. There was none available for anything with risk tied to it. This included the purchase of mortgage loan pools, particularly those that did not meet Federally standardized (Fannie Mae/ Freddie Mac) lending guidelines, including all those loans referred to as non-traditional. And, with that, there was no investor demand for non-prime product and the market died. At very least, it went dormant for several years. **This event reiterated one critical and inarguable truth… Investor appetite drives loan origination.**

Admittedly, not much was made at a national level of that crash in 1998. In part, this was because the non-traditional industry (including subprime, jumbo, Alt-A, 125 market, etc.) was relatively small. Most people did not even know about this little, boutique industry. From a capital markets perspective, the crash was not much more than a proverbial thorn in the side of Wall Street. So, they simply pulled that thorn from their collective side and stopped investing in these mortgages. Further, and as evidenced by the fact that no increase was seen in the occurrence of defaults and foreclosures, there was no obvious effect to existing borrowers. Presumably, this was because the Fed held rates fairly steady around the time of the crash and during the years that ARM borrowers had exposure to payment shock.

The lack of negative impact on consumers, in the form of payment shock and foreclosures, kept the industry out of the watchful eye of the consumer advocacy groups and Congress. If anyone was looking, they attributed the problems to the devaluation of the Russian ruble and its affect on tolerance to investment risk in America. No one was blaming the non-prime lenders. We were, in fact, the victims of the overnight shift in the marketplace. To those of us in that industry, the crash was a direct hit. Tens of thousands of people lost their jobs and most non-prime lenders went out of business, including the ten biggest lenders. There were, in fact, very few survivors of that crash.

And what about First Plus and the 125 market? Towards the end of 1998, one of my investor friends called me and let me know what had just happened at First Plus. All the employees were urgently escorted from their headquarters in Mission Viejo, CA at the sound of a fire alarm. Then, while they were out in the parking lot, they were told that the company had shut down. A few at a time, the (now former) employees were escorted back into the building to get their personal belongings. They had a few minutes each. While the other employees waited for their turn out in the parking lot, recruiters, who were given advance notice by First Plus solicited the newly unemployed. In an instant, the company that had been "all that" was no more. For the most part, the rest of the industry followed suit.

There were no winners. Yet arguably, the biggest impact was on the higher credit -risk homeowners who needed competitively priced, non-prime money but were unable to get it.

The recovery after the crash of 1998 was slow and steady. Over time, lenders came back as Wall Street and investors re-developed their appetite for subprime mortgages of all kinds. But lenders who had survived the crash were still licking their wounds and potential entrants into the lending industry were appropriately cautious. It would take a while for lenders to forget that their industry could turn on a dime due to circumstances far beyond their control.

With that, industry growth over the next few years was somewhere north of anemic and somewhere south of prolific. Lenders existed, grew and made some money. Borrowers had access to some capital. Investors had some limited appetite, which, in general, was being met by the supply of loans coming from the lenders. Very slowly, the market started coming back.

About three years after the crash, I turned thirty-eight on September 10, 2001. The next day I woke with a renewed sense of focus, purpose, dedication and enthusiasm. The market.... my market... was coming back. The worst was over. Then the phone rang, and I was directed to the news on TV. Like most everyone else in America, I stared at the TV for the rest of the day and went through the normal sequence of emotions in response to the most devastating terrorist attack in American history. Ironically, this horrific event would prove to be the single most significant catalyst of the forthcoming and unprecedented real estate boom that was not even anywhere in sight!

Within a few months, I had joined Saxon Mortgage, which was headquartered in Glen Allen, Virginia and which was one of the few survivors from the crash of 1998. It was owned by "old Dominion," which was, in fact, so old that its ticker on the NYSE was very simply "d." Mike Sawyer was the President and CEO of Saxon. Some years earlier in our careers, Mike and I had worked across the freeway from each other, and we had done some business together. With his background in capital markets, he coordinated the simultaneous divestiture of Saxon from old Dominion and the IPO (initial purchase offer) of Saxon Mortgage. In lay terms, he moved the company out of its parents' house and then took it public. Admittedly, we were a small publicly traded company, but the move was indicative of the recovery of the subprime and non-traditional mortgage industries.

Not long after joining Saxon, I was called to Virginia for a strategic leadership meeting. At the time, I was more than a little nervous about flying. It's worth noting that I don't really like to drink; I might have a glass of wine or two on Thanksgiving and Christmas, but that's about it. But to me at the time, flying across country was like the pig and chicken story. You know, the one about bacon and eggs where the chicken is involved but the pig has an entirely different level of commitment. I felt very much like the pig.

So, a few strong drinks, a couple xanax and a pre-arranged driver to the hotel later, I was on my way to Virginia. I (vaguely) remember waiting at the baggage carousel after landing. As fate would have it, Mike had just arrived at the same airport from some trip to who knows where. He kindly offered me a lift to my hotel. That's the last thing I remember about that.

The next morning, Mike addressed the leadership group. He opened with a story about how he had run into me in the airport the night before and that he had given me a ride to the hotel. I was starting to get a little nervous about what I might have said. Then he said that we had an insightful conversation in which I had said to him, " it's easy to do the right things when markets are down, but it's hard to do the right things when markets are booming." Oh, from the mouths of drunks.

This was Mike's way of letting us know that we were expected to do the right things, maintain credit quality, enforce all quality control procedures, etc., despite the fact that investors were loosening up and the market was improving. Renewed liberalism by competitors and investors would not, and could not, justify getting away from our core value of process discipline and loan quality at Saxon.

Like the immediately forthcoming and ironic lift created by the recent terrorist attacks, this little message would prove to foreshadow the unprecedented boom in the mortgage industry and its subsequent plunge into the crisis we face today.

Before we move on, let's review the roughly twenty-three years that we've already covered in the first few chapters of this book. To be sure, many other things happened during these same years and up until the present. We've had five different Presidents. Savings & Loans were de-regulated. That industry collapsed, as did the dot-coms a decade later. The junk bond market came and went. Both Houses of Congress changed hands - twice. Military installations were closed in large numbers nationwide as the military was greatly reduced in size. Along with it, the aerospace industry collapsed in on itself. Housing markets boomed and busted. We've been directly involved in three wars and an equal number of invasions.

All of these events, and others too, had some influence on housing and finance. But the key events related to the current mortgage and housing crisis, in chronological order, are:

Pre-1979:   Credit-worthy borrowers obtained loans from government regulated Thrifts. Less-credit-worthy borrowers were dependent on the unregulated, brutal consumer finance industry.

1979:   The Fed raised rates to combat runaway inflation while Thrifts hemorrhaged.

1981:   Congress passed a hefty tax bill to bailout the Thrifts.

The Thrifts unloaded their portfolios of about a trillion dollars.

Salomon Brothers bought the lion's share of that volume and lobbied Congress to use Freddie Mac and Fannie Mae so that loans ineligible for Ginnie Mae approval could still get a government stamp of approval. This allowed SB to convert those loans into bonds and sell them to institutional investors as government backed bonds.

The rest of Wall Street caught on to this trend and joined the game.

1983:   The first CMO (collateralized mortgage obligation) was invented.

1986-1988:   Congress passed the Tax Reform Act of 1986, which eliminated interest deductions on all personal debt with the exception of that paid on home mortgages. This created a strong incentive for homeowners to consolidate all their debt into their mortgages because the interest paid on mortgages would remain tax deductible.

CMOs had become the dominant mechanism on Wall Street for Fannie/Freddie qualified mortgages.

This mechanism drove down rates and created a mortgage and housing boom.

CFCs, which had been the only "legitimate" supply of money to less-credit worthy borrowers, went out of business.

A capital vacuum was created because no legitimate companies were left to meet the needs of these subprime borrowers.

1990:   Two investment banks on Wall Street created the first two subprime mortgage securities.

1991:   Wall Street's appetite for these subprime securities increased dramatically.

Some conforming lenders changed their business models and became non-conforming lenders. Others set up non-conforming divisions.

The need to reach critical mass, and other competitive challenges, forced these lenders to expand nationally and to reach down and out to even riskier borrowers.

1992:   The Co-Originated Securitization was invented.

Wall Street became fully addicted to subprime mortgage securities.

The industry exploded – in a good way. This increased competition continued to put pressure on rates, driving them downward for all subprime borrowers. Basically, this meant that the lenders would earn a lower premium (profit). At the same time, they continued to liberalize credit policy. But the product continued to perform and Wall Street wanted to keep buying it.

Rebate (yield-spread) pricing was introduced to the subprime market. This enticed loan brokers from the conforming industry into the subprime arena.

1994-1998   Prolific market growth, driven by national expansion, changed business strategies, new market entrants, higher LTVs, higher debt ratios, easier qualifying standards, YSPs, new products and program variations, etc.,

New markets were created, including Alt-A and 125s.

1998 (late): The Russian economy collapsed, the ruble was de-valued and the Russian government defaulted on its obligations to western bondholders.

This created panic on Wall Street, which triggered a "flight to quality" and away from risk- any risk. Investors were putting their money primarily in 30-year U.S. treasuries, which were a safe investment.

This created a liquidity crisis, as no one wanted to invest in anything associated with risk.

The Subprime Market crashed. There were very few survivors. Those companies that did remain stayed in a holding pattern for the better part of a couple years.

09/11/2001: Terrorist attacks were launched against the U.S..

The Fed stimulated the economy by dramatically lowering rates.

2002: The subprime market recovered and expanded..

The recovery of 2002 was expedited by the fact that the mechanism for subprime securitization already existed. It had simply been put on the back burner until it was needed, or wanted, again. But mostly, the subprime recovery of 2002 was triggered by the terrorist attacks of 2001 and by the response of the Fed.

Chapter Four: The Fed and the 2/28s

"It is well enough that people of the nation do not understand our banking and monetary system, for if they did, I believe there would be a revolution before tomorrow morning."
- Henry Ford

As the subprime market started to recover from the crash of 1998, most subprime origination continued to be 2/28 ARMs. By definition, all adjustable rate loans are set at some percentage, or spread, above some specific financial "index" such as COFI, prime rate, Fed Funds rate, discount rate and LIBOR to name a few.

LIBOR is the acronym for the London Interbank Offered Rate, which is the benchmark for interest rates on many adjustable rate mortgages, business loans, and financial instruments traded on global financial markets. LIBOR is determined by rates that banks participating in the London money market offer each other for short-term deposits. For all intents and purposes, it's the European version of our Fed rate. Because LIBOR tends to be the most stable index, the subprime market has always been indexed to the 6-month LIBOR. This allows subprime rates to remain relatively stable and not fluctuate by the day or hour, as often happens with conforming rates. This rate stability is important to borrowers, brokers, lenders and investors.

But the rate that we Americans are most familiar with, or at least those we hear the most about is the Federal Funds rate, which is determined by the Fed.

The Fed was created by Congress in 1913 to be the nation's central bank. It has four components:
-   A seven-member Board of Governors, who set monetary policy.
-   A 12 member Federal Open Market Committee (FOMC), who sets the Fed Funds Rate to be charged by Federal Reserve Banks. All Board members sit on the FOMC.
-   Twelve regional member banks located throughout the U.S.
-   Staff economists, who provide reports including Monetary reports to Congress.

In addition to the Congressional charter for the Fed to function as the Central Bank for other banks, the U.S. Government, and foreign banks, the Fed has three other primary responsibilities:

- Control inflation (rise in the cost of goods sold) without triggering a recession.
- Supervise the nation's banking system to protect consumers.
- Maintain the stability of the financial markets and constrain potential crises.

The Fed is further challenged by the fact that these objectives and responsibilities often contradict each other. Such is the case with unemployment, which is directly linked to the stability and growth of financial markets, and inflation, which indicates too much growth. This is why Economics 101 tells us that unemployment and inflation always move in opposite directions. Because the Federal Funds rate directly influences, and is used to maintain, the overall health of the economy, the Fed always has a close eye on the rate it sets.

The Federal Funds rate is the rate that banks charge each other for overnight loans. You might wonder why banks would want or need to borrow overnight cash from each other in the first place. The answer to this also goes right back to the Fed. Not only does the Fed set the rate that banks borrow money from each other, they also regulate the amount of money these banks must have in reserves.

The Fed requires banks to keep a certain amount of cash on hand or as money deposited in one of the twelve Federal Reserve banks. As these reserve requirements are changed, particularly increased, more cash must be kept on hand or on deposit with the Fed making it more difficult (and expensive) for funds to be acquired. This may force banks to borrow from one another in order to meet their reserve requirements with the Fed. But remember, the Fed controls the rate at which these banks can make these overnight loans.

This is why the Fed Funds rate is so important. Any increased cost to banks for borrowing the funds needed to meet their reserve requirements will be compensated for with an increase in that bank's prime rate, which is the rate they charge to their best customers. The same is true, in a reverse manner, if the Fed reduces reserve requirements or reduces the Fed rate. Regardless of direction, the banks pass the effects of the Fed rate changes (or reserve requirements) to the consumers in the form of rates on credit cards, auto loans, personal loans and mortgages.

It is also for this reason that there is no such thing as a single prime lending rate. Wells Fargo may have one prime rate, while Bank of America and Citibank may have another or even two others. Because of this dynamic, the most widely quoted prime rate figure in the United States is the one found in the Wall Street Journal. It represents a polling of the nation's thirty largest banks; when twenty-three of those institutions have changed their prime rates, the WSJ responds by updating the published rate.

A higher Fed Funds rate means banks are less willing to borrow money to keep their reserves at the mandated level. This means they will lend less money out and that the money they do lend will be at a higher rate since they themselves are borrowing money at a higher rate. Since loans are more difficult to get and more expensive, businesses will be less likely to borrow, thus slowing the economy.

In addition, mortgages will become more expensive so homebuyers can only afford smaller loans. This slows down the housing industry. Housing prices go down, homeowners have less net equity in their homes, less available equity to access and, therefore, less money to put back into the economy in the form of small and large consumer purchases.

When the Fed Funds rate is decreased, the opposite occurs. Banks lend more, businesses expand, more jobs are created, home loans are cheaper, the housing market improves, and homeowners obtain home equity loans. They usually use these loans to buy home improvements and new cars, stimulating the overall economy.

While the Federal Funds rate is not the only financial index to which the cost of money is tied, it does directly influence all the other indices. This includes LIBOR, to which all subprime ARMs are indexed.

As this book is not a dissertation on the structure and function of the Fed, we will not go into any more depth on the matter. The main point is to understand that the Fed controls the Fed Funds rate, which has ramifications to any and all other ARM loan indices, including LIBOR, as member banks adjust to recapture additional costs or pass through reduced costs to its consumers. This multiplier effect is the main reason that the Fed is interested in keeping the Fed rate as stable as possible.

To that point, consider that the Fed held rates at a flat 5.5% from April 1997 through September 1998. That's twenty consecutive months with no change in any direction or any amount. Then, things started to happen. From October 1998 through April 2001, the Fed rate went from 5.25 to 5%. A ¼% change in rate over the period of 31 months certainly suggests continued stability. However, the picture changes when you consider what rates did in between those two dates. During those thirty-one months, the Fed rate went as low as 4.75% and as high as 6.5%. The difference between these two rates is 1.75%, represents a 37% swing in the Fed rate over thirty-one months and demonstrates extreme volatility in the market. It also supports my earlier comments and helps explain why growth in the mortgage sector after the crash of 1998 was somewhere between anemic and prolific.

As an analogy, imagine (now, really imagine this) that you are flying comfortably across the country at 40,000 feet. Then somewhere mid-flight, the plane makes a sudden move down to 36,200 feet and then quickly climbs well above the initial cruising altitude of 40,000 feet all the way up to 49,600 feet before it erratically falls back down to about 38,000 feet. I suspect that not too many people, other than adrenaline junkies, would consider this to be a very enjoyable flight. For sure, the seat belt lights would be illuminated and even the flight attendants would be fastened in their seats. All activity, other than the flight itself, would come to a halt until the flight had stabilized. In rate terms, that's exactly what we did during those thirty-one months from October 1998 through April 2001. The uncertainty of the market was reflected in extreme rate volatility, both up and down, which resulted in inconsistent loan origination volume. The market simply did not know where it was going.

Towards the end of that volatile period between October 1998 and April 2001, George W. Bush (43) was elected President and took office. To this day, many economists (and Republicans) claim that Bush (43) inherited a recession left over from the tail end of the Clinton-Gore administration. While this could be debated ad nauseum, it is inarguable that the Fed Funds rate began a free fall starting in the very month Bush took office. Specifically, the Fed rate was 6.5% when Bush took office in January 2001. By September of that same year, it was down to 3.5%. That's a 46% decrease in the Fed rate within eight months!

Many people perceived these rate cuts were implemented as a means to offset rapidly decreasing consumer confidence in the financial markets and the corporate world resulting from one major scandal after another, including Enron, WorldCom, HealthSouth, Tyco and Adelphia. Whatever the cause or the intention, the Fed rate was clearly headed downward, and the Fed was trying to accomplish something with these drastic rate reductions even before we were attacked on September 11, 2001.

So, the Fed had picked a lane and the direction was clear. The only thing that would change would be the pace at which the Fed rate would continue to drop. As described above, rates had already dropped a phenomenal 46% between January 2001 and September 2001. Then, to stimulate the economy after the terrorist attacks, they were reduced another 50% down to 1.75% within just 4 short months. The Fed rate then stayed at that level through the end of 2002. Then they dropped another .5% to 1.25% where they held until mid-2003, when they dropped down to 1%. They stayed at 1% for a full year through the middle of 2004 (graph below).

These historically low Fed rates translated into the lowest mortgage rates in history and the greatest mortgage origination volume in history. Everyone was happy: the borrowers and their brokers, the lenders and mortgage bankers, the conduits and issuers of securities on Wall Street, the Investors who purchased them, the rating agencies that rated the bonds and even the servicing companies. Everyone benefited. This included industry-related participants like builders, title companies, home improvement contractors and consumers. And it included all industries that depended on customers with the cash to buy their products and services. That means that everyone, literally everyone, benefited from this unprecedented and sustained boom. **And the opportunities were not short-lived because, as shown in this graph, the Fed rate didn't return to its pre- 09/11/01 rate of 3.75% until October, 2005, over four years later!!!**

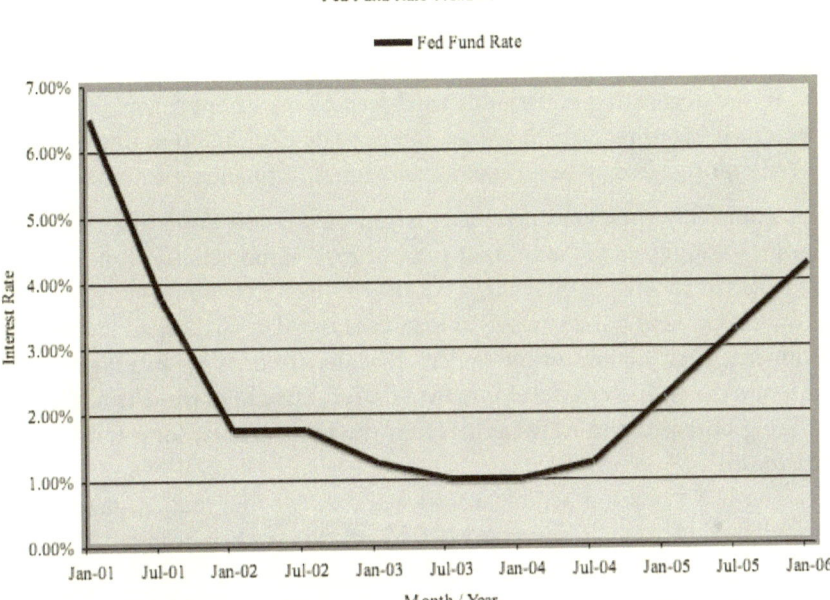

Fed Fund Rate Trend Jan 2001 - Jan 2006

These historically low rates, particularly those available when the Fed rate was held at 1% from mid-2003 through mid-2004, also triggered the sustained expansion of the lending industry itself. Lenders were again popping up everywhere across the country. Wall Street wanted more supply, and more lenders were working to fulfill that demand. But Wall Street wanted more borrowers, not just the same borrowers delivered from more lenders. In many ways, the market looked a lot like it did a few years before the crash of 1998. As we know, back then, the increased demand triggered the creation of new products that supported an entirely new population of subprime borrowers. Wall Street and lenders were looking towards the same solution this time around.

Timing was perfect. In February 2004, Alan Greenspan touted the significance of ARMs and more creative loan products in his speech to the Credit Union National Conference. In that speech he said:

"Indeed, recent research within the Federal Reserve suggests that many homeowners might have saved tens of thousands of dollars had they held adjustable rate mortgages rather than fixed-rate mortgages during the past decade, though this would not have been the case, of course, had rates trended sharply upward."

He then continued:

"American consumers might benefit if lenders provided greater mortgage product alternatives to the traditional fixed-rate mortgage. To the degree that households are driven by fears of payment shocks but are willing to manage their own interest rate risks, the traditional fixed-rate mortgage may be an expensive method of financing a home."

Admittedly, these comments are hedged with Teflon words like "suggests," "might," "though" and "may" that prevent total responsibility from sticking to the Fed or to Greenspan's words. Moreover, I certainly don't know anybody who went out and got a new ARM loan because Alan Greenspan made these comments. Yet, it's impossible to deny that **the effect of his message was to motivate the industry's development of alternative loan products, thereby enticing borrowers to move away from the more stable, long-term fixed-rate loans!**

The U.S stock market and world markets, for that matter, have always moved directly based on what the Fed Chairman says when he says it. Further, any such moves are generally more volatile and extreme if those statements are not expected and if they surprise the market. This would be no exception. In fact, **Wall Street received Greenspan's message loud and clear.**

Their appetite for creative loan products increased immediately, as did the premiums they would begin paying lenders for these loans. These increased premiums translated into lower rates that lenders would have to charge to earn the same profits, and this translated into even higher loan volume. Once again, the demand side of Wall Street went into action, and lenders moved to meet that demand with an increased supply of alternative loan products.

Greenspan never directly encouraged the loosening of credit standards. But lenders and investors know that loosening credit standards is exponentially faster and easier than developing and marketing new and innovative products, and the results often look like new products, or can at least be rationalized as such. Further, this was not an either/or proposition. The development of new products would soon hit full stride. But in the interim, the industry turned to the tried and true strategy of relaxing credit and income standards. Once some lenders started doing this (at the acceptance of Wall Street based on the comments from Greenspan), all other lenders needed to follow suit if they wanted to stay in business. All other things equal (like rate), why would any broker or borrower go to lenders that had tougher standards than other lenders? They wouldn't.

Fairly quickly, loan standards became almost moot. While most lenders did not generally tolerate fraud, it was often not looked for very thoroughly. Anything else, however, was generally good enough to get some type of loan. At a point in time, someone with a credit score below 600 (on a scale of 400-900) and no income documentation could get a loan at 100% of the property's value, even if it was an investment property. The credit standards simply didn't matter very much because the extraordinarily low rates were creating value appreciation that outpaced the structure of the loans.

In simple English, this meant that borrowers, almost regardless of their credit qualifications, paid any way they could in order to protect their growing equity. And investors knew that, as long as values continued to go up, these borrowers would be off the books in two years through refinancing their loans. Investors did not necessarily want the borrowers off the books at two years, but they expected borrowers to pay off at the first re-set. This would ensure that borrowers would not experience any payment shock that might otherwise send them into delinquency.

Unprecedented lending activity should be expected when the Fed rate is so low for so long. For sure, no one was complaining. The economy was being fueled by the Fed's rates. Their strategy had been effective. House prices were going up in amounts never before seen. People were cashing out their equity and spending their proceeds on everything from vacations to cars, other houses, durable goods, business ventures and on and on. The behavior perpetuated the behavior. Rates stayed low, values continued to go up, equity continued to accrue and people became even less concerned about possible payment shock.

They planned on riding the equity train until their prepayment penalties expired, when they could refinance and pull out even more equity. This is what the borrowers wanted and it's what the investors expected. Lenders were the conduits that connected the two interested parties. Even homeowners who didn't seek cash out were actively engaged in the frenzy. Millions of people were refinancing repeatedly to take advantage of rates as they continued going lower. Multiple refinances became something of a competitive bragging right amongst homeowners. And again, no one was complaining.

People who wanted to buy homes were also on the move. With rates so low, people could afford more expensive homes, even if only in the short run. With values increasing so quickly, they needed to get on board or be passed by. They "knew" that they could refinance at more favorable terms in a couple years when the values went up and they had acquired more equity.

But there was a snake in the grass. Remember that one of the main responsibilities of the Fed, if not the main responsibility, is to control inflation. Generally speaking, it represents a persistent increase in the level of consumer prices or a persistent decline in the purchasing power of money. The cause could be either an increase in money supply (increase in money available to consumers), a decrease in the value of money (devaluation) or a decrease in available goods and services that make prices go up. Because inflation is a rise in the general level of prices, it is intrinsically linked to money and leads to the informal definition that "inflation is too many dollars chasing too few goods."

This is exactly what happened when the Fed rate stayed so low for so long. Inadvertently perhaps, the Fed had created the very thing it is obligated to control. Inflation. In response, the Fed began raising rates quickly and dramatically. A funny thing happened as rates starting going up. For a while, even more loans were being made. Anyone who was on the fence and had not moved, began to move. And they moved in enormous numbers. This created the perception that the market was still heating up. So the Fed continued raising rates. In fact, after finishing its yearlong stay at 1% in June 2004, the Fed raised rates 425% (from 1% to 5.25%) within the span of twenty-five months between August 2004 and July 2005, inclusive. Eventually, the borrowers with 2/28s would be faced with the impact of these increased rates.

I'm not suggesting that the Fed shouldn't have lowered rates after the terrorist attacks or even that they shouldn't have held them at 1% for a full year. The Fed has access to information and resources unavailable to the rest of us, and they have responsibilities that often oppose one another. Inarguably, the drastic reduction in rates dramatically stimulated the economy and was presumably needed to stave off a possible catastrophic hit to the economy. It seems that it served its purpose and then some.

Nor am I suggesting that the Fed should not have raised rates so fast once that became necessary. Perhaps, had that action not been taken, the housing bubble would have continued to grow and the consequences might have been even worse than those that we are experiencing now. However, as recently as mid-2007, the only people in the crosshairs of responsibility for this disaster were the guilty, until proven innocent, lenders. Meanwhile, the Fed and its former Chairman Alan Greenspan, were nowhere on the radar. Since then, the Fed and Greenspan have steadily found themselves closer to center-scope. Greenspan himself recently defended his formerly untouchable and unquestionable credibility in an article he wrote, called "The Roots of the Mortgage Crisis," which was published in the Wall Street Journal, Asia on December 13, 2007. Some of the more interesting, albeit confusing, comments are included below:

> On Aug. 9, 2007 and the days immediately following, financial markets in much of the world seized up. Virtually overnight, the seemingly insatiable desire for financial risk came to an abrupt halt as the price of risk unexpectedly surged. Interest rates on a wide variety of asset classes, especially interbank lending, asset-backed commercial paper and junk bonds, rose sharply relative to riskless U.S. Treasury securities. Over the past five years, risk has become historically under-priced as market euphoria, fostered by an unprecedented global growth rate, gained cumulative traction.

> This crisis was thus an accident waiting to happen. If it had not been triggered by the mis-pricing of securitized subprime mortgages, it would have been produced by eruptions in some other market.

> Sharply rising home prices erupted into major housing bubbles world-wide, Japan and Germany (for different reasons) being the only principal exceptions. The Economist's [a financial publication] surveys document the remarkable convergence of more than 20 nations' house price rises during the past decade. U.S. price gains, at their peak, were no more than average.

> After more than a half-century observing numerous price bubbles evolve and deflate, I have reluctantly concluded that bubbles cannot be safely defused by monetary policy or other policy initiatives before the speculative fever breaks on its own. There was clearly little that the world's central banks could do to temper this most recent surge in human euphoria, in some ways reminiscent of the Dutch Tulip craze of the 17th century.

> I do not doubt that a low U.S. Federal-funds rate in response to the dot- com crash, and especially the 1% rate set in mid-2003 to counter potential deflation, lowered interest rates on adjustable rate mortgages (ARMs) and may have contributed to the rise in home prices. In my judgment, however, **the impact on demand for homes financed with ARMs was not major.**

> Demand in those days was driven by the expectation of rising prices - the dynamic that fuels most asset-price bubbles. **If low adjustable –rate financing had not been available, most of the demand would have been financed with fixed-rate, long-term mortgages.** In fact, home prices continued to rise for two years subsequent to the peak of ARM originations (seasonally adjusted).

The current credit crisis will come to an end when the overhang of inventories of newly built homes is largely liquidated, and home price deflation comes to an end. That will stabilize the now-uncertain value of home equity that acts as a buffer for all home mortgages, but most importantly for those held as collateral for residential –backed securities. Very large losses will, no doubt, be taken as a consequence of the crisis. **But after a period of protracted adjustment, the U.S. economy, and the world economy more generally, will be able to get back to business.**

I've read these excerpts repeatedly, and, while I do not have the opportunity to confirm my interpretation with Mr. Greenspan, nor to clear up any possible misunderstandings, I do love to interpret stuff like this; so here goes. The Fed had nothing to do with the problem, couldn't do anything to prevent it and we're screwed (at least until the "protracted adjustment" is complete).

In all seriousness, this is worth some critical analysis. The first contradiction in Greenspan's words appears when he talks about the market events starting "on August 9, 2007 and the days immediately following" as if they were the trigger of the crisis. He elaborates that, at that time, "the seemingly insatiable desire for risk came to an abrupt halt as the price of risk unexpectedly surged." This implies that around August 9, 2007, the market was suddenly hit with a liquidity crisis like the one that tanked the subprime industry in 1998. Frankly, that's more than the tail wagging the dog; that's more like the chihuahua's tail wagging the St. Bernard. The fact is that, by then, we were already deep into this mess. By August 2007, dozens of subprime lenders had closed down, tens of thousands of people had lost their jobs and foreclosures were skyrocketing. **Given the dates and dynamics involved, isn't it more reasonable that the appetite for risk tanked, and the flight to riskless treasuries happened as a result of the subprime collapse rather than being the cause of it?**

The next inconsistency is quite peculiar. Remember, Greenspan's article is called " The Roots of the Mortgage Crisis," not the roots of the current recession, the market collapse, global economic instability, the liquidity crisis or any other thing; just mortgages. He then says that this crisis was an accident waiting to happen, and it would have been triggered by other eruptions in some other market had it not been caused by the mis-pricing of securitized subprime mortgages. Where do you start with this one? Is that to say that if the mortgage crisis had not been caused by the mortgage crisis, it would have been caused by something else?

Further, **is there any recognition on the part of the Fed that the declared mis-pricing of risk (particularly in the subprime arena) may have been influenced by the Greenspan's encouragement in 2004 for the market to pursue new, creative alternatives to traditional fixed-rate loans?** If there is, I certainly don't see it. Then there's the contradiction between the phrases ".... price for risk surged unexpectedly" and "this crisis was thus an accident waiting to happen." Well, which one was it? If it was waiting to happen, then how could it have been unexpected? I don't know what the Fed could have done about the shift, but I do know that they can't have it both ways.

Let's keep going. He cites surveys from The Economist that suggest our housing bubble was remarkably similar to those experienced in more than other twenty other countries. Several questions come to mind. First, does that even matter? Is the Fed's responsibility to keep inflation similar to that experienced by other countries, or is it to control inflation? Is it possible that our Fed rate influenced the cost of money world-wide (by influencing other indices), which then led to their home price appreciation? If that's the case, then it's reasonable to conclude that our home price inflation was "remarkably similar" because we drove those markets as well. Whether the case or not, Greenspan declares that U.S. price gains (presumably means home prices) were no more than average.

Yet, less than four weeks after Greenspan's article was published, on January 4, 2008 Treasury Secretary Henry Paulson said in an interview on CNBC that "the current housing correction was inevitable and necessary following five years of an unsustainable boom which saw sales and home prices hit record levels." In theory, something (in this case, home price increases) can be both "average" and "record highs," but the likelihood is that there is significant disagreement between Greenspan and Paulson.

There is also the fact that while national averages might be similar, we had key economic regions like the northeast and the southwest that were realizing far above average appreciation rates, and these are the same geographies experiencing the greatest de-valuation and highest delinquencies and foreclosures. Statistics can say anything you want them to say. But I do know that the "average" is seldom the best representation of the true picture, and such is the case with home price appreciation in the U.S.

Greenspan then declares that human euphoria is the real driver behind this rise and crash, and loosely compares it to the Dutch tulip craze of about 400 years ago. The implication here is clearly that people's enthusiasm for the housing market was as irrational as the euphoria that drove a craze over flowers. While the tulip craze was truly irrational, you would expect people to wake up one day and say, "These things are only flowers." But the last time

I looked, our primary needs of food, clothing and shelter did not include the need for flowers, tulips or otherwise. People are generally not irrational about housing. They may stretch to get on the train lest it leave them in the distance and forever renting, but that's not necessarily irrational, just risky.

I'm not minimizing the role of consumer behavior, including fraud and euphoria, in this situation; I'm just saying that there is another way to explain it. It's called fear. Many people feared that the prospect of home ownership would get out of their reach and they stretched to buy before that option was gone. Some people of fortunate financial status do not have to worry about these kinds of things and have no fear about them. But the rest of us do.

Take a seat because it's time for a quick story. Just the other night, my wife and I were talking with our younger daughter, Andrea. She is eleven years old and has an extraordinarily high emotional quotient. Well, she got that look on her face and then told us that she was worried. She could not understand how people her age would ever be able to afford to live in California or afford a house like ours. We have a nice home, but it should not be out of reach of anyone's kids.

What my daughter does not know is that within one year of buying our home, almost every neighbor told me they could not afford to buy their same home "now." The price had already gotten out of reach for all of us. Good thing we bought when we did. While eleven-year- olds should not worry about things like this, her thoughts reflect an emotion that seems beyond the reach of certain economists who go by the initials of Alan Greenspan.

Maybe this emotion falls into the camp of irrational exuberance, but the implication is quite different. There's no doubt that low rates fueled the increase in prices, which subsequently fueled the market frenzy with exuberance and fear. The fact is that the euphoria was "enabled" by availability of low rates. There's no getting around that fact, regardless of what Mr. Greenspan might say and no matter what fancy words he might use.

The Fed made dramatic and rapid rate increases without full awareness or understanding of the subprime market and its affect on the economy. Mr. Greenspan's article really supports that point. This is no longer a theoretical argument: we know the consequences of those rate increases. Yet, in light of all the delinquencies, foreclosures, company closures, rise in unemployment to the highest level in years, rapid home price devaluation, decreases to the Fed rate, Federal economic stimulus packages to minimize the impact of the crisis, Greenspan still denies the Fed's role in this mess.

I can think of only three possible explanations. One, he never "got it" and still doesn't get it. He's just too far out of touch with the economy and the average American people who depend on it. Two, he knows the truth but is not willing to accept responsibility for it: in other words, he's in full CYA mode. Or three, he cannot afford to be candid because he still has the clout to create even larger and more negative consequences. I don't know which is the case here, but I do know that the Fed played a major role in this disaster.

To be fair, I acknowledge that there was a lot more information in that article and that I only selected relevant statements. I intentionally omitted references to the cold war, global savings rates, the negative arbitrage of equity premiums and real estate capitalization rates, the central banks' loss of control over longer term interest rates and the diminished scope of national governments to affect the paths of their governments. Such omissions were on purpose and stemmed from the fact that either they didn't really matter or, more likely, because they were confusing smokescreens that further deflected responsibility away from the Fed.

As far as this mortgage disaster is concerned, the real issue is not how far the Fed lowered rates or even how long the rates remained that low. Those are simply matters of opportunity duration, or said another way, the longer they stayed lower, the more time more people had to obtain loans. That's common sense. **The real issue is how quickly rates were raised after being so low for so long.**

The fact is that the Fed raised rates seventeen consecutive times from 1% in June 2004 to 5.25% in July 2006. This may have been necessary to slow down inflation and home price appreciation in particular. However, we know that the increases were made without full recognition, awareness and consideration for the magnitude of subprime loans that their previous policies had helped create nor the structure of these subprime loans that had saturated the market place.

Again, we know this is true because after these loans started to re-set and the pending damage became more real and more obvious, the Fed started lowering rates in October 2007. They have continued to lower them down to 2.00% through June 2008. We know the Fed Funds rate wasn't lowered for any other reason, because, while Wall Street had taken investors for something of a roller coaster throughout 2007, on whole, the market was up by 271 points by the end of the year.

Therefore, it's reasonable to conclude that the subsequent reductions to the Fed rate were driven primarily by the subprime crisis (as far as the Fed was concerned) and its possible affect on the housing market and on the rest of the economy. Had the Fed known they would need to lower rates again in the near future as a result of a pending mortgage disaster, would they have raised them so far and so quickly in the first place? Of course not. And that's why we know that the rapid and sustained rate increases were made without full awareness or understanding of the subprime market and its potential affect on the economy.

As described in the last chapter, the 2/28 ARM was designed specifically to meet the needs of the subprime borrower, and it had done so consistently for fifteen years. But it was not designed to accommodate such rapid, dramatic and sustained increases in the Fed rate. Through all of this expansion, 2/28s still represented about 85% of all subprime production. The only situation that could have created a real problem is if rates were increased dramatically during the two year introductory period and credit policies were substantially restricted such that borrowers became unable to refinance after two years. It was within the realm of possibility, but not anticipated. Then, exactly that dynamic happened, and the house of cards came tumbling down.

Understanding how 2/28 ARM loans are structured is key to understanding how the problem developed in the wake of rapidly increasing Fed rates. There's always a risk when painting an entire industry with one broad brush. So let me be clear that every lender did not do things as I am about to describe, and there was some industry variation on different aspects of loan structures and lending processes. But those would be exceptions to the rule.

Before getting into that, let's take another look at the Fed and LIBOR rate trends from 2001 and forward. Consider these trends in the context of a subprime market saturated by 2/28 loans that were especially vulnerable to such rate increases. The 2/28s that were originated between January 2003 and July 2004 began to re-set between January 2005 and July 2006, respectively. These latter loans originated around July 2004 were subject to a 320% increase (from 1.25% to 4.25%) by their first re-set! Now, that is payment shock!

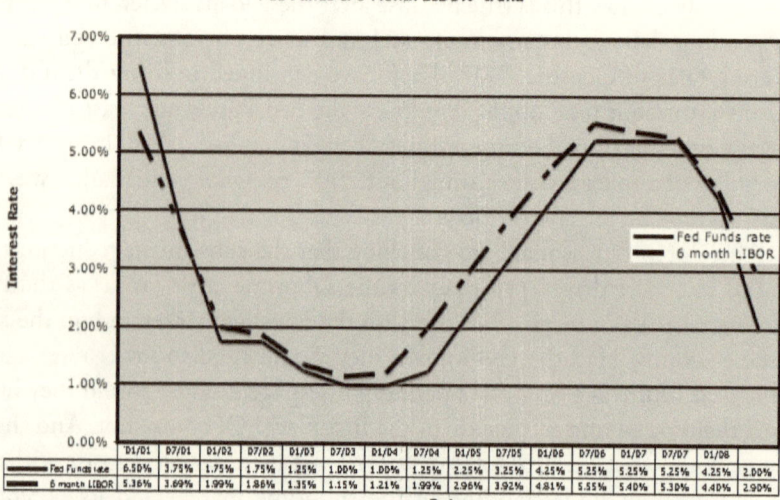

Fed Funds & 6 Month LIBOR- trend

	D1/01	D7/01	D1/02	D7/02	D1/03	D7/03	D1/04	D7/04	D1/05	D7/05	D1/06	D7/06	D1/07	D7/07	D1/08
Fed Funds rate	6.50%	3.75%	1.75%	1.75%	1.25%	1.00%	1.00%	1.25%	2.25%	3.25%	4.25%	5.25%	5.25%	5.25%	4.25%	2.00%
6 month LIBOR	5.36%	3.09%	1.99%	1.86%	1.35%	1.15%	1.21%	1.99%	2.96%	3.92%	4.81%	5.55%	5.40%	5.30%	4.40%	2.90%

Date

As a very general overview, most subprime loans were 2/28s, which means the rate was fixed at some discounted amount for the first two years, after which it converted to an adjustable rate loan for the next 28 years. During those twenty-eight years, the loan could adjust every six months. The new rate at each adjustment would be based on LIBOR when the loan funded, plus the margin that was established for the borrower based on their credit and risk profile ("grade"). While this spread would be different for different credit grades and borrowers based on their assessed risk, a 5% margin would have been considered typical.

In order to avoid significant "payment shock," or at least to spread it out into more manageable chunks, these ARM loans had three types of payment adjustment caps. Each of them influenced the amount of rate and payment shock a borrower would be exposed to at different adjustment intervals and over the life of their loan. A typical subprime 2/28 loan would have a 3/1/6 cap structure. This means that the first, or initial, rate cap would be limited to a maximum of 3% over the start rate. Then any future "periodic" rate changes would be limited to a maximum of 1% every six months. And finally, the rate could never exceed the "life cap" of 6% over the start rate.

This means that in a rapidly rising rate environment, these subprime 2/28s could go from the expiration of a discounted start rate to the ceiling with just four payment increases over a period of only eighteen months. In a worst-case scenario, the rate would increase by 3% at the two-year mark and then another 1% in each of the next three adjustments at six-month intervals. To make matters even more challenging, if the initial discounted start rate were anything less than 6% and rates went up at this pace, borrowers would be faced with more than a doubling of their monthly payment between months twenty-four and forty-two!

To illustrate the sensitivity of 2/28 loans to quickly rising interest rates, let's look at a hypothetical loan under three different market dynamics as shown in the following chart. For comparison, the loan amount is $150,000 with a 5% margin, a 2% discount for the first two years and a 3/1/6 cap structure. The rate increases used for comparison are based on the actual increases to the Fed rate over the measured timelines. For simplicity, a couple assumptions are made that have little to no real effect on the outcome.

The first example reflects the actual changes in the Fed rate between mid- 2003 when the Fed first lowered rates to 1% and mid-2005 when any 2/28s made in mid-2003 would have started to re-set. In this example, the payment associated with the discounted start rate would have been $729. The first re-set at two years would have taken the payment to $1,013, then to $1,116 six months later, then $1,233 six months after that and to $1,333 when the loan hit its life cap six months later. At this point, the Fed rate stabilized such that the payment would not have changed until a year later when it would have dropped back down to $1,250 as a result of a reduction to the Fed rate.

These payment changes caused incremental (at each re-set) payment shock of 39%,10%,10%, 8%, 0% and (6%) respectively, where "( )" represents a negative adjustment or a payment decrease. This corresponds to a 71% cumulative payment shock over the first four and a half years of the loan. More importantly, the borrowers would have experienced an 83% payment shock at the peak which would have lasted for a full year! Moreover, that 83% payment shock would have been realized within a period of just eighteen months following the first re-set.

It's easy to get lost in the numbers, but imagine what would happen if you had a $150,000 loan and the payment went from $729 to $1,013 and then went steadily upward to $1,333 before coming back down to $1,250. Even at that level, the payment would have been $521 higher than the initial payment of $729. In the interim, the loan would have been subject to foreclosure action at any point the borrower became unable to pay for the increase.

The second example reveals what would have happened with the same rate structure under the assumption that the Fed rate (and, therefore LIBOR) remained unchanged. The initial payment associated with the discounted start rate would have been $729. At two years, that would have adjusted up to $914 with the elimination of the 2% discount. Admittedly, this represents an initial payment shock of 25%; however, that's significantly lower than the initial payment shock of 39% shown in the earlier example, and it's drastically lower than the maximum payment shock of 83% in the example above. This is an extreme example because everyone expects the Fed rate and LIBOR to change. Yet, it shows mathematically that, increases in the Fed rate are clearly the driving force behind the payment shock.

Now, let's look at a hypothetical example where the 2% discount is removed while everything else, including the actual increase to the Fed rate, remains the same. This means that the ARM has a fixed introductory period of two years, but that rate is not discounted (no tease) from the initial fully indexed rate. **In this case, any and all increases in payments would be a function solely of increases to the Fed rate and not due to the structure of the loans.**

Our $150,000 loan would have an initial payment of $866 which would subsequently increase to $1,145 at the first re-set in 2 years and then to $1,241 six months later. This would be followed six months later by an increase to $1,322 where it would have stabilized to a large extent for about a year, along with the Fed rate, during which time it would have dropped slightly to $1,305 and then ticked back up to $1,350 six months later. It would have come back down to $1,196 as the Fed lowered rates simultaneous with the most recent re-set.

In this example, the borrower would have experienced 32%, 8%,7%, (1%), 3% and (11%) incremental payment shock respectively with each re-set. This means the borrower would have experienced a 38% increase in their payment from the initial payment, but only after enduring pay shock as high as 56% payment increase between the 5th and 6th adjustment.

This third example is extremely important because it takes away the initial two-year discount, which is the most criticized aspect of the subprime 2/28s. Further, it means that the majority of actual payment shock was caused only by the rate increases made by the Fed. Now, consider how many people could afford to increase their mortgage payments by 56%, or even 38%, and keep their loans current. I can assure you that in the subprime world, the number is very low.

We've all heard that a "picture is worth a thousand words." In the world of analytics, I'd say that a good graph is worth even more. The information in the previous three scenarios is shown on the following graph. It clearly shows that **the 2/28 structure exposed borrowers to some payment shock. It also shows that increases to the Fed rate had significantly more impact. It also shows that the big impact was caused by the combination of the two factors.**

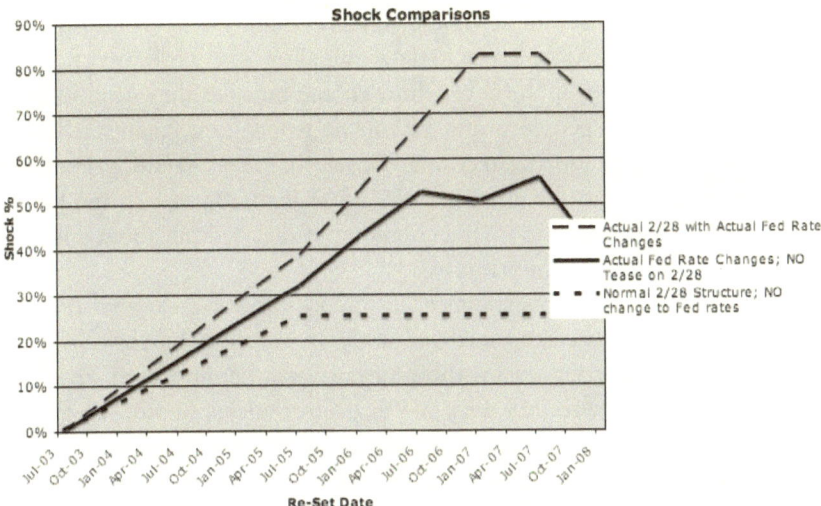

Ordinarily, none of these adjustments would have triggered massive delinquencies and defaults because the borrowers would have just refinanced to a new 2/28 loan at the first re-set. As a result, they would never have experienced the extreme payment shock shown in these examples. While their rates would have gone up on their new loan as a result of the increase in the Fed Funds rate, their payment would not have changed much. The discounted start rate for the first two years on the new loan would have kept the payment increase to a minimum.

For the record, we would see nearly identical results if we were to look at loans that funded around mid-2004 which represented the end of the Fed rate's stay at 1%, and mid-2006 when any 2/28s would have started to re-set. Even though the Fed rate increased faster and higher during that two-year period than during the mid-2003 to mid-2005 time frame, the results are virtually the same because the 3/1/6 cap structure of the 2/28s limited the effect of Fed rate increases.

This analysis, while somewhat technical, is very important. **There would have been two simple questions for the Fed to have asked and answered before increasing rates. First, if we make these changes, what will be the affect on subprime loans and more importantly, to the borrowers who are obligated to pay them? Secondly, how many loans and borrowers will be affected? In the light of the answers, the Fed may still have decided to raise rates.**

However, and this is a critical point, they would have had two years before the first re-sets to work with Congress, the Treasury Department, lending coalitions, Wall Street, rating agencies, etc., in order to develop a plan to avoid the inevitable payment shock suffered by these borrowers. With all the Fed's resources, it should have been fairly easy to measure the quantitative affect on ARM loans, to determine how many trillions of dollars in subprime loans were on the books, how far and how fast they would adjust, and also, how many people would be unable to pay as a result. Sadly, the Fed did not understand the affect that the rate increases would have on the mortgage industry and the existing 2/28 ARM loans already on the books. Either that, or they understood, but chose not to do anything about it during the two-year window of opportunity.

So let's wrap up all this technical mumbo jumbo. Here's what matters. 2/28 ARMs were created to meet the needs of subprime borrowers, which they did for about fifteen years without negative market impact or consumer pain. However, they were not designed to protect against rapid, drastic and sequential rate increases by the Fed over a very short period of time that started immediately after the Chairman of the Fed encouraged the market to create more of these product types. We know the decision to raise rates quickly was made without full consideration of the subprime market because, once the logical results occurred and the damage was done, the Fed started lowering rates again to correct the problem.

The Fed is in no way responsible for the structure of 2/28s that represent the vast majority of subprime loans. These loans existed and performed successfully over fifteen years while the Fed rate went up and down. However, the Fed did have three major influences over the mortgage market and resulting mortgage and housing crisis.

1) They fueled secondary market (investor) euphoria by touting the benefits of ARM vs. fixed-rate loans and encouraged the development of new and innovative products to function as viable alternatives to standard, long-term fixed-rates. As an aside, they later cited the mis-pricing of risk as the root of the crisis, but they made no connection between their own role in fueling the euphoria and the subsequent mis-pricing of risk associated with these new, innovative and expanded products.

2) They raised the rates by 325 basis points (3.25%) over twenty-four months and 425 basis points over thirty-six months. This slowed the housing market and, therefore, relieved some of the inflationary pressure caused largely by appreciation in the housing market. This dramatically slowed the appreciation rate of housing and, in some areas, even caused home price deflation. Either way, this made it much more difficult for people to refinance at the two year re-set. The cause and effect is fairly straightforward: as values flatten or decline, loan to value ratios (LTVs) go up (if for no other reason than to pay the fees associated with the new loan), and higher LTVs trigger higher rates because of the greater risk associated with having less equity.

3) Lower property values prevented existing borrowers from being able to refinance and exposed them to the payment shock associated with the loan structure and by the increase in the Fed rate over a couple short years. This created the increase in delinquency and foreclosures that generated the attention of consumer advocacy groups and Congress.

As a side note, the Fed has recently been making some noise about having lowered rates under the premise or assumption that lenders would engage only in responsible lending. This makes it worth repeating that the issue was not that rates were low or even for how long they were kept low. **The trigger is how quickly rates were raised once that cycle began.** Clearly, loan parameters and credit policies had become stretched, but that doesn't make a market crash. Having said that, **let's take a look at Congress, the Treasury and five Regulatory Agencies to understand how their efforts, combined with the Fed's decisions about rates, created a borrower trap that froze the market.**

Chapter Five: The IAG

"I don't believe in a government that protects us from ourselves."
- Ronald Reagan

Have you ever heard of the IAG? Do you know how it has influenced this mortgage and housing crisis? Most people do not. But they need to. Around the middle part of 2005, key representatives and executives from various government regulatory agencies started to openly discuss their collective concerns about non-traditional lending. These discussions specifically included so-called "exotic" products that involved the potential for negative amortization (where the loan balance can increase) and interest-only payments loans but specifically excluded subprime mortgages.

The member agencies were limited exclusively to the Board of Governors of the Federal Reserve System (the Fed), the Federal Deposit Insurance Corporation (the FDIC), the National Credit Union Administration, the Office of Thrift Supervision (the OTS) and the Office of the Comptroller of the Currency (the OCC). The OTS and the OCC are organized under the direction of the US Treasury Department, which, at the time, was led by Treasury Secretary John Snow. In turn, the Secretary of the Treasury reports to the President of the United States.

About six months later, on December 29, 2005 this group published for comment proposed Interagency Guidance on Non-traditional Mortgage Products. Over the next several months, the group considered and discussed various comments it had received from respondents. Then, on October 4, 2006 slightly more than nine months later, they released their "Final Interagency Guidance on Non-traditional Mortgage Product Risks."

This document quickly became known as the Interagency Guidance, or the IAG. But, no matter what it was called, it would immediately and dramatically change the world of lending for everyone. The "Final IAG" document and its attachments are forty-five pages long from which the Background section says:

> The Agencies developed this guidance to address risks associated with the growing use of mortgage products that allow borrowers to defer payment of principal and, sometimes, interest. These products, referred to variously as "non-traditional," "alternative," or "exotic" mortgage loans (hereinafter referred to as non-traditional mortgage loans), include "interest-only" mortgages and "payment option"

adjustable-rate mortgages. These products allow borrowers to exchange lower payments during an initial period for higher payments during a later amortization period.

While similar products have been available for many years, the number of institutions offering them has expanded rapidly. At the same time, these products are offered to a wider spectrum of borrowers who may not otherwise qualify for more traditional mortgages. The Agencies are concerned that some borrowers may not fully understand the risks of these products. While many of the risks exist in other adjustable-rate mortgage products, the Agencies' concern is elevated with non-traditional products because of the lack of principal amortization and potential for negative amortization.

That language should not be glossed over. **This document is *the* watershed event that triggered this crisis.** Do you see anything in the background section that refers to subprime loans or increases in delinquency, defaults and foreclosures? It's not there. Yet, consider the fact that the Agencies started working on this document in the middle of 2005, then released a draft by the very end of 2005 followed by over nine months of commentary and revision before the final IAG was published on October 4, 2006. Yet, in that span of one and a half years, the pending crisis in the subprime market was never their focus. In fact, subprime loans were not even covered by the Final IAG!

In no small way, there was another dynamic at play in this equation. In between the dates that the draft was published and the date that the Final IAG was released, there was turnover at the helm of the Fed and at the Treasury Department. Ben Bernanke stepped in as the new Chairman of the Fed in February 2006 and Henry Paulson stepped in as Treasury Secretary in July of that same year. Because Paulson was recruited out of the private sector, it's possible that he had little to no involvement or detailed awareness of the IAG when he stepped into office. Bernanke, on the other hand, was appointed to his new position from within the Federal Reserve System and was more likely to be familiar with the IAG project. Either way, three of the five Agencies involved in the IAG were ultimately overseen by organizations (the Fed and the Treasury) that were in the midst of leadership transition.

Looking again at the background section of the IAG for a moment, it's clear that the IAG was written in response to non-traditional products, not subprime products. In fact, the very mention of subprime loans was deflected by referring us back to years' old guidance that was published in early 2001. As a reminder, there are three types of mortgages. Conforming loans meet government standards and are Fannie Mae / Freddie Mac eligible and approved. Non-traditional loans are generally made to conforming quality borrowers, but with terms or documentation that might be considered "exotic." Subprime loans capture everything else but are not limited to people with credit and income problems. While there is no strict dividing line between non-traditional and subprime loans, the industry recognizes that they are two different things.

To that point, the Final IAG (October 4, 2006) said:

> Mortgage programs that target subprime borrowers through tailored marketing, underwriting standards, and risk selection should follow the applicable interagency guidance on subprime lending. Among other things, the subprime guidance discusses circumstances under which subprime lending can become predatory or abusive. Institutions designing non-traditional mortgage loans for subprime borrowers should pay particular attention to this guidance. They should also recognize that risk-layering features in loans to subprime borrowers may significantly increase risks for both the institution and the borrower.

Furthermore, their frame of reference was not a rise in delinquencies or foreclosures. Rather, it was the dramatic rise in the number of institutions offering non-traditional products along with the possibility that these borrowers did not, or would not, truly understand the lack of principal reduction and the potential for negative amortization on these loans.

Because this is a critical point, it bears repeating. **The five Regulatory Agencies spent *over one and a half years* finalizing the IAG, which was published in October 2006. The IAG was limited to non-traditional mortgage products and *excluded* subprime mortgages altogether.** The driving force was not delinquency nor foreclosures, but a concern in the number of institutions offering these non-traditional products.

This is very interesting because, by that time, delinquencies on subprime loans had started growing in numbers that could not be missed or ignored. As shown in the graph from the previous chapter, the first payment re-set shock would occur around the middle of 2005 on ARM loans that were originated when the Fed rate was originally reduced to 1% in mid-2003. As would be expected for most borrowers exposed to a 39% increase in their monthly mortgage payments, these loans started going delinquent in droves.

Yet, at this time (late 2005-early 2006), the IAG had already been drafted and was out for comment. It was still the better part of a year from being finalized. Still, nothing was being done in response to the surge in subprime delinquencies and foreclosures even though they were beginning to flood the market. The Agencies were staying true to their concern about non-traditional loans, even though these loans were not going delinquent or into foreclosure in unusual numbers. So what were the Agencies so worried about that they would stay the course on non-traditional loans and disregard the groundswell in the subprime industry?

The answer is found in the background section of the IAG. They were concerned about the rapid proliferation of alternative products, which were taking over the marketplace. Option ARMs, Neg Ams, Interest Only, Alternative Income Doc loans and Stated Income loans were the uninterrupted rage.

The Agencies knew this was true because they regulated, evaluated and audited the lending practices of their member institutions. They also knew it because nearly two years earlier Greenspan delivered his speech to the National Credit Union Association at which he said, as cited earlier:

> "American consumers might benefit if lenders provided
> greater mortgage product alternatives to the traditional fixed-
> rate mortgage. To the degree that households are driven by fears
> of payment shocks, but are willing to manage their own interest
> rate risks, the traditional fixed-rate mortgage may be an expensive
> method of financing a home."

Paradoxically, Greenspan had given the green light for the development and proliferation of non-traditional, exotic and alternative loan products and then got to work, along with the Fed's Interagency counterparts, on methods to minimize and restrict the production of those products. In the interim, however, those products were dominating the market. Unfortunately, this would not be the last example of illogical steps made in the wrong order.

During the creation of the IAG, arguments were raised by some politicians, consumer advocacy groups and the lending industry that the proposed IAG was too restrictive and prescriptive. Others argued it didn't go far enough, and still others voiced concerns that the guidance would not apply to all lenders since all lenders were not regulated by at least one of the agencies.

The IAG addressed issues regarding collateral dependence where borrowers would "need" to sell their home once the loan re-set, regarding risk-layering where non-traditional features are combined such as interest-only amortization with reduced income documentation and regarding non-owner-occupied loans.

The most significant requirement of the guidance included the expectation that interest-only ARM loans and payment-option ARM loans should be underwritten and qualified at the fully indexed rate and not at the discounted start rate. This would obviously put a significant hit on borrowers, lenders and investors who had all become familiar with the latter approach. This brings us to the word "guidance" which is included in the title of the document and which implies some level of flexibility and voluntary adoption. The reality, however, is that "guidance" is just a politically correct word for "mandatory."

Because the IAG is quite lengthy and detailed, several key passages have been isolated for simplicity and discussion:

> Given the potential for heightened risk levels, management *should* carefully *consider* and appropriately *mitigate* exposures created by these loans.
>
> Institutions *should* use this guidance to ensure that risk management practices *adequately* address these risks.
>
> Institutions with *sound* underwriting, *adequate* risk management, and *acceptable* portfolio performance will not be subject to criticism merely for offering such products.
>
> Underwriting standards *should* address the effect of a *substantial* payment increase on the borrower's capacity to repay.
>
> Loan terms *should* be based on a disciplined analysis of potential exposures and *compensating* factors to ensure risk levels remain *manageable*.
>
> An institution's qualifying standards *should* recognize the *potential* impact of payment shock, especially for borrowers with *high* loan-to-value (LTV) ratios, *high* debt-to-income (DTI) ratios, and *low* credit scores.
>
> The criteria *should* be based upon prudent and appropriate underwriting standards, considering both the borrower's characteristics and the product's attributes.
>
> Loan approvals *should* include an evaluation of their ability to repay the debt by final maturity at the fully indexed rate, assuming a fully amortizing repayment schedule.
>
> The analysis of repayment capacity *should avoid over-reliance* on credit scores as a substitute for income verification.

The *higher* a loan's credit risk, either from loan features or borrower characteristics, the *more important* it is to verify the borrower's income, assets, and outstanding liabilities.

An institution *should* demonstrate that *mitigating* factors support the underwriting decision and the borrower's repayment capacity.

Clear policies *should* govern the use of reduced documentation. For example, stated income *should* be accepted only if there are *mitigating* factors.

Loans with *minimal* or no owner equity generally *should not* have a payment structure that allows for delayed or negative amortization without other significant *risk mitigating factors*.

Non-Owner-Occupied Investor Loans *should* qualify based on [the borrower's] ability to service the debt over the life of the loan. Loan terms *should* reflect an *appropriate* combined LTV ratio that considers the potential for negative amortization and maintains *sufficient* borrower equity over the life of the loan. Further, underwriting standards *should* require evidence that the borrower has *sufficient* cash reserves to service the loan, considering the possibility of *extended* periods of property vacancy and the variability of debt service requirements associated with non-traditional mortgage loan products.

In addition to these excerpts, there is also a bunch of language about portfolio and risk management practices, policies, concentrations, controls, third party origination, secondary market activity, management information and reporting, stress testing, capital and allowance for loan and lease losses, consumer protection issues and legal issues.

Lenders quickly determined that the "guidance" had three main implications. First, lenders knew that individual states across the country would likely use the IAG as a framework from which to establish their own tightened and restrictive lending laws and regulations. Second, they expected the guidelines to be viewed as the standards for unfair and deceptive loan practice lawsuits which might be brought about in the future at the state level. And third, lenders accurately expected investors to require that loans they purchased to be written in accordance with the guidance.

The mathematical implications for lenders were easy to measure. Each lender could simply determine what percentage of applicable loans they had funded that would no longer qualify at the fully indexed rate. While the percentage varied from lender to lender, the range was about 30%-60% fallout from this one, single restriction. The impact of risk-layering criteria was more difficult to measure as the criteria were not exact and because they were subject to offsetting factors, such as low LTVs and higher cash reserves. But, if nothing else, the new criterion made lenders and investors more cautious and less flexible.

Worse than the rules themselves is their vagueness and ambiguity. The italicized words in the selected excerpts from the IAG offer a significant amount of wiggle room and flexibility. While those things are good for regulators and politicians, they are nightmares for lenders. And while the "guidance" looks reasonable, it's not really guidance at all. From a lending perspective, it's the law. And it's vague law, exposing lenders to open-ended responsibility and litigation.

Because the potential consequences were unacceptable to lenders, the new standards were never truly implemented by the industry. Instead, lenders just threw in the towel and stopped offering any products and features that could fall under the umbrella of the IAG. Even if they had not done that, the products still would have gone away. The fact is that few, if any, non-conforming borrowers would qualify under the new criterion. Therefore, even if lenders wanted to offer the products, they would not do it because there would be too much loan fallout (loans funded as a percentage of applications received) and too much inefficiency. Lenders would have no cost-effective way of offering the products, which would cause them to lose money and, ultimately, go out of business.

This deadly combination of ambiguity, consequences and inefficiency was too much for the industry to stomach. So away went all non-traditional products and features, including jumbo loan amounts, loans to self-employed borrowers, reduced income documentation, alternative income documentation (Alt-A), Neg Ams, Option ARMs, non-owner occupied loans, second trust deeds (lines, loans and simultaneous 2nds) anything with non-conforming (layered) credit risk and almost all ARM loans. Away went almost everything except conforming, long-term fixed-rate loans to borrowers with strong credit and fully verifiable income from an employer.

Most of the lenders regulated by any of the five Agencies shifted their resources and business strategies back to the conforming industry exclusively. Technically speaking, however, subprime loans were still undefined by, and excluded from, the IAG. Therefore, the subprime industry was scratching its collective head. Unlike most regulated lenders who had delved down into the non-traditional and subprime markets, the subprime lenders did not have the ability to immediately shift all resources to conforming products because these were never even part of their product menus.

Subprime lenders knew that everything they funded met the characteristics included in the IAG but they did not know if the IAG would apply to them as most of these lenders were non-regulated. These lenders were trying to determine if they needed to abide by the IAG and whether investment banks would continue to buy subprime loans if the lenders continued to fund them. This was no conceptual or philosophical debate. This was about survival. The lenders knew they would suffer a knockout blow if it were determined that they needed to abide by the IAG.

They also knew there would be no lead time if the investment banks simply decided to stop buying subprime loans. The industry was just waiting for that final punch. Meanwhile, they were fighting for market share, to control costs, to stop losses, to fend off repurchase demands and to keep their doors open. Virtually every subprime lender who had not shut down was for sale. The ship was sinking.

Then, within six weeks after the release of the Final IAG, the national mid-term elections were held on Tuesday, November 7, 2006. By the end of the night, it was clear that both Houses of Congress were going to be turned back over to the Democrats for the first time in more than a decade. Key committee chairs were established by inauguration day on January 4, 2007. This included Barney Frank (D-MA) as Chairman of the House Financial Services Committee and Christopher Dodd (D-CT) (who, until early 2008, was a Democratic Presidential candidate) as Chairman of the Senate Banking, Housing and Urban Affairs Committee.

Even before Inauguration Day, however, the Congressional wheels were already in motion. On December 7, 2006, about five weeks after the IAG had been finalized, six members of the Senate Committee on Banking, Housing and Urban Affairs sent a request letter to the heads of each of the Agencies. The recipients included Ben Bernanke, the new Chairman of the Fed, and the letter was signed by Senators Sarbanes (of Sarbanes –Oxley fame), Allard, Dodd (the Committee's incoming Chairman), Bunning, Reed and Schumer.

Their objective was to convince the agencies to amend the IAG and include subprime lending within its scope. As with most government memos, there was a lot of rhetoric about nothing. Then there's the important stuff that is sort of buried in the text. This memo was no exception. They went through the obligatory applause of the agencies' efforts, the value of their decisions, etc. But the essence of the document was to request that the Agencies include subprime 2/28s within the context of the IAG. Logically, that's no great stretch and an argument can be made for including it. But there was something bigger going on.

It may sound like a good thing to American homeowners that some members of Congress finally had the necessary evidence to support their objectives so that they could stop predatory lenders and help the perceived victims – the subprime borrowers. But let's take a closer look.

Philosophically, you can decide for yourself whether people should have the right to make their own financial decisions and have access to equity they have acquired. These may seem so basic and fundamental that you might take them for granted. I will offer a word to anyone who does take these rights for granted: **don't.**

If you think I might be making something out of nothing, consider a couple cases in point. Neither of them had anything to do with Congress itself, but they have everything to do with the potential affect of legislative action - in these cases, at the state level.

The first example has to do with the state of Texas. Until 1997, homeowners had no ability to access their equity by any means other than selling their homes. Cash out equity loans were prohibited by the state constitution. In order to change this, they needed to do more than create a new law. They had to amend their State Constitution, which speaks to the importance of lifting the restrictions placed on homeowners. This took years of lobbying from various groups, but, ultimately, it happened. The result was that "overnight" billions of dollars in acquired equity was unlocked, and people started to access it.

But lenders were not yet so eager. Many rules were attached to the new lending laws, including different disclosure language, expiration periods, required documents and limits on the number of times borrowers could refinance in a specific period of time. They implemented a unique concept that once they obtained any cash out from their acquired equity, any subsequent loan with those owners on that property would also be considered a cash out loan, even if there was no cash out received. While all of this was new to the lenders and took some getting use to, the potential consequences were immediately clear. Lenders knew that any violation of the state's requirements would be considered non-remedial. This meant that the lenders would not have the ability to correct even minor and /or unintentional mistakes. The penalty for those mistakes could be the lender's forfeiture of the security on the loan.

The upside to lenders was the possibility of accessing an un-tapped market. The down-side was forfeiting their security if they made a mistake. While I never heard of this happening, lenders understood the situation. So, growth in Texas took longer than expected. But eventually, it ramped up. In order to be closer to the front line, and to minimize the possibility of such costly mistakes, many lenders relocated to Texas. Others opened branches there or acquired companies that were already there.

The second, and even better example, involves the state of Georgia. On October 1, 2002, Georgia enacted the most stringent anti-predatory lending laws in the country. The Georgia Fair Lending Act (GAFLA) had a complicated three-tiered loan classification system including "home loans," "covered loans" and "high cost loans." The act allowed for different provisions for each of the three types of mortgages, but in all cases applied a unique definition of points and fees that was difficult if not impossible to implement consistently in practice.

Further, GAFLA clarified that any person who purchased or who was otherwise assigned a high-cost loan was subject to all affirmative claims and any defenses with respect to the loan that the borrower could assert against the original creditor or creditors of the loan. Simply interpreted; anyone who touched the loan downstream was as financially liable as was the original lender.

In response to this punitive system, by January 2003 all three major rating agencies, including Moody's, Fitch and Standard & Poor's, announced that that they would not rate any mortgage securities (pools of loans held by investors) that had any loans in them which were secured by properties in the state of Georgia. Notice I did not say subprime loans. GAFLA, in fact, applied to all mortgages. As a result, the rating agencies would not touch them, whether they were originated by some little Correspondent lender or by Bank of America, Wells Fargo or Countrywide.

The reaction of the rating agencies had nothing to do with the lenders. It had everything to do with the restrictions, ambiguity and penalties associated with the new laws. Lenders, knowing that they could not get their securities rated (and therefore, traded), backed out of the market, which quickly froze. In three short months, legislators in Georgia had found a way to create a devastating liquidity crisis (as no lenders were going to make any loans) that brought the market to a complete halt. People could not sell their homes, buy homes, refinance for lower rates or get cash out. Realtors, lenders, title companies, appraisers – everyone tanked. Some companies decided to continue paying employees to stay with their companies in hopes that the legislature would reverse its decision.

Eventually, that did happen as the state government realized the consequences of their earlier decisions (which of course were made without lender involvement). The reversal process was hostile and volatile. It was a classic case of government thinking they knew what was best for consumers. And, in the process of implementing those "best practices," they (temporarily) destroyed the market by removing the ability for consumers and borrowers to get any loans.

These most certainly are not the only two examples, as the city of Oakland (CA) took its case all the way to the Supreme Court before they were required to remove its city-level restrictions. Stories similar to that in Georgia happened in New Jersey, Ohio and Providence, Rhode Island. Any number of additional examples can be used to illustrate the same point of what can happen when the legislature, at any level, moves too fast, doesn't understand the implications of what it is doing, and doesn't trust or seek the cooperation and involvement of the lending industry.

In the face of seemingly unsolvable problems, it's tempting to do something, even if it's wrong. But the potential magnitude of this crisis was enough reason to make sure we did not just do something. This was the time to do the right thing. **Political leaders needed only to look at the fallout from the Georgia fiasco in order to understand the impact of poorly designed legislative initiatives.** Yet, they proceeded with their request to have the IAG updated to include subprime loans.

Two things stand out about the request. First, as described earlier, the Agencies worked on the document for about one and a half years from the middle of 2005 until October 4, 2006, but intentionally deferred the subject of subprime loans to the subprime guidance that was last published in 2001. This reinforces my earlier message that the decision makers and powers did not fully understand the impact or significance of the subprime marketplace, nor did they give it full consideration while making their decisions. The subprime industry continued to fly under the radar.

I'm not suggesting that subprime loans should have been included in the IAG because they should not have been. Rather, I'm pointing out the Agencies specifically excluded subprime loans primarily because they did not recognize the importance of the industry as indicated by cumulative volume and the number of borrowers who held these loans.

Second, and even more importantly, is the excerpt from the letter written by the six Senators. It speaks to the actual reason they made their request. In writing to the regulators, they said:

> The Guidance cites as examples of such loans payment-Option ARMs and interest only mortgages. However… we were informed about other products that also result in significant payment shock to consumers. Specifically, Mr. Michael Calhoun, President of the Center for Responsible Lending, cited certain subprime hybrid adjustable rate mortgages (ARMs) known as 2-28 ARMs. … Mr. Calhoun then goes on to give a typical example of such a loan in today's marketplace:

> "… the initial payment would be based on an interest rate of maybe seven-and-a-half or eight percent; however, after the end of that two-year fixed–rate period, the fully adjusted rate would be in the range of 11-and-a-half to 12%, even with…market rates remaining the same. This produces a payment shock …of 40% to 50% for the borrower."

The letter from the Senators continued:

> …borrowers should not be forced to refinance their mortgages to pay off these mortgages,… the Guidance should apply to mortgages such as subprime 2/28 mortgages.

Clearly, the six Senators were heavily influenced by Mr. Calhoun and his statements. This would have been fine if Mr. Calhoun's statements were true. But they were not. Further, I wonder how many borrowers these six Senators talked to in order to determine that they "had to pay off these loans" vs. the probability that they wanted to in order to get more cash out, consolidate more debt, get a renewed lower rate, etc., whether or not they would have qualified for the existing loan at the fully indexed rate.

They finished by writing:

> Again, we ask you to move quickly to issue a clarification to the Guidance to ensure this result.

This letter from the six Senators solidifies my point that the government, collectively speaking, had made their decisions without full awareness or understanding of the role of non-traditional and subprime loans in our economy. We already know that the IAG was written and finalized over the period of one and a half years and that it purposely excluded subprime loans. We also know that it was not written in response to increased delinquencies, even though subprime loans had long since been going delinquent in numbers that could not be missed. Incredibly, this letter reveals, in their own words, that these key Senators did not even know about the existence or structure of hybrid 2/28s as late as December 2006! Yet, within four weeks, they went from a position of total ignorance to a knee jerk reaction based on the statement of one person.

Within three weeks of that letter, the Consumer Mortgage Coalition (CMC), to which I indirectly contributed some input and feedback, reached out to the six supposedly open-minded Senators who were anxious to have their request approved.

> We are writing to express strong concern about the possibility that the Interagency Guidance on Non-traditional Mortgage Products ["Guidance"] could be expanded to cover well-established

hybrid adjustable-rate mortgage ["ARM"] products such as the 2/28 ARM and to provide [them] with additional information about current industry practice with regard to hybrid ARMs.

…We share your concerns.…But including traditional hybrid ARM products such as the 2/28 ARM in the Guidance could have serious negative consequences for borrowers, the mortgage market and the entire economy.

… Bringing hybrid ARMs under the Guidance, which is intended for a different type of product that can present more risks to borrowers and lenders, would force lenders to restrict their offerings of these loan products by imposing underwriting standards that are stricter than what is needed to cover the lender's risk. The result would be that many borrowers who currently qualify would no longer be able to obtain financing. Ironically, the most immediate victims of such a change in policy would be borrowers who have experienced a sudden change in their financial circumstances and can benefit from the ability to reduce their monthly payments, pay off other obligations, or in some cases accomplish both at the same time.

There are two things worth noting here. First, the CMC was being very polite in their reference to borrowers' changing circumstances. As phrased, it implies that borrowers may have taken on more debt, lost their job, or realized some other event that raised their cost of living (like medical and education expenses). While all these things are possible, what they really meant was the fact that borrowers were experiencing dramatic payment shock since the Fed had raised rates 300 bps., or 3%, over the two most recent years!

Second, let me remind you that this letter was written way back on January 2, 2007. For sure, subprime loans had long since been going delinquent and into foreclosure. Yet, this letter was making it crystal clear that the situation would become much worse if the six Senators' request was honored. The picture was handed to the Senators on a silver platter and they could not, or would not, allow themselves to see it.

To make the picture even clearer, the CMC went on to address the false and misleading statements from Mr. Calhoun that so greatly affected the Senators' perception. The CMC wrote:

It appears your request for an expansion of the Guidance to cover 2/28 ARMs may have been prompted by testimony … by Michael D. Calhoun, President of the Center for Responsible Lending ("CRL").

Not only does the example cited by Mr. Calhoun not reflect the characteristics of most 2/28 ARMs in the marketplace today, his claims are based on the specific allegations included in a lawsuit filed by one borrower. The lawsuit is in its very early stages, awaiting even the submission of an answer, and the case had not even been officially filed at the time of the testimony. In any event, the allegations in the complaint address unique circumstances of fraud involving multiple parties in which both the borrower and the lender may have been victimized; not a typical situation with a 2/28 ARM.

In a typical subprime hybrid ARM, the maximum rate increase after the fixed period is limited by the lender expressly to prevent "payment shock" from forcing the borrower into default....

There is a very practical reason for such a conservative policy – lenders lose money when a borrower defaults..... Thus the potential for negative amortization that concerned the Agencies in issuing the Guidance is not present in a traditional hybrid ARM.

Not more than a week later, Sheila Bair, chairwoman of the FDIC spoke at the Reuters Regulation Summit in Washington DC. She addressed the updated request from the six Senators and said, "We don't want to bring in all ARMs, but that it is just in the subprime area that we're thinking about." She then continued, "[We] want to do this sooner rather than later." In non-political language, this means they weren't "thinking about it"; they were doing it.

More importantly, **the prophetic memo from the CMC had fallen on deaf ears,** and the Agencies continued to process the request for clarification around subprime lending. Not only was the letter of January 2, 2007 from the CMC ineffective, it seemed to trigger an even heightened response from the Senate Committee for Banking, Housing and Urban Affairs.

Chapter Six: The Baby and the Bathwater

"A fanatic is someone who can't change his mind and won't change the subject."
- Winston Churchill

On February 7, 2007, Christopher Dodd (D-CT), the newly appointed Chairman of the Senate Banking, Housing and Urban Affairs Committee, initiated open hearings on predatory lending, as it had become known. Chairman Dodd, who was one of the six Senators who wrote the letter to the Agencies, opened the hearings. Dodd said that "predatory lending and irresponsible lending practices are creating a crisis for millions of American homeowners." Amazingly, only three months earlier, he did not even know that 2/28s were subject to payment shock.

The target of his attention was *not* non-traditional lending. Non-traditional lending was covered by the IAG. Non-traditional loans were no longer being originated to any significant extent, while existing non-traditional loans were performing as expected to that point. Dodd's target was the subprime industry. But if the objective of this new-found attention around subprime lending was to create meaningful solutions, he and his group were off to a bad start. **The subprime ship was sinking quickly, and Dodd threw them an anchor.**

Let me reiterate that **only a few months earlier there had been no mention of subprime nor of delinquencies in general. Now, the entire industry was tagged as "predatory."** Remember, at the time, the Agencies were still (officially) mulling over the request from the Senators that subprime loans be included directly into the IAG. Now, hearings were being held on predatory lending, using the term synonymously with subprime. What do you suppose the odds were that the Agencies would do anything but include subprime loans? Not surprisingly then, and a full five months after the release of the "Final IAG," the Agencies published a revised draft for comment on March 2, 2007. They allowed sixty days for industry and consumer responses.

By this time however, subprime lenders were already on their heels just trying to stay in business. The secondary (investment) market had already responded to the increase in delinquencies and foreclosures by lowering the prices that they were willing to pay for loans, by rejecting more loans, refusing to buy certain types of loans and by conducting aggressive audits on non-performing loans that they had already purchased.

In other words, the lenders were eyeball deep in repurchase demands from investors in regards to loans that had already gone delinquent. Lenders were frantically strategizing to balance volume requirements with credit quality, operational costs, investor demand and repurchase liability. In a nutshell, subprime lenders were already struggling so hard just to keep their doors open that most of them were not very receptive to another potential dagger in their heart.

This was not the first time that Congress or their friends in various consumer advocacy groups and the regulatory agencies were looking at the subprime industry. In fact, the subprime industry had been involved in legislative push and pull over various issues from the inception of its modern era in 1992. However, this was the first time that the industry was so vulnerable that the legislative and consumer advocates could deliver a final knockout blow.

The wheels were in motion and political leaders on both sides of the House were looking for anything that would help them fuel their attack on the subprime industry. On March 28, 2007, they got it. On that day, Fed Chairman Bernanke made the following statement to Congress:

> "Although the turmoil in the subprime mortgage market has created **severe financial problems for many individuals and families**, the implications of these developments for the housing market as a whole are less clear. The ongoing tightening of lending standards, although an appropriate market response, will reduce somewhat the effective demand for housing, and foreclosed properties will add to the inventories of unsold homes. At this juncture, however, **the impact on the broader economy and financial markets of the problems in the subprime market seems likely to be contained.**"

I find it difficult to even get past this statement. In March 2007, the mortgage industry was already on the verge of the collapse and was ready to take the housing market and the economy with it. Who knows whether ignorance, optimism, fear, political correctness, denial or some other factor fueled this statement. Regardless, Bernanke may have just won the award for delivering the understatement of all understatements with "…will reduce somewhat the effective demand for housing." He was talking to Congress, including both Representative Barney Frank and Senator Christopher Dodd, as they were pushing initiatives to effectively eliminate all loan products other than fully income-documented, fixed-rate, conforming loans.

Perhaps this would have been a good time for the Fed Chairman to advise the misguided Congressman and Senator that their efforts to legislate away all non-traditional and subprime loan products, if successful, would put an immeasurable strain on the mortgage market, the housing market and on the overall economy. It would cause millions of families, and millions of voters, to lose their homes. Why didn't he deliver that message? Did he still not get it?

Apparently, the Fed Chairman thought the damage was limited to "individuals and families" while the impact to the economy had been "contained." Well, that's reassuring, isn't it? Then he followed it up by keeping the Fed rate at 5.25% for the next six months just to make sure (tongue planted firmly in cheek) that the combined effect of high rates and tight lending standards would clear up the uncertainty regarding the "implications...[to] the housing market as a whole."

Apparently, Bernanke's speech gave leaders the additional boost they needed. The very next day, Representative Barney Frank, the Chairman of the House Financial Services Committee, sent out a "Dear Colleague" letter to all other members of the House of Representatives in regards to a series of hearings that his committee was going to hold. His objective was to rally even more support against the subprime industry. And why not? The Fed had just raised rates seventeen consecutive times, and the Chairman was saying the problem was limited to subprime and contained to individuals and families so as to not affect the rest of the economy. As far as anyone could tell, the economy was rolling right along and had to be throttled back with higher rates, except for the subprime industry. This was a good time to pile on because the Fed Chairman just made it safe and validated badly misguided perceptions.

Barney Frank's letter started with this paragraph:

> As you know, there are serious problems in the country's mortgage lending market. Foreclosure rates are rising, housing prices are stagnating and too many consumers are surprised to find out that their monthly payments are spiking. The difficulties have been concentrated in "subprime" loans, which generally go to borrowers with limited or damaged credit, although there is evidence that some borrowers are shifted into the subprime category because they are African-American or Hispanic. Real damage has been done to families and communities as many adjustable-rate mortgage loans "reset" to higher interest rates and monthly payments.

This introduction is nothing less than stunning. Remember, the subprime industry was purposely omitted from the Final IAG, which took over one and a half years to finalize. Yet, it took Mr. Frank less than one paragraph to play the race card before he went on to describe the four objectives of the hearings, along with "the discrimination aspects of these activities." Despite

Frank's comment, the fact is that some African Americans and some Hispanics are subprime, just as are some Whites, Native American Indians, Japanese, Chinese, Christians, Muslims, Jews, young people, elderly, men, women and even some politicians. But, that doesn't mean that they were racially steered into subprime loans, as is clearly implied by Frank's statement.

Ironically, one of the constant criticisms of the subprime industry has been that it discriminates against minorities and turns down a disproportionate percentage of minority applicants. As it turns out, this is untrue as proven by detailed and in depth investigations based on HMDA reports (Home Mortgage Disclosure Act) which say exactly the opposite. Nonetheless, it is the perception. Yet, while the subprime industry is accused of discriminating against minorities, Barney Frank is saying that some minorities are being steered into it. Go figure.

Mr. Frank went on to explain the eight guiding principles around which the meetings would be conducted. Yet, by this time, the two Chairmen (Frank in the House and Dodd in the Senate) had already slapped the industry with labels of being racist, predatory and discriminatory. With all this emotion, who could possibly have gone into these meetings with an open, solution-oriented mind? By contrast, imagine how these meetings might have proceeded had the leaders said something to the effect that the market was in disarray as a result of the involvement of all parties from the borrowers to the investors and everyone in between, including the Fed and Congress. The letter continued:

> Our legislation will be drafted with several key principles in mind: Consumers should get "good credit." The best thing we can do for consumers currently in bad loans – and for future borrowers – is ensure that they can get good loans.

Perhaps the Chairman should understand that borrowers don't "get" credit - good or otherwise. Rather, they earn it; and this is an important distinction because it implies a victim mentality. It implies that if borrowers didn't "get" good credit that somehow, they were ripped off. The fact is that not everyone has good credit. People with poor credit should have access to competitively priced, and structured, capital. They should also have the opportunity to rebuild their credit rating. In the interim, however, they just don't have good enough credit to get the lowest rates in the industry.

The second part is even more important. **He acknowledges that the best thing we can do for consumers currently in bad loans – and for future borrowers – is ensure that they can get good loans. <u>Yet, the only thing that happened is that people with "bad loans"</u> (as Mr. Frank calls them) <u>no longer have access to any loans. And that is why they are stuck.</u>**

The next premise of the letter was that:

> Credit availability must be preserved especially in a troubled market. We will take a measured approach that cracks the whip on abusive lending but preserves a robust system that boosts sustainable home ownership.

This is very much like the previous premise. Yet, credit availability has not been preserved. In fact, it's been eliminated. Cracking the whip sounds good, doesn't it? The problem is that the term "abusive lenders" has not been defined. It sounds like subprime lenders are generally considered abusive. So, he cracked the whip on an industry that served millions of people per year primarily because he didn't understand it. Maybe if he were more like the people he was seeking to protect, and had their needs, he'd understand better.

The next premise said that:

> Mortgage originators should not have incentives to steer consumers into bad loans. Borrowers should be assured that they receive a loan at the best terms they qualify for - financial and other incentives for those who originate mortgages should serve that goal.

Again, sounds good. But who decides? Maybe the best terms they qualify for involve conditions that cannot be met or involve terms they do not want. Does this mean they shouldn't be able to get a loan? Shouldn't borrowers be able to decide what loan is the best for them? Contrary to some liberal thinking, people need to be empowered (or allowed) to make their own decisions.

The letter then says:

> We cannot return to redlining. **We will remember that before predatory lending provided too much bad credit, many communities had little access to credit at all.** We must end discriminatory lending practices.

Once again, **Mr. Frank saw the correct issue and then went the wrong way.** This gets back to the years long pressures that Congress put on the consumer finance and subprime lending industries to open up capital to under-served markets. And that was good. Mr. Frank literally made the connection between previous efforts and consequences and still drove forward with his initiative to wipe out subprime lending. Somehow, we needed to crack the whip and restrict lending without changing the services provided to the formerly underserved. Can someone explain to me how that happens?

The open market can and will only take on so much risk. Is the government going to guarantee payments to investors of conforming loans made to higher-risk subprime and non-traditional borrowers? If the answer is yes, are you willing to subsidize that with higher taxes? That's a key question. Are you, as a taxpayer, willing to pay higher taxes so that less credit-worthy borrowers can have access to the lowest priced conforming loans? That is the implication of Frank's statement.

The letter continues:

> The Committee is intently focused on these issues and is working toward a balanced solution that stops abuses, preserves access to credit, and aids stable homeownership. If you would like to monitor our activity on these issues, after the April District Work Period we will have additional information available in a "Predatory Lending" section of the Committee's website.

Once again, the presumption is that subprime is predatory. Politicians often talk about reaching across the aisle to work with parties on the other side. Yet, they are not working with the subprime industry. The Democratic leadership just labeled subprime lenders as abusive, predatory and discriminatory. I'm not sure what aisle they're reaching across.

In short, the leadership in both Houses of Congress appears to suffer from a severe case of cognitive dissonance (no one with a degree in Psychology, myself included, could avoid discussion on this). Cognitive dissonance refers to the ability of a person to simultaneously hold at least two opinions or beliefs that are logically or psychologically inconsistent with one another. In some cases, the believer is aware of the contradiction. In other cases, he or she is only conscious of the two beliefs separately, in different contexts. People who feel dissonance tend to try to reduce the dissonance by changing either one of their beliefs or their actions.

Mr. Frank has reduced his cognitive dissonance by acknowledging all the things that should exist in a balanced solution, but then ignores them in practice. And that's why none of the solutions are balanced, and it's why the market has frozen up. For over twenty years, the Democrats have wanted all lenders to become conforming or look that way. Yet, they want the market served by these lenders to continue to be served. Reality check: all risk is not the same, and all loans are not conforming. The only way they can be is if the government agrees to insure them through their Fannie and Freddie lending standards.

Short of that happening, the message is that the Democrats expect the private lending sector to pick up the dime (or trillions of them) to make loans where price is not aligned with risk. If I recall correctly, this is exactly what Greenspan said was at the root of the mortgage and housing crisis. While I disagree with him, things would certainly go farther in the wrong direction if the private sector did take these actions. Fortunately they won't because they can't afford those losses. The recurring message is that the leaders expect the lending industry to offer all borrowers the same products and price, regardless of risk.

There are only two ways that could happen. One is that we as taxpayers subsidize the lenders for their losses caused by legislated under-pricing of credit risk. The second way would include charging higher rates to better borrowers so that lenders could offer lower rates to riskier borrowers. Neither of these outcomes are reasonable or palatable. But that's where the strategy of the Democratic leadership takes us. They know what they want ideologically, but their actions won't get us there in the real world.

Fast-forward a few months from March 2007 to July. While the Final IAG was never amended to include subprime loans, the market had made its position clear. The IAG was hanging over its head, such that there was too much risk and not enough reward to continue subprime lending. The Chairmen, their committees and the regulatory agencies had what they really wanted. The non-traditional market had essentially disappeared. The subprime market, 2/28s and all, was gone. Within a single year, it had gone from a $600 billion per year market serving some three million households to zero.

Since then, repossessions, foreclosures and delinquencies have risen to historic levels and continue to get worse. Unemployment has jumped by the greatest amount in twenty-two years. Home prices have fallen at the fastest pace in history to match the greatest decline in home sales in history. And yet, the worst is still out in front of us because another thirteen million mortgages will experience their first rate re-set over the next few years. All of this has put our economy on the brink of a serious recession. Wasn't this exactly what the letter from the CMC, which was ignored by the Agencies and by the Senate, had predicted and warned them about?

Apparently, the Democrats did not find a remedy for their cognitive dissonance. Rather, their self-described quest for balance fell woefully short of their desire to squeeze the lending industry down to a conforming-only market.

Conspiracy theorists could have a field day with this one. Would the Democratic leadership in both houses of Congress knowingly create a recession just to increase the likelihood that Americans would vote for a Democratic President in the next election? Admittedly, that's a stretch; yet something has to explain this irresponsible legislative action. Was it a philosophical issue that some leaders don't think that people can be responsible for their own decisions and finances? Was it a lack of awareness regarding how much loan product would leave the market (remember, their original and first "final" guidance didn't even include subprime, so it was not a subprime issue)? Did they know what the effects would be, but moved forward anyhow out of arrogance? Did they think they were helping homeowners, or were they looking for an issue on which to base their re-election campaigns? Who knows? The only thing that matters is that they did what they did, and it created the consequences we face today.

Very simply, the IAG as it was designed and implemented, is the reason the market fell off the cliff. It is the reason foreclosures shot up so dramatically and why so many people have lost their jobs. It is why people have little to no access to capital. It is why we continue to spiral downwards despite all the economic efforts to stabilize us.

I'm sure Congress and the Agencies would deny this was their intention and would say that they only wanted to protect people. But by imposing vague and ambiguous rules for approving 85% of the loans issued by subprime lenders (interest only loans and 2/28s), they effectively shut it down. Lenders who had built themselves up over the years to support the financial needs of millions of people were suddenly stuck with the cost structure associated with large organizations that were now only able to fund about 15% of what they could previously fund. Then, with the resulting deterioration in property values, the bottom fell out on their ability to fund all but the slightest amount of the remaining 15%. And even if they could fund it, there was no secondary (Wall Street) appetite for the product because it was crippled with the stigma of subprime. Lenders could no longer reach the critical (or any) volume levels necessary to issue mortgage securities. They quickly went bankrupt or just closed down.

It was as if Congress and the Agencies had forgotten all their efforts over the previous two decades to get lenders to reach out to lower income and higher risk borrowers who were primarily from underserved, minority markets. Maybe even more important in the immediate term is that the borrowers who had obtained 2/28s in anticipation of refinancing two years later had become unable to execute their strategy. Simultaneously, they became unable to pay their mortgages when they were hit with the significant rate shock caused by the drastic increases to the Fed rate over two years. They were trapped.

And then there's the affect on otherwise would-be homeowners. By early 2007, homeownership had approached its highest level in history up to almost 70%. This included a 5% increase in homeownership between 1989 and 2006. Much of this growth was due to the expansion of subprime lending, which grew from $35B in 1994 to $665B in 2005. And from 1998 to 2006, subprime originations grew from 10% of total mortgage originations to about 20% of total originations. Think about that for a second. One in every five mortgages loans originated was subprime. But Congress took the loans away because they quickly and conveniently determined that the industry was predatory and that only subprime lenders were responsible.

Meanwhile, the five Regulatory Agencies were still working to clarify the IAG in regards to an already dead industry. We have already seen the vague and ambiguous language that frightened lenders into removing their products from the marketplace. One of the key aspects of the IAG was supposed to be "plain language disclosures." I could not possibly support that objective more strongly because that is exactly what we need to open the market back up. If you, and every other borrower, knew exactly what you were getting in a loan, clearly understood how it worked and what the risks were, is there any reason that we couldn't allow all products back into the marketplace? Not from my perspective.

I suspect the Agencies behind the IAG would agree with me on this. If the IAG were clear, specific and binding, then the market could open back up to the extent that lenders could meet the rules and borrowers could qualify for the terms. That's exactly why they stopped fifty yards short of the goal line on plain language disclosures. They simply do not want the market to open back up. Rather, they want all lenders and borrowers to be conforming. To do this, they keep the guidance vague and ambiguous.

As evidence, the IAG is supplemented with a document called "Illustrations of Consumer Information for Non-traditional Mortgage Products." The three Proposed Illustrations consisted of (1) a narrative explanation of non-traditional mortgage products, (2) a chart comparing interest only (IO) loans and Payment Option ARMs to fixed-rate and traditional adjustable-rate loans, and (3) a table that could be included with any monthly statement for a Payment Option ARM providing information on the impact of various payment options on the loan balance.

The Agencies noted that there would be no Agency requirement or expectation that institutions use the illustrations in their communications with consumers. Instead, the Agencies intended to illustrate the type of information that the Interagency NTM Guidance contemplates. Institutions would be able to determine whether or not to use the illustrations and whether and how to tailor them to their own circumstances.

One of the three illustrations is shown here. Notice how (un)clear and non-specific the statements are.

Illustration 1

Important Facts About Interest-Only and Payment Option Mortgages

- Whether you are buying a house or refinancing your mortgage, this information can help you decide if an interest-only mortgage or a payment option mortgage is right for you. These mortgages can be complicated. If you do not understand how they work, you should not sign any loan contracts, and you might want to consider other types of loans.

- Interest-Only Mortgages allow you to pay only the interest on the money you borrowed for the first few years of the mortgage (the "interest-only period").

- If you pay only the amount due, then at the end of the interest-only period:

   -You will still owe the original amount you borrowed.
   - Your monthly payment will increase because you must pay back the principal as well as interest. Your payment could increase even more if you have an adjustable rate mortgage ("ARM") and interest rates increase.

- Payment Option Mortgages allow you to choose among several payment options each month during the first few years of the loan (the "option period"). The option period will end earlier than scheduled if the amount you owe grows beyond a set limit—for example, 110% or 125% of your original mortgage amount.

- During the option period, the payment options usually include:

   - A payment of principal and interest, which reduces the amount you owe over time.
   - An interest-only payment, which does not reduce the amount you owe.
   - A minimum payment, which may be less than the interest due that month. If you choose this option, any unpaid interest will increase the amount you owe.

- At the end of the option period, depending on what payment options you chose:

- You could owe substantially more than the original amount you borrowed.

- Your monthly payment could increase significantly because:

   - You may have to start paying back principal, as well as interest.
   - Unpaid interest may have increased the amount you owe.
   - Interest rates may have increased (if you have an ARM).

Additional Information

▶Home Equity—If you make interest-only payments, your payments are not building home equity. And, if you make only the minimum payment on a payment option mortgage, you may be losing home equity. This may make it harder to refinance your mortgage or to obtain funds from selling or refinancing your home.

▶Prepayment Penalties—Some mortgages require you to pay a lump-sum prepayment penalty if you sell your home or refinance during the first few years of the loan. You should find out if your mortgage has a prepayment penalty, how it works, and how much it could be.

▶No Doc/Low Doc Loans—"Reduced documentation" or "stated income" loans usually have higher interest rates or other costs compared to "full documentation" loans that require you to verify your income and assets.

Do you notice something interesting about the proposed illustration #1? Take a moment and think about it.

Look closely and you'll see there is nothing about the predatory, abusive, unscrupulous subprime loans or the vilified 2/28 re-sets. How could this possibly be, since those were the things that supposedly triggered this disaster? Some of the respondents mentioned this concern, and here is how the Agencies replied:

> Finally, two commenters suggested that the Agencies include in these illustrations information about two additional products – 2/28 and 3/27 adjustable rate mortgages. These are "hybrid" ARMs that start with a fixed interest rate for two or three years, respectively, and then reset to a variable rate, which generally will be higher than the introductory fixed-rate. Because the Interagency NTM Guidance does not cover fully-amortizing mortgage products such as hybrid ARMs, the Agencies are not including information on these products in the NTM illustrations. However, when the Agencies finalize the "Statement on Subprime Mortgage Lending," which was proposed on March 8, 2007, and which provides guidance concerning hybrid ARM products, we expect to issue for public comment disclosure illustrations appropriate for that guidance.

What?! There were only two comments, from more than thirty respondents, about this (probably, the most significant) issue? Furthermore, **the technicality that the IAG doesn't cover fully amortized loans is nothing more than a lame, bureaucratic excuse. We are in the middle of a disaster, and they are getting hung up on whether the IAG does or does**

not cover fully amortizing loans. This is exactly why we can't depend on the government alone to solve this problem.

Another Final IAG specific to subprime loans was released to the market on June 28, 2007. Interestingly, it (still) didn't define subprime, and it didn't provide any illustrations. **This is exactly what made lenders nervous because they feared being accountable for something even the regulators couldn't define.**

But let's be honest. The real reason that subprime loans were not clearly defined or simply disclosed is that that might open the door to making some subprime loans. If all borrowers knew exactly what they were getting and fully understood their loan, there would be no objection to providing those loans. But that's not what the Agencies want. They only want conforming loans and conforming lenders, even if that keeps us stuck in the financial mud for many years to come, while millions of American families (and voters) continue to lose their homes.

Isn't this amazing that the cornerstone of the IAG, including protection against predatory, abusive lenders and clear disclosures, addresses neither of these things together in the context of subprime loans. That's simply because ambiguity is much more powerful than clarity. If lenders are afraid, they pull back. If they know the rules, they operate within them. But that's not what the Agencies want in the subprime world.

Having said that, let me draw your attention to one particular and critical area having to do with the workouts of existing, troubled subprime loans. These are the next wave of foreclosures, so check out this logic:

> Workout Arrangements
>
> The Agencies specifically requested comment on whether the proposed statement would unduly restrict the ability of existing subprime borrowers to refinance out of certain ARMs to avoid payment shock. The Agencies also asked about the availability to these borrowers of other mortgage products that do not present the risk of payment shock. The majority of financial institution and industry group commenters who responded to this specific question believed that the proposed statement would unduly restrict existing subprime borrowers' ability to refinance.
>
> However, most consumer and community groups who addressed the issue expressed the view that allowing existing borrowers to refinance into another unaffordable ARM was not an acceptable solution to the problem and, therefore, that eliminating this option would not be an undue restriction on credit. Some commenters mentioned that certain government sponsored entities and lenders have already committed to revise their lending program criteria

and/or create new programs that potentially may provide alternative mortgage products for refinancing existing subprime loans.

To address these issues, the Agencies incorporated a section on workout arrangements in the final text that references the principles of the April 2007 interagency Statement on Working with Borrowers. The Agencies believe prudent workout arrangements that are consistent with safe and sound lending practices are generally in the long-term best interest of both the financial institution and the borrower.

I have no clue what that third paragraph is saying about what to do in the real world. But once again, **the first two paragraphs make it crystal clear that the warnings of the lending industry were ignored in deference to the opinions of the consumer groups. The homeowners are continuing to pay the price for that "protection." This has to be comforting to millions of homeowners who have been trapped by rising rates and product elimination to know that consumer groups don't think that a two-year extension at lower rates would be of benefit to them and be better than losing their homes. We homeowners need to speak up because the consumer protection groups are not protecting us; they're hurting us because they don't understand what they're talking about!**

But the pressure did not stop there. After the Final IAG had been clarified, after the Subprime IAG was updated and after the market had already collapsed, both Senator Dodd and Representative Frank proposed similar legislation to further regulate the non-traditional and subprime lending industries. Frank threw his support behind HR3915, which would serve to cement the IAG into law and throw the mortgage industry off the plank to sink to the bottom.

This Bill had seven parts to it, and they are all technical. In general, however, the effective purpose of HR3915 was to get the IAG more specific and for that to become law. This would clearly take us in the wrong direction.

Over the latter half of 2007, HR3915 kept working its way to the floor. Leading up to that debate, some other people had the opportunity to voice their opinions. On October 24, 2007, Kurt Pfotenhauer, Senior Vice President of Government Affairs and Public Policy for the Mortgage Bankers Association (MBA) testified before the House Committee on Financial Services. He made the following statements (excerpts) in regards to HR3915.

"This bill is well thought out, and if enacted, it will be extraordinarily consequential. That comment does not, of course, signal agreement, but is intended to recognize the thought and the effort that went into this ambitious proposal and to concede upfront that your hard work justifiably gives you some insulation from the common industry charge that your bill is fraught with the danger of unintended consequence. **Indeed, I rather suspect that you intend much of the consequence that would result from this bill.** Which begs the question, is your approach, the right approach?

Members of the committee, if they don't understand, should understand that if HR3915 becomes law, some people will be locked out of the mortgage market, many of whom would have been successful homeowners. The question for this committee is whether the protections that this bill provides are worth that price.

85% of subprime borrowers are paying their mortgages on time. It's an open question; how many would even qualify for a loan under the proposed regulatory construct. The alternative to eliminating borrowers from the market is to prepare them for the market. In that respect, we urge the Chairman to tackle the lack of transparency in the origination space. Streamlining the mortgage process and improving disclosures are essential to helping borrowers help themselves.

This bill as currently drafted is not pre-emptive. As the Committee already knows, this prevents MBA from offering our support.

Despite our lack of support, we would like to continue to work with you in a constructive way to improve this bill. My written testimony suggests a number of fixes that will make the bill a better product. Some of them merely clarify what is in HR3915. Others are alternative approaches to the same goal. Still others are areas where we may have to agree to disagree. I do not think there should be any surprise here today that the Mortgage Bankers Association is going to oppose some elements of this bill. But I hope that there is likewise no surprise that the Mortgage Bankers Association will continue to work with you in a spirit of constructive good will, to make this bill better."

Doesn't this sound very much like the prophetic response from the Consumer Mortgage Coalition to the six Senators who wanted the IAG updated to include subprime loans? If you remember, that request was honored while the response from the CMC was ignored. We now know that their warnings were accurate. What about this time? Would the warnings of the MBA be heeded? Not a chance. Three weeks later, the bill passed Congress by a vote of 291 Y and 127 N and was submitted to the Senate a couple weeks later on December 3, 2007. Fortunately, it stalled in the Senate.

At about the same time all that was happening over on the House side of Congress, Dodd in the Senate announced in September 2007 that he would draft bipartisan legislation that would protect homeowners and borrowers. On his own website, Dodd says that legislation is needed to reform mortgage lending practices that have created problems for homeowners and investors in the subprime market. He also said:

> "Let me be clear: affordable home loans are a good thing; predatory lending is not. Predatory lending needs to be stopped, which is why I intend to introduce legislation that will put an end to the practices that have forced thousands of Americans into foreclosure and put thousands more in danger of losing their homes."

This is our tax dollars at work, folks. **The subprime and non-traditional markets were dead and gone by mid-2007. Yet the Finance Chairmen in both Houses were introducing future legislation to regulate the market several months after the collapse.** They were still equating subprime to "predatory" lending and they were badly underestimating the significance of the situation. The fact is that millions, not thousands, of people had gone into foreclosure. Likewise, millions, not thousands, more homeowners and their families are at risk. Most importantly, Dodd still sees the cause of all this as the industry itself, as opposed to the overly dramatic involvement and response by the government itself.

Nonetheless, as a result of the fall of non-traditional and subprime lending, we started to hear a new term called "credit crunch." It's a catchy buzz-phrase that people generally don't understand. It simply means that little to no capital is available to most consumers. While catchy, a credit crunch is a serious problem, and it's a man-made one at that. Make no mistake, the overall mortgage and housing crisis has resulted from the cumulative actions of about a dozen different groups of participants. However, in a subtle but powerful distinction, the credit crunch itself has resulted from the regulatory agencies that created the over restrictive and under clarified guidance (IAG). Meanwhile, despite their efforts over decades to open the mortgage market to more borrowers and socio-economic groups, some in Congress leveraged the opportunity to make the guidance even more restrictive. They were successful and it has destroyed the market. **Not only did Congress, the Treasury and the Agencies throw out the baby with the bathwater, but they denied the baby ever existed at all.**

Chronology on InterAgency Guidance (IAG) and Congress:

03/01/1999: Subprime Guidance released for comment.

01/31/2001: (Almost two YEARS later) 02/07/2003 the Subprime Guidance was published.

mid - 2005: Work began on InterAgency Guidance on Non-traditional Mortgage Product Risks (IAG).

12/29/2005: IAG was released for comment.

10/04/2006: Final IAG was published.
- Proposed Illustrations for IAG released for comment.

11/04/2006: Mid-Term election day; Democrats won back both Houses of Congress.

12/07/2006: Six Senators sent letter to request that subprime be added into IAG.

01/02/2007: CMC sent letter to six Senators advising them to withdraw their request and to exclude subprime loans and, in particular, 2/28 hybrid loans.

01/04/2007: Inauguration day for new Congress.

01/10/2007: Chairwoman of the FDIC, Sheila Blair spoke in Washington, D.C., and said, "We don't want to bring in all ARMs, but it's just in the subprime area that we're thinking about."

(Tip of the Day: never underestimate the meaning of the word "just.")

02/07/2007: Senator Dodd opened first hearing on "predatory lending."

03/02/2007: Proposed (Revised) IAG Released for comment (now, including subprime loans).

03/28/2007: Fed Chairman Bernanke testified before Congress.

03/29/2007: The very next day, Barney Frank sent out his "Dear Colleague" letter playing the race card.

05/02/2007: End of Comment period for revised IAG proposal.

05/31/2007: Proposed Illustrations to support IAG were published (8 months after it was opened for comment!). They excluded subprime loans under the premise that a revised Subprime Guidance was to follow shortly.

06/08/2007: Revised Guidance on Subprime lending was published.

July 2007: Basically all non-traditional and subprime products were gone.

Late 2007 + Senator Dodd and representative Frank push legislation to further regulate the industry.

Chapter 7: The Players' Club

"Success has many fathers, but failure is an orphan."
- John F. Kennedy

The credit crunch has trapped millions of borrowers in higher rate loans with no refinance alternatives or options. However, the overall mortgage and housing crisis resulted from the cumulative actions of several different types of market participants.

We started with the Fed, the Treasury, Congress and the five Regulatory Agencies because they have played the most significant roles in this disaster by collectively creating the "credit crunch." Yet most people have minimal, if any, awareness of those roles and actions. Likewise, these same groups will continue to have the greatest influence and power moving forward. Like it or not, they are at the helm. This is true, despite the fact that none of them have acknowledged anything but the very slightest of responsibility for this mess.

On the other hand, these participants were certainly not alone. We couldn't paint a complete picture of this crisis unless we gave due justice to all the other players. While it's convenient to point the finger of blame at one or maybe two primary parties, and the need to deflect responsibility is strong (albeit pointless), the reality is that the overall mortgage crisis is the result of a true team effort.

Borrowers: We have already discussed this group at some length. Some borrowers have been victims of unscrupulous lenders and greedy brokers. Others intentionally rode the equity train as if it would never come to a stop. They knowingly and strategically obtained the lowest possible discounted rate for the first two years expecting to refinance again when the rates adjusted and the discounts expired. In a growing market, they would always have more equity by then, and they would tap into it. Agree with them or not, their plan was to pull out their equity and get a new discounted start rate every two years.

Borrowers had no way to understand the rules by which lenders were approving their loans and specifically that they were being qualified at the start rate. Furthermore, they didn't care. They wanted their loans and the benefits of them. Any potential difficulty in paying an increased rate two years down the line was a lifetime away and heavily outweighed by the perceived benefit of cashing out their equity and having the lowest possible rate and payment in return.

Additionally, the Fed had held the Fed Funds rate so low for so long, most people would not have believed that significant rate increases were on the horizon. Had these borrowers been more risk averse, they easily could have obtained long-term fixed-rate loans that were about 3 1/2% higher than the discounted start rate on a 2/28. While this sounds like a significant difference, remember that most subprime borrowers have experienced 3% payment shock at their first re-set followed by 1%, 1% and 1% in six-month increments. Had they taken the longer-term fixed-rate loans, they would not have had to worry about the re-set rate. They would not have had to worry about the inability to refinance their 2/28 in two years, and they likely would not have been able to borrow more than they could afford.

In fact, lenders even offered rate incentives to get more borrowers into long–term fixed- rate loans. Because about 85% of subprime production was from 2/28s, lenders often provided price incentives on fixed-rate loans in order to balance their loan origination across various product types. While this balance would help lenders achieve maximum profitability, the other products usually did not meet the needs of most subprime borrowers. These borrowers most certainly had access to safer, reasonably priced, fixed-rate loans, but those did not meet their needs that were usually measured in two-year increments.

Other borrowers saw the rapid increase in equity and leveraged that equity in order to finance the purchase of non-owner occupied properties. They would then rent out these properties and enjoy the market appreciation on them over the next couple years. Eventually, they would either profit on the sale of the property or refinance into another 2/28 and use the proceeds to buy other non-owner occupied properties. This strategy did not happen by accident; these particular borrowers were financially savvy and knew exactly what they were doing and understood the risks that were involved.

Unfortunately, these borrowers were not only putting themselves at risk but prospective tenants as well. The nation has become littered with eviction notices served to good, paying tenants because the property owner became unwilling or unable to pay as their loans re-set.

Some borrowers took it a step further and committed outright fraud in order to obtain their objective. It's now becoming common knowledge that fraud was rampant during the peak of the market. But fraud doesn't usually surface until loans go delinquent and audits are triggered. And voila, fraud. Borrowers can be very creative when they want money. They can distort income records, bribe appraisers, transfer properties back and forth between related parties, increasing the transfer value at each stage. They can pay people for their credit histories, and they can steal other people's credit histories. This partly explains why identity theft has become the fastest growing crime in the U.S.

Many borrowers strong-armed creditors into removing derogatory credit from their reports by exploiting a technicality that requires creditors to abide by a very specific and unreasonable process. While the credit information was accurate, it would get scrubbed on a technicality. As a result, no subsequent lender would see the derogatory credit and could not appropriately grade, or price, for credit risk. By definition, this is not fraudulent. Yet, it misled lenders into underestimating the risk of lending money to certain borrowers.

Some borrowers have claimed they didn't understand the loan documents and that's why they got into trouble. In a prolific market, I could see this happening. It was normal for people to wait anxiously for their loan documents to be prepared. The lender typically contracted a signing service, and the process was faster than getting a cavity filled at the dentist. It was sign, sign, and sign. Not too many borrowers got hung up on the details; they just wanted their loan.

The flip-side is that all owner-occupied refinances require a three-day right of rescission (cancellation) before the loan can even fund. This allows borrowers time to ask their lender any questions, remove their confusion or even cancel their loan. Some companies even required double rescission periods in some states. I'm not blaming these borrowers, but I also understand that the other parties involved are in a hurry and are so familiar with the terminology that they can just skim over it when perhaps they should not. While loan documents and disclosures need to be simpler and more transparent, wouldn't you take personal responsibility for understanding the terms of a 30-year obligation to the tune of hundreds of thousands of dollars?

Loan Brokers, Real Estate Brokers and Appraisers: We've all heard the stories. And they have merit. In the state of Florida alone, over 5,300 persons with criminal records became loan originators between 2000 and 2007. More than 2,200 had been convicted of financial crimes. While this is a relatively small population compared to the number of originators, they can do some real damage.

Industry-wide, most origination was wholesale, meaning that a licensed loan broker originated it. Among other things, the broker completed the four-page loan application on behalf of the borrower. While some of this was automated through processing software that automatically populates credit information from the repositories onto the application, most of the information was taken verbally. The broker and the borrower may never have even met one another. In fact, they rarely did. Likewise, because the broker originated the loan, the lender could not (they're not licensed to) work directly with the borrowers.

Brokers knew the lenders' rules and underwriting criterion regarding income, debt ratios, etc. If they needed to make changes in order to get the loan approved with the lender who offered the best rate and least conditions, they often took the liberty to adjust the information before they submitted the loan. I'm sure that, most of the time, they could justify this as a necessary step in order to serve their client and get the borrower their loan. Other times, however, it was outright fraud where the broker knew the borrower could not meet the terms of the loan. But these types of brokers did not care, so long as they got paid when the loan funded. In these cases, neither the borrowers nor the lenders knew the brokers lied.

In this world of technology, so much is automated that almost anything can be fabricated. W-2s can be printed on a computer where they are virtually indistinguishable from the real deal. Information is transferred electronically. Even signatures can be scanned. Lending in the techno-age allows for brokers to reach out to borrowers far away from them and far away from the lenders. As a result, the first time that borrowers might see their loan package is at signing. They would never know if the broker replaced their W-2s, changed their "stated" income or did anything else that would compel the lender to approve a loan they would have otherwise declined.

While the borrowers needed to sign the loan application at document signing, they never went through the details. The lender, escrow company, signing service or whoever is signing the borrower will say something like this: "We need you to sign the loan application in order to obtain your credit report, which, of course, we already did. You're not signing as to the accuracy of the information on the application, because we know that things like income, debt balances and credit histories change all the time."

So the borrowers signed without looking to see that the broker might have changed key information. Or, they may have known that the broker changed information but were led to believe that it didn't matter to anyone.

Then there are real estate brokers. One story paints this picture the best. A couple years ago, my youngest son and I were out riding our bikes. We stopped at a model-match of our house in the cul de sac above our street. The original buyers had never taken possession (due to a divorce), and the house was for sale. I just wanted to see the flyer on it. The broker who had the listing was well known in our neighborhood and he had a reputation for getting the highest price in the market. It seemed like almost every property on the market around my house had his sign in the yard.

Anyhow, as I was getting a flyer out of the advertising box in the front yard, the broker/realtor pulled up out of nowhere like some sort of real estate ninja. I knew who he was, but he didn't know me from Adam. He didn't know I lived one street away or that I am an ethical mortgage guy by profession. Here's how the conversation went.

He introduced himself and told me the property was in escrow and then told me the agreed upon sales price. That was the first no-no, as the property had not yet closed escrow. But I immediately knew the price was well above the current market and asked him how he got that price. He told me that he sought buyers who were relocating to southern California from somewhere else because they expected price shock, they just didn't know how much. Then he relied on his relationship with particular appraisers (to whom he gave a lot of business) who would find some feature to attribute a large value adjustment. The result was a price about $80,000 more than the most recent sale- every time!

No wonder he had so many listings. On this particular property, the appraiser gave a $100,000 positive adjustment in value for the view. I suppose it does have $100,000 view of the surrounding hills, mountains and valleys if you're walking down the upstairs hallway or in the one bedroom on the second floor. However, from the main living area and from the back yard, the owners would have a beautiful view... of a concrete wall that was placed there by the builder in order to block some of the sound coming from the main road immediately behind the house.

This is not a win-win situation. The real estate broker, the seller and the appraiser win, to greater or lesser extents. However, the buyer overpays and the lender over-lends. And guess what is more likely to happen when a borrower realizes that they owe more than their property is worth? If fallen upon hard times, they might stop paying their mortgage. Then the lender has a non-performing, over-leveraged asset. Nice.

Let me remind you that I'm writing about the exceptions here. Most people in this industry are much more ethical and service oriented. I'm writing about the people that Congress and the regulatory agencies should have focused on, instead of having buried the industry. Yet, while these people are the exception, I only had to travel one block to find this guy. I suspect guys like him exist across the country, and, collectively, their results figure into this crisis.

Perhaps no one has more opportunity than appraisers to commit mortgage fraud. This is hard to demonstrate without pictures, but I will give it a shot. The fundamental problem with appraisers is that they are paid by the brokers and lenders who give them the work. This is a serious conflict of interest as appraisers often feel the pressure to come in with the number that the lender needs. This is so prevalent that the highest appraiser designation, MAI, is often called, "made as instructed" by brokers and lenders.

The other fundamental problem with appraisals is they only show what they show. Lenders do not usually know what information is being left out. They normally find out when they have to foreclose due to non-performance. While most lenders have appraisal review policies, they also have tolerances that allow for many loans to fund without thorough reviews. This creates another opportunity for fraud. Wholesale origination in particular, is vulnerable to this fraud because the lenders do not order the appraisals; the brokers order them. Lenders order appraisals when the loans are generated retail, which is why there is usually less appraisal fraud through the retail origination channel.

Mortgage Bankers and Lenders: Let me tell you about a true predatory lender. While preparing my business plan for GMAC/RFC back in 1994 (as described in chapter three), I noticed that RFC had purchased a significant amount of loans from one particular lender. This bundle of loans had one striking similarity. They were cash out loans to retired people on a fixed-income (typically social security). Worse yet, that fixed-income was "stated" on the loan application and not verified.

I'm a big believer in stated income documentation loans under the right circumstances. However, making "stated doc" loans to elderly, fixed-income borrowers is not one of those circumstances. Generally, these types of borrowers receive all the benefits of a fully income-documented loan by providing nothing more than a standard award letter from the Social Security Administration. It's that simple. Further, there is so much benefit to the borrower for providing it to the lender, that there is no good reason to make a loan without getting a copy of the letter. Unless someone is lying.

Not only is there a moral problem with making stated doc loans to retired, fixed-income borrowers, there may be some legal exposure, as well. At very least, the last thing a lender / servicer would want to do is foreclose on an elderly person who never had to verify their income, even though it was extremely easy to do.

So we ceased our relationship with that lender, a move for which I took some grief from certain executives. At the time, that lender was considered one of RFC's better lender-customers. That's because customer value was determined mostly by volume and virtually not by any other factors. From some people's perspective, all I had done was cut off the volume.

Then, a couple years later, while at Investors Mortgage in Seattle, I got a phone call from one of my friends at RFC. That lender, from whom RFC had stopped purchasing loans, had made the headlines. The lender was committing fraud, but some senior people in their company were trying to stop the practice from happening. Legend has it that these people had blown the whistle on their own company and were summarily fired. This led to a tip to the FBI, which led to an investigation and indictments.

Now, I'll tell you about the vast majority of non-prime lenders. In the world of kids' games, they were the "monkey in the middle." They spent their business activities bouncing back and forth between two sets of customers, including the brokers and borrowers on the front end and the investment banks and investors on the back end.

All retail, wholesale and correspondent lenders literally depended on the inefficiency in the market for their survival. The same was true for loan brokers. In a truly efficient market, individual borrowers could obtain the lowest rate and best loan by working directly with investment banks on Wall Street. But, as yet, there is no efficient way for that to happen. So, in reality, the only thing that lenders and loan brokers do is fill the void created by that inefficiency. As Angelo Mozilo, CEO of Countrywide said "There are only two customers, the borrower and the investor; everyone else is just noise." And that's the truth.

The first set of customers includes the borrowers and brokers who were looking for the best deal they could find. And if you as the lender could not provide it, they went somewhere else. In fact, the brokers and borrowers generally did not wait until the lender provided their answer. Over the past few years, the advent of technology-driven automated underwriting (AU) made the process virtually instant for many lenders. An application would get submitted electronically, and the lender's AU engine would evaluate and spit out a list of approval options, which involved different combinations of rates, conditions, loan amounts, etc.

Lenders who were, shall we say, technologically challenged were at a significant disadvantage. If they wanted to compete and to survive, they needed to make up for their shortfall in other ways. That usually meant lower rates, fewer conditions and better service. Better service is an interesting concept because it can mean whatever you want it to mean. It certainly meant many, many different things to different people, but it always involved more employees and the higher cost of employing them.

At Option One, we were truly passionate about customer service, and, in order to measure it, we paid big money to outside companies who specialized in gathering market feedback. Year after year, we found that we were ranked the highest, or amongst the highest, in all categories that the broker-customers defined as most important to them (like "do what you say you'll do, return phone calls within one hour, don't add conditions, honor mistakes made by the sales people, etc."). Yet we were losing huge market share to numerous competitors who were all ranked towards the bottom in all of those "most important" categories. Why was this happening?

Obviously, we ranked high in the areas that were most important to the brokers and lenders who completed the survey. But I argued that we were losing market share because the market was being driven by a different and much bigger group of "high-tech" brokers and lenders who did not fill out the survey and who had a very different definition of service. Mostly, they wanted fast answers, low rates and minimal conditions. The things we did best mattered, too; but they were not as valuable as fast answers, low rates and minimal conditions. We heard what we wanted to hear because it was consistent with our passionate values, and we continued to sell "service" as we had defined it over the years. After all, it was that "service" and our performance that had allowed us to be one of the top lenders in the entire industry.

But we were blind to the truth that the market had changed and the definition of service had changed. This explained why we were losing market share. A colleague of mine and I discussed the survey and its implications with respect to survival in the mortgage market. Months after my friend left the company, he sent me a quote from some unknown source. It said, "If the rate of change inside your company is slower than the rate of change outside your company, then your company's days are numbered. You just don't know it yet." Options One's days were numbered.

This story is not peculiar or specific to Option One. All lenders understood the market dynamic and knew the competitive forces they were up against. This put significant pressure on them to lead with the best possible deal, meaning the most aggressive approval they could stomach. In many cases, that approval would be even better than the borrower or broker requested. There was no opportunity for lenders to hold anything back because they would not get a second chance. The whole dynamic was sort of like a blind auction or a seller's market in housing where prospective buyers offer a higher than listing price.

This pressure was real for all lenders from the smallest correspondent to the largest originator. Even retail originators, who worked directly with the applicants, were not immune to this competitive pressure. Retail origination was quite inefficient and expensive. Every loan had to be originated at the borrower level and, therefore, generally involved high levels of advertising and higher cost structures. The flip-side is that the rates on retail loans were significantly higher than those of their wholesale counterparts. When firing on all cylinders, the retail business was a true cash-cow. As a result, many lenders adopted a similar business strategy. They would use the high-profit margins of the lower volume retail business to subsidize the thinner margins of the higher-volume wholesale business channel.

This is exactly why so many companies had retail and wholesale channels like New Century and 123.com, same for H&R Block Mortgage and Option One, same for Ameriquest and Argent. This last one is particularly interesting in its history. In chapter two, I described how Long Beach Bank (LBB) had almost accidentally helped create the market for subprime securitization. Later, LBB became Long Beach Mortgage (LBM) and the owner, Roland Arnall sold it to Washington Mutual (WAMU). He took the cash to fund the acquisition (from another small lender) and national expansion of Ameriquest, who at its height was marketed in nearly every professional baseball stadium in the US. They even advertised on the Superbowl to the tune of $2M per minute. He then took the proceeds from the high margin retail originator, Ameriquest, and built the wholesale channel, Argent. The latter sponsored everything from professional golf tournaments to Indy racecar drivers (Danika Patrick) and teams (Andretti Green) to Olympic swimmers (Michael Phelps) and various other high-profile events.

Even if lenders didn't operate retail and wholesale under two different companies, they typically operated two separate channels under one business name. This is true for companies such as Countrywide, Wells Fargo, Fremont Investment & Loan, Saxon, Aegis, IndyMac, and Aames, to name a few. Regardless, the retail originators felt the same exact pressure. If they didn't provide the best possible approval, then they knew that every other lender, broker and correspondent in town was hunting down that same applicant.

Exceeding the expectations of brokers and borrowers was made more challenging by the fact that employees of lenders had conflicting responsibilities. None of us wanted to admit this, since we were all there to serve customers. But the fact is that internal company friction was a constant in all companies. Salespeople wanted fewer conditions, lower rates and faster service. Operations wanted more conditions and cleaner packages. The trading desks and finance departments always wanted higher rates and couldn't understand why the salespeople couldn't sell them better.

Perhaps the greatest fallacy of the lending industry is that it's a "relationship" business. I can immediately think of a few thousand people who would disagree with me, but the business was not about personal relationships. If lenders generally gave borrowers and brokers what they wanted, then the lender got the loan. If they did not, some other lender got the loan. Brokers and borrowers wanted some combination of the most aggressive products, the lowest rate, fastest processing time and fewest conditions. If the lender didn't provide these features, there was no "relationship."

Yet, the perception of it being a relationship business never changed or even wavered. So, at many companies, the AEs (Account Executives) who developed these "relationships" typically had quite a bit of authority and an awful lot of power. If they had any level of professionalism, they never made this obvious, yet everyone knew they had it. In a good market, there was no downside to this dynamic. If they facilitated the funding of a weak loan, rarely would anyone take a hit. The market would just keep moving north and equity would be created. That increased equity became the great equalizer for weak loans, and it justified doing more of the same.

Loans funded during bad times were a different story. Yet, ironically, as times got worse and lenders became more desperate to fund loans in order to stay in business, AEs became even more powerful. And they used that power more openly. They were doing what they had become accustomed to doing over the years, and they were doing what they truly believed was in the best interest of their customers.

The AEs also had another strong incentive called personal compensation. Compensation differed from company to company. I cannot prove this, but I would make an educated guess that the average AE across the country made about $35,000/ month. Weaker, or newer, AEs were probably in the $10-15 thousand/ month range. Stronger AEs were pulling down $250,000-$300,000 per month! In every company I've worked for, we've had AEs making more money than the President and CEO of the company and even of the parent company, if there were one.

Therein lay the potential conflict. Companies desperate for business were not going to lose people who were perceived to have the relationships that would keep the doors open. No, they were going to accommodate those people.

Understand that I'm not blaming the AEs, and I will tell you that the vast majority of them were honest, hardworking and professional. Maybe more than anyone else, they felt the squeeze of a shrinking market and paid the highest personal price. They didn't create the rules or the compensation structures. They just played by them and did a good job. Nonetheless, their "relationships" gave them a lot of power, which made it difficult for many companies to enforce standards in challenging markets. The only way to change that was by getting AEs to "feel" some level of personal accountability and responsibility for loan performance and loan quality. Very few companies even made an attempt at that objective. Fewer were successful at it.

The second set of customers included the investment banks on Wall Street. Lenders developed reputations based on the manner in which the loans they sold performed within traded securities. This included how quickly, or slowly, they paid off, how much fraud was found in the deals, how many loans had to be repurchased, etc. That reputation, while volatile, could affect the price the investment banks paid for the loan pools, how much tolerance they allowed for underwriting exceptions and even influenced how the securities were ultimately rated.

Fraud is typically defined very loosely as "any material misrepresentation of income, value, property condition credit, verifications and documentation, etc., whether intentional or otherwise." Using this vastly open-ended definition, investment banks could find some evidence of fraud on virtually any loan on which they wanted to find it. The lender's greatest protection against this possibility was for the loans to meet, but not exceed, established guidelines and, more importantly, for the loans to pay on time and not go delinquent. Under these conditions, it is likely that investors would never have audited the loans in the first place.

This was a major liability because lenders were not allowed to use other credit lines to repurchase existing loans from investors. Instead, they had to use their own cash reserves. This expensive remedy made it critical for lenders to sell "investment quality" loans to these buyers. While investment banks didn't pull this trigger very often in good markets, lenders knew they would get an itchy trigger finger if the market changed course.

This left lenders walking the tightrope strung between the two sets of customers. And while those two sets of customers were far removed from one another, the common bond of the lenders connected them. The balancing act was delicate and never-ending, as long as the lender remained in business. Loans that completely favored the brokers and borrowers would have little value to Wall Street. Conversely, loans that had the risk profile that Wall Street wanted would be of no use to brokers or borrowers.

The higher up the food chain the lenders were, the more day to day decisions those lenders made. For sure they made the credit, funding and pricing decisions. But they only did that within the context of a market dynamic that required them to meet the needs of two different sets of customers.

In that respect, lenders did not call the shots; they didn't even deliver a product. All they did was provide a service, which was to connect two sets of customers who needed each other but had no other way of making contact. If either set of customers went away, the lenders knew they would go away, too.

This may be a far cry from the perception that lenders create the rules and act as profit-seeking predators in search of a quick buck. Perhaps that would be true without competition, but the lending industry, if anything at all, is hyper, hyper-competitive.

Investment Banks and Investors: In order to fully understand the causes behind the mortgage crisis, we need to look at four distinct types of investors.

We've already talked quite a bit about the first group, the investment banks. These are the lifeblood of Wall Street and include companies like Goldman Sachs, Bear Stearns, Morgan Stanley, Credit Suisse, Lehman Brothers, Wells Fargo and Merrill Lynch. So as to not do injustice to companies with less or more than two words in their name, it also includes companies like Citigroup, Wachovia, Bank of America and Nomura. This list is by no means exhaustive and isn't meant to imply that all of these companies are deeply entrenched in the situation. But they do represent the investment group known for purchasing giant pools of mortgages and issuing them into securities.

I've been clear that this group represents the demand side of lending, meaning that if they don't demand the loans, then efficiently priced loans cannot be originated by lenders or obtained by borrowers. But to be fair, and like the lenders they purchase loans from, investment banks don't operate in a vacuum either. They can make or break a market, but they also face the same competitive pressures as lenders. They evaluate the data that describes the loans in any particular pool that mortgage bank wants to sell. Based on that data, and based on the reputation of the lender selling the loans, the investment banks establish a price that they would be willing to pay for that pool of loans. They also identify the loans they are not willing to purchase at all and kick them out of the pool. Lenders usually send the loan pools to the investment banks that offer the best price, kick out the fewest loans and have a reputation for executing the purchase quickly.

This process was summarized most succinctly by one of Option One's senior leaders at a meeting in Florida. His real job was to determine which loans and loan pools would go to what investors. He told us that his kids had asked him what he did for a living and he replied, "I pick the highest number."

This dynamic applied a significant amount of pressure on potential investors, as Wall Street is also a hyper-competitive environment. Potential buyers knew they could lose hundreds of millions or even billions of dollars in loans if they priced a smidge too high or kicked out a few too many loans. Worse yet for them was that the loans didn't just go away. Rather, they would be purchased by the investment bank's biggest competitor next door or across the street, city, country or world.

The investment banks then sliced and diced the pools into seemingly endless structures based on risk, price, etc. and sought investors to purchase the bonds created for these loan pools. They made BIG money on the spread between what they paid the lenders and what they received from investors. But it took a while for the profit to be realized. The typical turn time (when a deal turned profitable) was about eighteen months. With that, two things happened. One, they needed to have really deep pockets to put out billions of dollars without turning positive for a year and a half. Second, because the 2/28 loans always paid off at two years anyhow (as described throughout this book), the investors basically earned a profit for six months.

Investment banks exist for one reason. To make money. So when investor appetite for mortgages (or any asset) dries up, there is a reason for it. If Wall Street could make money by buying mortgages, they would buy them. So what makes them stop or makes them reverse direction? The answer lies with the second group of investors.

This second group includes the people and entities that invest in the securities themselves. These include pension funds, trust funds, international funds, individual investors and the like. The bottom line is that the investment banks slice and dice the deals to create the greatest possible mixture of investor appetite and return on investment (ROI). Anything can change investment appetite, as distinguished from investor (investment banks) appetite. You might recall from an earlier chapter that the crash of 1998 was triggered by the devaluation of the Russian ruble, which frightened investors worldwide. As a result, potential investors pulled their money out of anything with risk associated with it and put their money in the "riskless" US treasuries.

Similarly, in Chapter Four on the Fed, Greenspan explained that this current crisis is due primarily to the prolonged mis-pricing of risk that ultimately needed to correct. While I don't agree with his short-sighted, and ironically overly complex, assessment and conclusion, I do agree that there was (is) a flight away from credit risk and back toward riskless US treasuries. Without investment (trust funds, pension funds, etc.) appetite, investor (investment banks) appetite goes away. Along with that appetite goes the product and the availability of it in the open market.

Let's take a look at Stated income loans to see how this concept works in the real world. Stated Doc loans were loans made to people without any written income documentation. The additional risk on the loans was typically offset with slightly higher rates, reduced LTV positions (more equity), higher credit scores (less credit risk) and the like. Further, lenders typically did not allow brokers or borrowers to change the amount of stated income once it was submitted in the application. This was often a point of friction as circumstances on a loan could change such that higher income was required to get the loan approved again. However, this was not allowed and, without additional income, the rate could go up, the loan amount might go lower or the loan might even be turned down.

Further, most lenders required the stated income to be reasonable and consistent with the borrower's source of income and with their credit profile. While this was subjective in nature, it killed many, many loans to applicants who needed to claim much more income than was reasonable for their particular source.

As I described earlier in this chapter, few if any legitimate subprime lenders, would make stated income loans to borrowers on a fixed-income like social security or retirement. This was for the protection of the borrowers with fixed-income and in recognition of the fact that full income documentation, which would get a lower rate, required nothing more than an award letter from the Social Security Administration.

Having said all of that, there were two meaningful types of stated income loans. The first included those loans made to wage earners who were people with typical jobs and who received regular paychecks. The other type included loans made to people who were self-employed and generated their own income. As you might suspect, lenders and investors were much more skeptical about stated loans made to wage earners - simply because their income should have been quite easy to verify through readily available documents like pay-stubs, W-2s or tax returns.

Nonetheless, stated income loans had been a mainstay of the subprime industry since 1992, and they had been equally commonplace in the conforming and alternative loan markets. More importantly, these loans had historically performed well over the previous fifteen years. Perhaps, that's a result of all the filters I mentioned above.

Whether the case or not, in the early part of 2007, investor appetite for stated subprime loans disappeared overnight. In response to this absence of investor demand for stated loans, my company provided some major investment firms on Wall Street with actual loan performance data. It showed that "Stated Wage Earners" performed better in every delinquency category than "Stated Self-Employed" loans. Interestingly, they even performed better in two of the three significant delinquency categories than fully-documented loans. These facts were counter-intuitive, and possible explanations were bantered about. But it didn't matter. We could not change the mind of one single investment bank. Although, one of them was candid enough with us to say that, regardless of the facts, "investors are dry-heaving on stated self-employed, and they're vomiting on stated wage earners." Like I said, the product disappeared from the marketplace.

The third type of investor includes investment banks again, but from a very different perspective. While the market was booming, lenders were making big money. Obviously, the investment banks profited greatly from their role in the process, but they were leaving money on the table. From a financial perspective (there is no other), lenders were standing in between the borrowers and the investors, thus absorbing profits that "should" belong to the investment banks. Second, they were leaving competition in play by not having first rights to a given lender's origination volume. This created two tremendous opportunities for investment banks, both of which could be achieved by one strategic move. Simply buy the lenders. So that's what the investment banks and private equity firms started to do.

For example, Merrill Lynch bought First Franklin and OwnIt. Morgan Stanley bought Saxon. Shearson bought Aurora and B&C Mortgage. GE Capital purchased WMC. HSBC bought Decision One. Bear Stearns bought Encore and on and on.

There is yet another fourth group of investors. Most of the major subprime lenders are (or were) publicly traded companies like Countrywide, Wells Fargo, New Century, Fremont and Saxon. Alternatively, if they were not publicly traded themselves, they were often owned by parent companies that were publicly-traded. For example, Long Beach Mortgage was owned by WAMU; Option One was owned by H&R Block, First Franklin was owned by GE, while both B&C Mortgage and Aurora were owned by Shearson.

Either way, being publicly-traded brings more people with higher expectations into the equation. Individual investors like you and I can purchase stock in any publicly traded company that we want. Further, we can invest in funds that diversify through acquisition of stocks from various companies. Either way, and for some reason that I truly cannot understand, these companies are valued more on their growth than on their proven sustained profits. Individual investors look at companies making money year after year and determine that's not good enough.

At Option One, we made about $700M net pre tax in fiscal year 2004. We weren't even into the new year and we were already talking and strategizing about what we needed to do to grow in the following year. This is true even though we represented the upper end of market share in the industry and even though we expected the market to shrink as rates were going up.

We were bringing in hundreds of millions in profits to our corporate parent, H&R Block, but we were perceived as a shackle around the stock price of Block. This is not a Block issue; every company faced the same issue. And when you have to grow to maintain or increase your company's value, lenders have to become more aggressive to achieve that growth. There is an optimum point of return at which increased growth is more than offset by the risk of the loans that created that growth. It was the "greater fools theory" in real life. Individual investors were willing to pay higher stock prices expecting growth, even though the market should not have warranted that value nor support that growth.

Interestingly, and with full hypocrisy, Warren Buffet delivered a lengthy message at his most recent annual Berkshire Hathaway shareholders meeting on May 5, 2008. He called every group mentioned in this chapter to the carpet for their role and responsibility in this crisis. He only omitted one group: individual investors. He mentioned nothing about the expectation of individual investors for publicly traded companies to continuously grow and to increase market share. This is particularly important because Warren Buffet, via Berkshire Hathaway, was the majority shareholder in H&R Block, the parent company of Option One Mortgage (top 5 subprime lender).

If things were so out of control, shouldn't a person with the power and influence of Warren Buffet have delivered a message to all H&R Block shareholders not to push so hard for continued growth at the expense of credit quality and long-term stability and profitability? To the best of my knowledge, no such thing happened. The full court press was on H&R Block and, therefore, on Option One Mortgage. So the blame game continues.

People might want to question whether the mortgage debacle of 2007 and beyond stems from the same factors that drove corporate scandals in 1991-1992. Shareholder pressure to grow, along with the highest levels of personal greed, largely caused several major corporations to falsify their balance sheets. The Sarbanes-Oxley Act virtually guarantees that cannot happen again. Yet, the companies still have the same pressure. While I don't know any lenders who ever padded their balance sheets, I know many who continued stretching production, guidelines and prices in the face of shareholder pressure to grow.

Rating Agencies: Investment banks could not issue securities for any investment without the involvement of the rating agencies. The business of rating agencies is highly complex, very proprietary (secretive), expensive and riddled with huge potential liability, government and regulatory oversight, and responsibility for market perception. In short, there are extremely high barriers of entry into this industry, and, as a result, there are relatively few companies who do this work. The market is dominated by two major rating agencies including Moody's and Standard & Poor's, while Fitch follows in a distant third and D&P lags much farther behind in fourth. There are others as well, but the securitization of mortgages rely almost exclusively on the first three mentioned.

Without them, there would be no securitization of mortgages, no acquisition of lenders by publicly traded companies or investment banks and no ability for private investors to buy stock in those companies. Most importantly, there would be no institutional investors like pension funds, trust funds and international investors. In effect, without rating agencies and bond insurers, this industry, as we know it, would not exist. The same can be said for all the benefits we have received from this industry over the past twenty years. So this raises two important questions. First, what do they do? And second, what role have they played in this mortgage and housing fiasco?

Due to the complexity of rating agencies, I'm going to remain admittedly light on this topic. If you want more information on the subject, you may want to go buy any number of books that Frank Fabozzi has written over the years on capital markets. He is the master.

In order to understand what rating agencies do, we need to think like an investor. Investors in bonds, including mortgage securities, which could be either asset-backed securities (ABS) or mortgage backed securities (MBS), face three risks. The first is interest rate risk, which is the risk that interest rates could rise. The second is purchasing power risk, which involves the possibility of market inflation eroding the value of the bonds. The third is credit risk. It is this credit risk that rating agencies measure and communicate.

The primary responsibility and function of the rating agencies is assessing and communicating the credit-worthiness of the underlying bonds that they rate. Credit ratings are rankings of a bond's ability to withstand various types of financial and economic stress compared to that of other bonds. Ratings are intended to help provide forward-looking opinions regarding the probability that bonds will pay, or fail to pay, full interest on time over the course of the investment.

Stress testing these securities involves the application of different economic models. For instance, the loans might be measured with respect to the Great Depression, the Texas oil crash of the 1980s or the recession of 1991-1992. The objective is to determine how many of the loans will continue to perform under those circumstances and how many will not. From that analysis, the rating agencies grade, or rate, the bonds.

Each of the rating agencies uses letters, or combinations of letters, to communicate their assessed risk. To keep complex measurement simple and useable for potential investors, the grading is done much like we had in school, with A being the highest and moving downward from there as measured risk increases. While no "F"s are allowed, the assigned grades do place bonds into one of two general categories. They are either considered investment grade bonds that carry a lower probability of default (not paying on time) or non-investment grade "junk bonds" which are expected to demonstrate a higher probability of default. By law, institutional investors are not allowed to invest in these lower grade "junk bonds."

The letter grades can be further separated by numbers in order to create even more distinction, but the purpose is the same. In order to measure this risk, the rating agencies conduct a very thorough review of the bonds that they rate. There are numerous considerations that are weighed, the most important of which is a bond's cash flow. Bonds with high credit ratings have quick-turning, high quality accounts receivable, meaning that they are getting paid on time and getting all that they are due. Rating agencies therefore deploy dozens of mathematical formulas and financial ratios to aid them in their rigorous examinations. But rating agencies take pains to meld both quantitative and qualitative analyses in order to get the most complete picture of a bond.

Rating agencies must always consider external factors such as the economic cycle, but the fundamentals of the bonds that they rate always get first consideration and have a far greater bearing on a bond's overall rating. Nevertheless, rating agencies have increased their responsiveness to, and consideration of, the economic cycle in recent years, given the large impact that the economic cycle has on many bonds.

To gather this quantitative and qualitative information, rating agencies depend on data and information provided to them by their customer, the investment banks. This is an obvious conflict of interest, given that the investment banks will want the highest ratings possible and may be pressured to withhold information that might compromise that objective. A thorough investigation into this conflict of interest has been triggered by the mortgage and housing crisis.

For example, right now, authorities in New York and Connecticut are investigating whether Wall Street banks hid crucial information about high-risk loans bundled into securities that were sold to investors. As is typical and customary, all these loans were sold by subprime lenders to Wall Street firms. Those firms bundled them with other, less risky loans into securities. Now, some investigators want to find out whether the investment banks properly disclosed the high risk of default on those loans when selling those securities to other investors.

This is not to suggest that investment banks withhold critical information from rating agencies and investors, just that there is an inherent conflict of interest in the process. This is not a new problem. But it gets a lot more attention when bonds go south at a pace or extent greater than that predicted by the rating agencies in their risk assessment and grading.

Earlier this year, the FBI said it was investigating fourteen companies for possible accounting fraud, insider trading or other violations that could result in criminal charges. The FBI didn't identify companies, but said the probe involves firms across the financial services industry. Further, the FBI is working with the Securities and Exchange Commission (SEC), which has civil enforcement powers. The SEC said in January that it had about three-dozen active investigations under way.

It's also important to understand that while securities of mortgages are large pools of loans, they are not the same exact pools of loans the investment banks purchased from any individual lender. Rather, investments banks slice and dice pools and mix and match volume from different originators in the same security. In this way, they get maximum investor appetite and premium based on the overall credit quality of that security. In a like manner, each security made up of different loan pools will be rated differently from AAA to D. This process of stratifying and assessing credit risk has many significant implications to lenders, investment banks and investors. But those are highly complex and far beyond the scope and purpose of this book.

There are two other participants on the back end of the loan process. They are the bond insurers and the loan servicers. Both are critical to the loan industry, and they both have substantial, but indirect, influence over how loans are made. Bond insurance is a service whereby holders of a bond can pay a premium to a third party, who will provide interest and capital repayments as specified in the bond in the event of the failure of the issuer to do so. The effect of this is to raise the rating of the bond to the rating of the insurer; accordingly, a bond insurer's credit rating must be almost perfect. This has become a problem in the wake of the non-prime and subprime crises, as contracted bond insurers have had to pay up in huge amounts to keep insured bonds performing. As a result, the rating agencies have been evaluating whether they need to downgrade the very bond insurance companies who insure the bonds that the Agencies rate.

Servicers can affect loan performance based on their infrastructure and ability to collect timely payments and to minimize foreclosures and losses. Some servicers are rated significantly better or higher than others, such that an investment bank may require the seller of a pool of loans to have those loans serviced by one of that lender's competitors. This was often the case at Option One, as we were highly rated and became the largest sub-servicer (serviced loans in someone else's behalf) of subprime loans in the country.

Servicers obtain a nice fee for their services and, if run efficiently, can and should be a profit center for the company. They do this not because of gains made on foreclosures but as a result of the difference between their servicing fees and their costs of servicing those loans.

To come back full circle, many participants played a major role in this debacle. Borrowers, loan brokers, appraisers, correspondent lenders, mortgage banks (lenders), investment banks, institutional and private investors, rating agencies and bond insurers all share responsibility along with the Fed, the Treasury, both Houses of Congress and the agencies involved in the creation of the IAG.

Perhaps the best evidence of this claim is wrapped up in the events of June 17-19, 2008. In those three days alone we learned that two Democratic Senators, including Senate Finance Committee Chairman Christopher Dodd and Senator Kent Conrad, were on Countrywide Financial's VIP list and received preferential loan treatment from the lender. Conrad acknowledged that he spoke with Countrywide Chairman Angelo Mozilo directly. Both Conrad and Dodd claimed they knew they were on Countrywide's VIP list but did not think they received any preferential treatment.

This might surprise you, but I think they should have received preferential treatment. Like I've said all along, all risk is not the same. Lending is a for-profit business, so I'm assuming that Countrywide did not take a loss on any loan they made to these Senators. However, because the risk associated with lending to these people was lower, and because the cost of processing their loans was lower, the lender could offer slightly lower rates and/or faster processing. There is nothing wrong with that. Everyone, even Senators, needs to borrow money.

Not more than a few days later, we learned that Senator Obama's head of Vice Presidential Search, James A. Johnson had also benefited from the VIP program. Johnson resigned from his position immediately upon that information becoming public. Then we learned that Obama himself had obtained a better than market deal from his lender, Northern Trust. His campaign immediately replied by calling the rate "consistent with Northern Trust policies, and it reflected the base rate set for that period discounted to address the competition for the account and other opportunities, such as personal financial services, that the relationship would bring to Northern Trust."

These responses are much more interesting than Dodd's and Conrad's veiled attempts to feign ignorance. We are biting off our collective nose to spite our face, if we are more concerned about any politicians getting sweetheart deals than we are about the really big problems in this crisis. Johnson had no need or responsibility to resign. Furthermore, Obama immediately and squarely hit the nail on the head. When it came to his own loan, he completely understood the power of relationships, competitive pressure and market behavior. The amazing thing is that many of his counterparts in the Senate and House cannot see these same market forces are in play when it comes to the people they are elected to serve, including subprime and non-traditional borrowers!

I suppose that just about every politician can be bought for some price. But I also suspect that that price would be well above the benefit they might receive from some mildly discounted mortgage rate. Maybe I'm not shrewd enough to see this at any deeper level, but this just seems like much ado about nothing. It's a red herring that pulls us away from the big picture.

That picture includes the legislation that Dodd conceptually introduced in September 2007, several months after the crash of the subprime and non-traditional markets. That bill screamed through the Senate. The bill includes about $300B for foreclosure rescue. Because the government had a key role in all three circumstances that drove this crisis (**low rates with aggressive products, quickly increased rates, removal of alternative products from the market**), it makes sense that they are stepping up to he plate.

However, the proponents of the bill say that taxpayers will not pay for it. I'll let you in on a little secret that these people do not want you to know. ALL money in the government comes from taxes (or printing, I suppose). Presumably, much of that money will ultimately benefit lenders and investors who would otherwise have to take a great hit by foreclosing on properties worth less than their loan amounts.

Ordinarily, I would not have too much sympathy for these lenders and investors. However, it is critical to understand that these parties have been forced to hold the loans on which borrowers became unable to pay. These borrowers became trapped by the uncoordinated and irresponsible governmental actions that simultaneously raised rates and took products away from the market. But these loans do not just disappear. The lenders hold them and are taking monumental losses on them. They became trapped just like the borrowers did.

Here's the conflict I see and the problem I have with the situation. Senator Dodd was instrumental in driving all non-traditional loans and subprime loans from the market. This largely caused the collapse of the mortgage industry and serious financial hardship for any lenders that remain. Then he wastes taxpayer dollars by continuing to kill something that is already dead. He then receives VIP treatment from one of the very lenders he is blaming for the crash. Meanwhile, he initiates legislation that will help support that lender and others by subsidizing borrowers on the backs of taxpayers. Everyone, except Dodd, loses to the tune of $300B. He is like the firefighter that commits arson so that he can be the hero by putting out the fire.

But I digress; so back to the three days at hand. Within the period of these same three days, the FBI announced that it had arrested 406 people in a sting named "Operation Malicious Mortgage." They said that the most common type of mortgage fraud was misstatement of income or assets, followed by forged documents, inflated appraisals and misrepresentation of a buyer's intent to occupy a property as a primary residence. Except for appraisals in some cases, how much of this fraud could have been committed by lenders? Little to none. In a separate sweep, two former Bear Stearns managers in New York were indicted Thursday, becoming the first executives to face criminal charges.

Meanwhile, Frank and Dodd keep beating their mantra that this whole thing was caused by predatory, subprime lenders. The FBI said it had been investigating an estimated 1300 mortgage fraud cases over the past several months. This included only nineteen involving subprime lending practices by U.S. financial institutions. To be clear, 1300 cases of investigated fraud and four hundred six arrested people did not create this enormous disaster. At the same time, nineteen out of 1300 does anything but suggest that subprime lenders were the only culprit.

During those same three days, Moody's became the first major rating agency to downgrade the biggest bond insurers of their highest ratings. Moody's stripped both Ambac and MBIA of their Aaa ratings. Moody's said the high cost of accessing the debt markets made it challenging for the two largest bond insurers to raise new capital. In simple terms, this means that they have become victims of the credit crunch and solvency problem. What they did not say was that Ambac and MBIA were directly involved in creating the credit crunch and solvency problem. Suspicions are that the other rating agencies may follow suit.

These four events that happened within a few days of each other prove that this crisis was a team effort. This crisis is not an orphan. It has many fathers.

Chapter 8:   The Scapegoat's Been Milked

"You can sleep in the garage and call yourself a Buick. But it doesn't mean that you are one."
  - Al Rantel, Radio Host KABC

By now, the myth that this situation was caused by selfish, unscrupulous and predatory lenders should be sufficiently de-bunked. We know that, in fact, it was created by the uncoordinated, cumulative efforts of many different parties all acting in their own best interests. And to be clear, the disaster would not have happened without the participation of every single one of those parties. Had any one of them backed out, stepped down or declined to participate, the market would have slowed immediately.

Now it's time to unveil some dirty little secrets. **First, we have not reached the peak of the subprime problem nor of its consequences. Second, subprime is not the big problem that will drive this market down and keep it there for years to come (unless we do something about it). That honor belongs to all the non-traditional products that were wiped out by the IAG.** Subprime loans and the subprime industry went down first because the majority of these loans had two-year re-sets. Meanwhile, **the cumulative volume of non-traditional loans is almost three times greater than the subprime universe. These loans will not see their first re-set until three to five years after the loans were originated.**

In other words, these loans have not re-set. But they will, and when they do, they will follow the exact footsteps of the subprime industry. This is why subprime has been the scapegoat used by the Fed, the government and Wall Street, in order to deflect attention away from their involvement and, more importantly, to calm markets by making the problem seem isolated.

I know this may be hard for many people to accept because all we hear about is the subprime crisis, but that is not what it is. We need not look much farther than IndyMac, Bear Stearns and Countrywide to know that's the truth. So, we can call it a subprime crisis, but that doesn't mean it is one. If you are skeptical, just start watching the stock prices of Fannie Mae / Freddie Mac and banks that focused on Option ARMs and Alt-A loans. WAMU, Wachovia and Downey Savings might be a good place to start.

In addition to these other non-traditional products, keep in mind that the mortgage industry is not as isolated as you might think. In fact, the financial system that created the mechanism for non-traditional and subprime mortgage securitization is the same one responsible for all other financial industries, including commercial lending, automobile lending, and unsecured lending like credit cards. They use the same risk management tools, the same pricing and compensation models and are essentially run by the same people. None of these industries or market segments fall under the umbrella of the IAG and have not been legislated out of the market.

Yet, all these market sectors are at significant risk because their customers have become financially strapped as a consequence of the IAG. What do you think the likelihood is that certain industry sectors were run exceedingly well while others were allowed to become crises? What do you suppose the likelihood is that people will lose their homes but continue to buy cars or pay on their credit cards?

The final reason we know this is much more than a subprime crisis is because the foreclosure estimates do not reconcile. Estimates range from twenty-five hundred to eight thousand per day through the end of 2009. If we compare these numbers to the number of subprime loans still on the books and subject to rate re-sets involving an increase in the Fed rate, we see that the projections exceed the total number of loans that meet that criterion. Since it's mathematically impossible to have more foreclosures than loans, we know that the foreclosure estimates must include other types of loans other than just subprime.

As mentioned in the first two chapters, there are three general categories of mortgages: the first is conforming or prime, the second is non-traditional and the third is subprime. Conforming loans meet Fannie Mae/ Freddie Mac lending guidelines, or more specifically, get approved by Fannie/Freddie automated underwriting (AU) engines.

Many people believe that Fannie Mae / Freddie Mac are lending arms of the government. The fact is that they are neither the government nor lenders. Confusion may stem from the fact that Fannie Mae was originally created under Franklin D. Roosevelt in 1938. However, Fannie Mae was re-chartered in 1968 when it became a publicly traded company funded solely by investors on Wall Street and around the world. Further, they operate only in the secondary market. They do not lend money themselves; rather, they invest in pools of loans which meet their criterion and that were originated by approved lenders.

As a publicly traded company, they are in business to make money and to grow and return reliable profits. Therefore, they are under the same pressures as all other publicly traded lenders. However, there is a big difference between them and all other publicly traded companies. They establish the rules by which loans are considered to be conforming. So, if they need more business, they just loosen their credit policies so that their lenders can originate more business.

The story with Freddie Mac is different, but similar enough that it doesn't need to be repeated. What is important is that both companies have seen their stock prices plummet by more than 80% over the past year. As a result, the President, the Treasury and the Fed have all stepped into the arena in order to shore up Fannie Mae / Freddie Mac and avoid a full-scale economic catastrophe. Their efforts are unprecedented but certainly constitute the pre-commitment of an industry bailout. Remember, Fannie Mae / Freddie Mac are not the government. Rather, they are government-sponsored enterprises that happen to be publicly traded companies.

Here's a great question. Why would lenders, who only make conforming loans to lower risk, better-qualified borrowers across all socio-economic populations, need that kind of support in the face of financial collapse? There are two related answers to this question.

First: **They do not just buy conforming loans.** For many years, **Fannie Mae / Freddie Mac** were the largest securitizers of subprime and non-traditional loans in the world! The pressure of being publicly-traded worked on them, too. They could grow and be more profitable by investing in loans that performed - regardless what type they were. In a related manner, they also **purchased massive amounts of subprime loans just by calling them something else.**

This can only be appreciated by understanding how technology fits into the picture. Lenders that sell loans to Fannie Mae use an automated underwriting engine called DU or Desktop Underwriter. Freddie's version is called DO or Desktop Originator. As a whole, the industry refers to these loans as conforming, prime, DU approved, DO approved or Fannie/ Freddie approved. They all mean the same thing. To the best of my knowledge, printed copies of Fannie/Freddie guidelines are still available. They publish actual loan tolerances regarding everything from loan amounts, debt ratios, liquid assets, net worth, required documentation and countless other criterion and combinations of criterion that determine whether a loan is conforming-eligible or not. But those written guidelines do not matter because no one uses them.

No one uses them because all Fannie/Freddie loans must be submitted through and be approved by DO or DU. The lender's job is then to obtain documentation from the borrowers that meet the requirements of the DO/ DU approval. The DO and DU engines are commonly known as "black boxes," because everyone has some general sense of what they do and why. However, very few people actually know what is in them and how they work.

I personally have a pretty good idea because I helped them create their engines. While at RFC, we were asked by Fannie Mae / Freddie Mac to share our credit expertise with them as part of their objective to become technology based. Those meetings went on for some time and became very detailed. We got a good look at the template they were building and came to better understand their lending philosophies and credit logic. Even without any personal involvement like that, lenders and brokers know that information from the borrower's application can be tweaked until the engines issue an approval that works for the borrower.

Users can modify the application electronically as many times as they want or need to until they get the right approval. Lenders and brokers don't know exactly what makes the deal work or not work, so they just keep changing the input fields until it does. For example, they can change a borrower's years on the job or net worth or cash reserves or income or whatever. Only property values and credit must be verified and are absolute. **Changing any and all other fields does not necessarily mean that criteria will need to be proven or verified.**

For example, if a lender or broker inputs an artificially high dollar amount of liquid assets, in other words - they lie, but DO or DU do not condition for (require) verification of those assets, then everyone's happy. If, on the other hand, the approval conditions for verification, then different criteria get changed in the AUs until they issue the best possible combination of rates, terms and conditions.

To be sure, **conforming loans** typically involve very good credit (although the definition of that has moved around), full income documentation (tax returns, W-2s, pay stubs, etc.) and the lowest possible rates. However, they **do not reflect some specific and exact written criteria that need to be met in every way. Rather, they meet the established *combination* of risk tolerances as determined by the AU engines and based on the information *input by the broker, lender and obtained by third parties, such as the appraiser and credit repositories.***

As a function of the policies and input procedures, Fannie Mae / Freddie Mac end up with a lot of subprime loans. Back in the late 1990s, my business partner at the time and I ran a small broker shop. Like all brokers, we would seek out interested borrowers and work with them to complete loan applications. Mark and I both had very strong backgrounds in subprime and non-traditional lending, so we both knew subprime loans when we saw them. But right about that time, DO and DU were being marketed to the broker community heavily, so we gave it a try. We started with applications that were on the subprime fence. Invariably, they would get approved by either one of the two engines with fewer conditions and a lower rate than we would have received had we submitted them to any subprime lenders.

Let me be clear; we never falsified information from, or on, a loan application. We input the information honestly and accurately such that any approvals and conditions we received met the criteria inside the AU engines. In our minds, however, they were subprime loans.

With that success, we kept moving down the credit ladder deep into the subprime world as we knew it. And we kept getting approvals with lower rates and fewer conditions than we would have obtained from subprime lenders. We did not know why exactly, but we did know that our borrowers were getting fast (automated) approvals with the best possible terms, conditions and rates.

To some readers, this may seem questionable. Understand that we were using the established rules in order to get the best loans for our customers. That was our job. It was not our responsibility to conduct due diligence on Fannie Mae / Freddie Mac credit policies. If we had implemented a higher standard than Fannie Mae / Freddie Mac required, then we would have lost the loans to some other broker who would have provided the borrowers with a conforming loan. That other broker would have been paid and the borrower would have obtained their conforming loan anyway. But Mark and I would have been out of business had we done that too many times.

As loans continued to perform, or failed to perform, up to the standards expected by DO and DU, Fannie Mae / Freddie Mac simply tweaked the insides of the black boxes. They didn't need to change guidelines necessarily or publish any statements; they just updated their technology. All of this was very efficient and very good. It greatly reduced the cost of originating loans, which allowed lenders to operate on thinner and thinner margins and it provided borrowers with the best possible deals in the least amount of time.

Second: Fannie Mae / Freddie Mac are obligated to make the monthly payments to investors on a cumulative $5.1 TRILLION in outstanding loans. In theory and in practice, conforming borrowers pay better and have less loan delinquency than do their non-traditional and subprime counterparts. But even conforming borrowers stop paying as well when they lose their jobs or when their homes become worth less than their debt against it.

So, in an ironic twist of fate, the government turned the screws on their own charters when they enacted the IAG that wiped out the market. Whether they understand that or not, the bottom line is that Fannie Mae / Freddie Mac are smack in the heart of this mortgage crisis!

There are very few absolutes in conforming lending, but there is one worth mentioning. Even if a loan qualifies in all other ways, it is not conforming if it exceeds Federal loan limits. As a result of the recently signed economic stimulus package, this amount may be higher in some areas at least through the end of 2008. This appears to be an area of significant misinterpretation as many people think the amounts have been raised categorically. Unfortunately, this is not true.

In fact, the conforming loan limit is still $417,000, but it can temporarily go as high as 125% of the median price for a residence in that area. However, in no event shall that amount exceed 175% of the 2008 limit, or in other words, $729,750. Clearly, this is a step in the right direction and opens key markets up for higher loan amounts. At the same time, its lift is minimal because it is restrictive and temporary. People are reluctant to buy properties for a higher price if they believe that the price will come down by next year, simply because conforming loan limits will be lowered back down.

While conforming loan limits have temporarily changed in some areas, the premise is unchanged. Anything over the conforming loan amount would be considered "Jumbo" and almost always require a higher rate. While people may not know exactly what the limits are for their area, the AU engines have been updated, and qualified borrowers do have access to this capital.

Nonetheless, **the removal of non-traditional and subprime products from the marketplace essentially equates to government <u>price-fixing</u>. In general, qualified borrowers are limited to conforming loan amounts.** Except in the most unusual cases where people have a tremendous amount of cash reserves that they want to put down on a purchase, the price is severely restricted. In effect, property values went up as a result of capitalism and came down as a result of government interference.

As a case in point, there is a house on the street behind mine that previously sold for about a million dollars. The owners became unable to pay and the bank foreclosed. The bank just sold the home for $439,000. Why? The market had a lot do with it. But so did the fact that conforming loans are limited to $417,500 in Riverside County. That house sold quickly in a down market because it was "under-priced" for market appetite. However, the artificially low and restricted loan limits prevented the market from working normally according to supply and demand.

It should be understood that there is nothing specifically in the IAG that prevents the funding of jumbo, non-traditional loans. However, there are significant restrictions on the available product variations, which would have previously been available on jumbo loans. Perhaps more importantly, the market freeze on products not specifically included in the IAG demonstrates the power of legislation, just like that described earlier regarding Georgia and other states.

People should also understand that some financial institutions have the enormous financial capacity to hold on to their loans rather than having to sell or securitize them. This is a special and select breed who has access to a very low cost of funds and who has very high liquidity. With this, they can sustain profitable operations without having to get their principle back right away and instead, earn a higher return over a longer period of time in the form of monthly mortgage payments that include principle and interest.

It's kind of like the lottery; if you win it, you can take a reduced or discounted lump-sum distribution, or you can get the full amount paid in equal monthly installments over a much longer period of time. Most lottery winners choose the discounted, lump-sum distribution because they want their cash now. For the same reason, most lenders sell or securitize their loans. But, if you were already extraordinarily rich, and then won the lottery, it may not be so important to get cash today. So you might select the full amount over a longer period of time. The same is true for portfolio lenders. To be clear, nothing requires lenders to pick one channel over another. They can portfolio some loans, securitize other loans and sell others "whole loan."

These lenders (typically large banks), who can and want to portfolio loans, have more flexibility in what they call conforming or non-traditional loans. For example, most people would probably think or assume that Wells Fargo makes conforming loans to conforming borrowers. And that would be true. But it's also true that in late 2006, they re-categorized massive amounts of their "conforming" loans as subprime. I'm not sure why they did this, but I do know that by reclassifying these loans, overnight Wells Fargo became the largest subprime lender in the country.

But again, that's the exception rather than the rule. So, with the knowledge that conforming loans have very few absolute limits and represent a fluid and evolving combination of risk criterion, the subprime world takes on a whole new look. Technically, every loan that doesn't DO or DU qualify, is (by definition) non-conforming which includes non-traditional and subprime. That's a big, big world, and it speaks to the scope of this mess.

We already know that big world includes "jumbo" loans, which exceed Fannie Mae / Freddie Mac loan limits. It also includes "stand-alone" second trust deed loans ("HELOAN") and "stand-alone" second trust deed lines of credit ("HELOC"). It also includes the 2nd trust deed part of purchase money combo loans like 80%/20% (1st/2nd "piggybacks"). It also includes loans that fall somewhere outside the credit box. We all know about the subprime market, but there are others.

The most prolific of these markets has been the Alt-A market, which is designed to support borrowers who are neither conforming nor subprime. Alt-A loans are typically made to people who have strong credit that meets Fannie/ Freddie standards, but who need or want to use alternative sources of income documentation, such as bank statements instead of tax returns.

High credit quality borrowers might also drift towards Alt-A loan products if they don't meet Freddie/ Fannie requirements regarding property type, LTV or debt ratios. In effect, Alt-A loans fall somewhere in between subprime and conforming, while sharing characteristics of both sectors.

As the Alt-A market had increased over the past decade, Wall Street had begun slicing and dicing the credit distinctions ever finer. Names like Alt-A minus and Alt- B started circulating about the marketplace. Wall Street had enough cumulative volume to begin making these distinctions, but few lenders actually offered Alt-A minus or Alt-B as separate products. They may have marketed them that way, but they were nothing more than subsets of the Alt-A product they already offered.

Regardless of what Wall Street did with the Alt-A product, how finely they sliced it and what they called it, the loan characteristics generally involved borrowers with very good credit, but less (or alternative) income documentation. They were able to obtain very high (100%) combined 1st and 2nd LTVs and rates between conforming and subprime. Some market participants searched for an exact product definition as if it were the Holy Grail. But the fact is that there are as many definitions of Alt-A as there are originators and investors of the loans.

Like the subprime market, Alt-A loans offered borrowers a wide variety of different payment structures. They could be 30-year, fixed-rate loans or ARMs that adjust monthly or semi-annually. Most often, however, they were set up with a fixed-rate for the first 2,3,5 or 7 years followed by a 6-month adjustable structure for the remaining term of the loan. In other words, these loans also have re-sets and are vulnerable to interest rate fluctuation.

It should be clear by now that the non-conforming market reaches far beyond subprime loans and includes jumbos, heloans, helocs, Alt-A (and the entire family of "alt"ernative products), and piggybacks. But that's not the full picture either. Within the world of conforming lending, there are features or products that are considered to be non-traditional or "exotic." These include stated income documented loans, interest-only loans and variable payment option plans ("Option ARMs"). Option ARMs came into the marketplace in about 2002, and while everyone who was anyone offered them by 2005-2006, they are generally recognized as the brainchild of Washington Mutual (WAMU) and World Savings. By 2006, Option ARMs were the IPOD of lending. They had all the hype, they were totally different, they changed the way the industry worked and they allowed borrowers to enjoy the benefits of lending like never before.

In short, they were the greatest thing out there. At least, if you were a borrower who couldn't qualify for the loan size you needed or if you expected your income to go up dramatically or to be earned in large, uneven chunks throughout the year. It also worked for people who "knew" that the market was moving so fast and would continue appreciating at a rate that would outpace the structure of the loans.

As with all loan structures and features, there was some variance in the marketplace, but at a very high level, here's how these worked. Option ARMs were adjustable rate loans with rates set at some margin (say 2.25%) above a selected index like MTA (Monthly Treasury Average), LIBOR (London Interbank Offered Rate) or COFI (11th District Cost of Funds). They were designed to adjust monthly as the index changed and could be amortized over 15 years or 30 years. To this point, they sound just like any other conforming ARM loan.

From this point, things change. The Option ARMs offered a very short, very low introductory (start) rate and corresponding payment. The introductory rate usually ranged from about 1.25% up to 4%, based on the LTV and income documentation on the loan, but were as low as 1% for the better part of a year when index (MTA, LIBOR, COFI) rates were at their lowest points. This rate and payment was good for 1-3 months based on the structure of the loan. Once the introductory period expired in 30-90 days, the rate increased to the fully indexed rate (index + margin) based on the current index rates. From there, the loan allowed borrowers to choose from one of four payment options (thus the name).

First, the borrower could elect to make the minimum payment, which was defined as the payment they were making at the discounted start rate for the first one to three months. The difference between that minimum payment and what the payment would have been had they been paying at the fully indexed rate would then be added to the principle loan amount each month. This is known as negative amortization because, with this approach, the loan balance increases instead of decreases.

There is also an additive affect because the deferred interest, which was added to the principle loan amount, also accrued interest. So, by not paying at least the interest due on the loan, the balance increased, which increased what would otherwise be the new interest-only payment. In other words, any deferred interest increased the loan balance and increased the amount of interest that was required for that new, higher balance.

Assuming the borrower continued to make the minimum payment for the first twelve months, the balance kept going higher for the two reasons mentioned above. In order to keep this feature from getting out of control, the loan was typically limited to maximum of 7.5% negative amortization. So, in theory, the borrower may not have been able to stay at the minimum payment for a full year, but generally they could.

The second payment option involved interest–only payments. As suggested by the name, the borrower would pay an amount equal to the interest that had accrued in the past month at the fully indexed rate on the outstanding balance. With this approach, negative amortization could not happen. On the flip side, loan balances would not go down either. Generally, Option ARMs allowed borrowers to make interest-only payments for a maximum of five years. At that point, the loan would be re-cast so that the outstanding balance would be paid off over the remaining term of the loan at the fully indexed, adjustable rate. It bears repeating that the balance, on which the loan would be re-cast, would be the same (if interest only payments were made) or even higher (if the minimum payment was made for the first twelve months) than it was at origination.

The third option looks more like any other conforming, fully amortized loan where the monthly payment includes principle and interest such that loan would be paid off by the end of its term (thirty years). These fully amortized payments would be subject to monthly changes if, and as, the index changed.

Fourth, the borrower could choose to pay more than the normal fully amortized payment, thereby decreasing the life of the loan and the interest paid back to the lender over the life of the loan.

This product quickly morphed into other similar looking products with slightly different features, like longer introductory periods, longer amortization periods, longer adjustment periods, different asset documentation requirements and different income documentation levels. But they all shared the same basic benefits: borrower choice, borrower flexibility and easier qualifying standards.

When Option ARMs originally hit the market several years ago, they started out like any other new product. They were originated and purchased somewhat conservatively. At the very least, they required full income documentation and the borrowers were qualified at the fully indexed rate (index + margin). With these parameters, it's no wonder the loans performed at least as well as expected. Then, over time, the rules loosened up; income documentation requirements went down and borrowers began to be qualified at the interest-only (not the fully-indexed) rate.

Then, as the market began to really heat up, Option ARM borrowers were qualified at the minimum (negatively amortized) payment, and their income didn't need to be documented at all. Let me say that again; borrowers were qualified based on their stated income and at the minimum (initial) payment, even though that was known to include negative amortization and would change within one year!

All of these features and benefits came with a price. Borrowers typically paid about 1% more in order to get this flexibility (options), the increased access to capital based on the easier qualifying standards and to cover the lender's risk of providing those very same things to the borrower. So here's the $64,000 question. If borrowers qualified for lower rates, why would they pay more for these features?

The answer is simple. The borrowers needed these features. They certainly didn't pay additional rate in order to make fully amortized or extra payments. They paid the premium in order to be able to pay less than interest-only payments and to watch the appreciation in the value of their property outpace the negative amortization that was accruing on their loans. That's great when it works. The problem is that the appreciation they were watching was due largely to the existence of the product itself which was making homes much more affordable. In that manner, the Option ARM product was dependent on itself to continue fueling the increase in home prices. If something were to happen to the product, then something would happen to the home prices.

To be fair, Option ARMs didn't have a corner on that market. The same was true for all the products that were collectively driving home prices up at historic rates (notwithstanding Greenspan's earlier comment that our appreciation rates were "remarkably average"). The longevity of all the products was dependent on the home price appreciation that the products were creating. The continuation of that appreciation, or, more importantly, the prevention of the collapse of home prices, was dependent on the continued existence of the products. Without one, the other disappears and all realized profits get erased.

It's normal for people to want simplicity and clear dividing loans. But lending does not allow for that clarity. Any of these products and features could overlap with one another. Subprime and non-traditional mortgages could have involved Option ARMs, 2nd trust deeds (loans or lines), Alt-A, negative amortization, stated or reduced income documentation, and jumbo loan amounts to name a few features.

However, all of these products and features have one thing in common. For all intents and purposes, they don't exist any more. That is why they were all written about in the past tense. Directly or indirectly, every one of these products were wiped out by certain shortsighted Congressional and regulatory agency efforts to end pre-determined, and alleged, predatory lending.

The vast majority of loans are NOT conforming, fixed-rate loans. This means that one way or another, they were caught up in the web of the IAG. This conclusion is reinforced by the attached bar graph painstakingly created by Charles Hugh Smith as seen on his website www.oftwominds.com. He obtained the information from three separate data sources. I understand that these numbers are not fully exhaustive, and the data can be sliced and diced, challenged, refuted, reconciled, etc. Regardless, these data are the best I've seen in the market, and they clearly illustrate a point that cannot be denied.

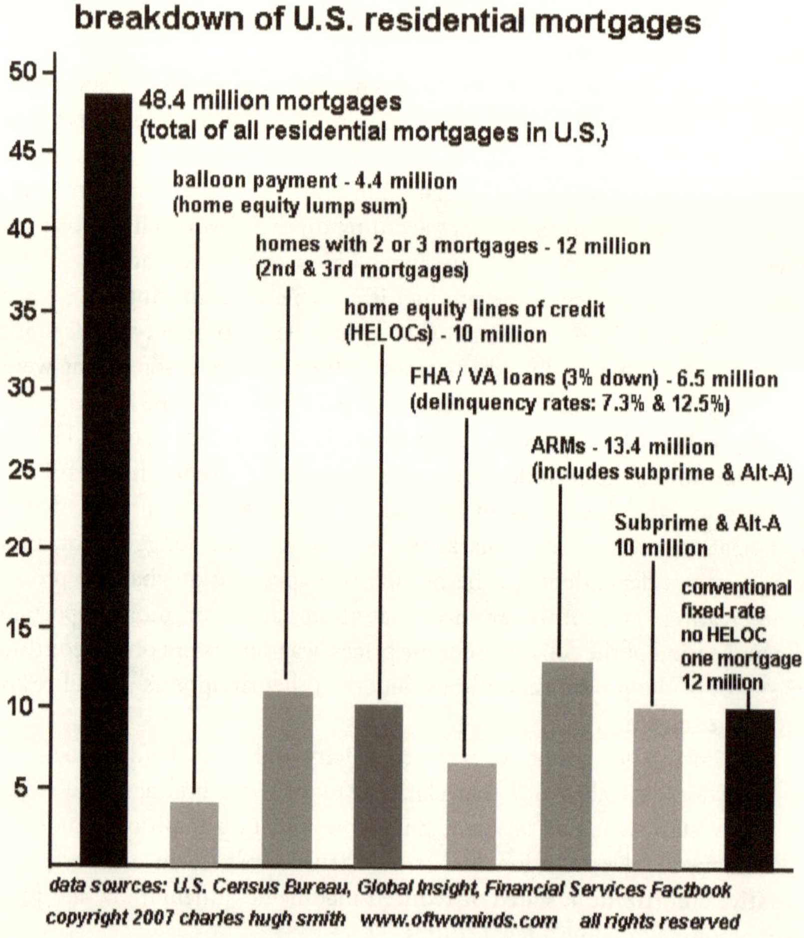
breakdown of U.S. residential mortgages
50
45
40
35
30
25
20
15
10
5
48.4 million mortgages
(total of all residential mortgages in U.S.)
balloon payment - 4.4 million
(home equity lump sum)
homes with 2 or 3 mortgages - 12 million
(2nd & 3rd mortgages)
home equity lines of credit
(HELOCs) - 10 million
FHA / VA loans (3% down) - 6.5 million
(delinquency rates: 7.3% & 12.5%)
ARMs - 13.4 million
(includes subprime & Alt-A)
Subprime & Alt-A
10 million
conventional
fixed-rate
no HELOC
one mortgage
12 million
data sources: U.S. Census Bureau, Global Insight, Financial Services Factbook
copyright 2007 charles hugh smith www.oftwominds.com all rights reserved

For the most part, all product lines in between the bars on either side of the box are gone from the marketplace. Assuming that some smattering of these products exist out there somewhere, this equates to about 70% of the total market!

This analysis is further supported by the fact that, before the IAG was published, $480B in non-traditional (excluding Option ARMs) and subprime loans was funded each quarter. That represented 64% of the market. By 2008, that number had dropped by 77% to $110B per quarter. Because 64% of the market was cut by 77%, the market fell by 50%! This is not yet

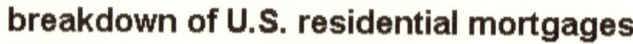

consistent with the bar graph that suggests the number is more like 70%. But that's because we have not yet included Option ARMs into the equation.

In 2006, about $535B in Option ARMs were funded, equating to 19% of the total market. That number had dropped by about 78% by the middle of 2008. That's a net loss of another 15% of the market (.19 x .78). And that takes us to a total market reduction of 65%.

By now we have settled down into a range of 65%-70% of the market that has gone away since the IAG was published on October 2006. This is offset by an increase in the production of conforming loans. That increase helps a little bit by shoring up availability of capital- any capital. However, it does not help the specific borrowers who are in the most trouble and who are key to getting the market stabilized for all of us. For this reason, the increase in production of conforming loans will be excluded from this discussion.

Having said all that, we have a suffered a 65% hit in the availability of capital for purchases and refinances of homes. We needed to cut out *some* of that production because it had clearly pushed the limit of sound underwriting and credit policy. But **a 65% hit equates to $1,937B or $1.9T in lost production! That is about 8.6 million loans, at an average loan amount of $225,000. With about 2.5 people per household, this has had a direct impact on about twenty-two million Americans!**

Who is most at risk as a result of this staggering product void? The answer is the homeowners who are trapped in their existing mortgages, while being subject to interest rate fluctuations and while not being able to execute their mortgage exit strategies. That is why nearly a million homes have already been foreclosed upon since this all began, why three to four million more are currently in foreclosure and why that number is growing to the tune of eight thousand loans per day!

To reiterate, these represent fallout from all loan types. But, if for some reason you are trying to sell your home while market value is being driven down by a relative flood of foreclosure listings (REOs) in your neighborhood, does it matter to you why those houses were foreclosed upon? Does it matter to you whether the previous owners were subprime, Alt-A or conforming? So, about eight million loans cannot be made and four million loans have gone into foreclosure. This is not a coincidence.

Having said that, what is the foreclosure risk in the Alt-A and Option ARM markets? As of mid-2008, we had just seen the peak of the subprime re-sets. However, we had not even begun to see the beginning of re-sets on Alt-A loans or Option ARMs! Approximately $600 billion in subprime loans experienced their first re-sets during 2007 and 2008. By comparison, approximately $500 billion in Option ARM re-sets and Alt-A loans will experience their first re-sets between 2009 and 2011. The bottom line is that we were only about half way through all loan resets as of mid-2008. The remaining half will play out over the next three years.

As if these numbers were not bad enough, the Rating Agency, Fitch added more darkness to the picture. They announced that approximately 80% of these loans were paying at the minimum level and realizing no principle reduction. They also determined that the average payment would increase by over $1,000 month once the resets began.

Some leaders would tell us not to worry about this next wave of re-sets because these borrowers, with better credit profiles, will be better able to withstand the re-sets. We need to poke some serious holes in that logic. First, remember that these borrowers were willing to pay a significant rate premium to get the structure and features they obtained with these loans because they didn't qualify for the long term, fixed-rate loans. Second, they may have paid the rate premium because they wanted the flexibility and then planned to refinance out at the first re-set. However, if that was their intention, they will no longer be able to do that since the products are gone. Third, the IAG specifically addressed these two types of loans because the regulators recognized the pending risk of the proliferating products. While they came up with the wrong solution, they certainly recognized the right problem. Fourth, these loans have never been "stress-tested" in the real world to see what will happen in an economic downturn. Given the extraordinarily low savings rate of Americans, I would say that this creates a huge question mark.

It is these loans that fueled the expansion of the HopeNow program into the LifeLine program to cover non-subprime loans. It is also these loans that partially explain why the agreed-upon "rate freeze" was done for five years because most of these loans will re-set within those five years. Of course, this is another red herring, as the Fed has lowered short-term rates (so lenders don't need to) and because freezing rates will not freeze loan terms. These loans are still subject to being re-set for terms and amortization, such as to eliminate negative amortization. I'm saying this to emphasize that we have not yet solved the problem. We have barely even pecked away at it.

You might buy into the idea that the damage is already done, that we're taking our medicine and the government is stepping in to solve the problem. If so, I would encourage you to re-evaluate your position. **Leaders need to say things to calm the market and to avoid panic. I understand that. But the risk is that if we actually believe what they're saying, we're bound to expect less of our leaders and we're bound to absorb much more pain in the near, but sustained, future.**

Chapter 9:   Red, White or Blue

"The road to hell is paved with good intentions."
  - 16th Century Proverb

Have you ever been involved in a car crash when the airbags deployed? If you have, you know they are not soft or comfortable. They are quite painful and designed as the last line of defense to save our lives. Economic bubbles are like airbags. They are not pleasant things that little kids chase around or blow into the air. They are, in fact, indicative of a market crash, and they hurt like hell. They also trigger a long list of equally painful consequences that will be taken care of over time.

Having said that, we have to wonder why people say the things they say. Maybe it has something to do with the powerful combination of denial, optimism and ignorance. Maybe it has something to do with the knowledge a few very powerful people have that they can shape and affect entire markets by simply uttering a few words.

We've already covered the inaccurate, untimely and inconsistent messages delivered by Fed Chairmen Bernanke. Not to be outdone by the Fed, on May 17, 2007, Secretary of the Treasury (the nation's Chief Financial Officer, a member of the President's Cabinet and 5th in the Presidential line of succession) Henry Paulson said in an interview with Jim Lehrer:

> "That correction (housing) was inevitable; that correction has now been significant. **We think it is near the bottom**. It will take a while to work its way through the system. Fortunately for us, we have a very diverse, healthy economy. There are other things that are positive that are offsetting that.
>
> So **my very strong view is that we are near the bottom and that this will be contained as the housing market will be contained**, and we're fortunate that we have a diverse, healthy economy."

There's that word again; "contained." Does the Treasury Secretary understand the connection between the mortgage-driven housing market and the overall economy? Surely, he does. Was he aware of the impact that the IAG could have on the mortgage industry given the fact that two of the five Agencies involved reported up through the Treasury Department over which he is the Chair? I would think so.

Interestingly, only ten months after Bernanke's statement of "containment" to Congress, and only eight months after a similar statement from the Treasury Secretary, former Fed Chairman Greenspan delivered an entirely different message in an interview with Die Zeit on January 30, 2008. In that interview, Greenspan said that the Fed or political policies could "probably not" keep the US economy from sliding into a recession. He said that "the influences of the global economy today are stronger than almost any monetary or budgetary response" and that the turmoil was "entirely the result of market forces at a global level."

Did we go from a contained subprime mortgage problem to an eminent recession within ten short months? If so, how did that happen? Was it never just a subprime crisis? Or, is Greenspan attributing the crisis to something bigger (the global economy) than our ability to handle it, just so that he can protect his own legacy? In that same interview with Die Zeit, Greenspan also said that he found it hard to understand that "the Federal Reserve policy [under him] had somehow allowed housing and stock prices to rise." Maybe this book will help Mr. Greenspan understand how the policies of the Fed did, in fact, fuel the increase in home prices and, more importantly, how they contributed to the crash of the housing market.

Clearly, these three people are not singing off the same sheet of music. In fact, they're not even in the same concert hall. That's a real problem since we're not going to get out of this mess if the former, but still influential, Fed Chairman is saying a recession is inevitable and the cause is global, while the Treasury Secretary is attributing the blame to the lenders. Meanwhile, the current Fed Chairman was so blind to the problem that he thought it was contained, until the point that emergency measures were needed to stave off recession or, at the very least, to counter the damage created by the Fed's lack of action to that point.

Let me further illustrate how disconnected these leaders are from each other. As recently as July 2007, Chairman of the Fed Bernanke put the subprime-related "exposure" at $50-$100B. Meanwhile, Goldman-Sachs has put the total projected price tag of mortgage-related losses at $400B! Not only were these projections off by 300%-700%, Goldman-Sachs also projected that these losses would trigger a $2T retraction in mortgage lending. These differences are especially significant because the most recent Chairman and CEO of Goldman-Sachs was none other than the current Treasury Secretary, Henry Paulson! Granted, we're not exactly comparing apples to apples, as there may be a real difference between subprime-related exposure, mortgage-related losses and market retraction. Yet, the numbers are extremely far apart and result from someone being wrong or from someone intentionally downplaying the scope of the situation.

In order to put a $2T retraction into perspective, consider the fact that the President recently submitted the largest budget in history to Congress. It was the first time that the $3T mark was hit or surpassed. So, according to Goldman-Sachs, the market retraction may equal two thirds of the submitted national budget! As another comparison, consider the total cost of the war in Iraq. Through 2008, the total cost will be $611B, or about $100B per year since the war started in March, 2003. That is not chump change. However, the retraction in the mortgage market is projected to equal 3.25 times the total cost of the war through 2008!

Furthermore, if $50B-$100B subprime loss is an accurate projection from the Fed and $400B total mortgage loss from Goldman-Sachs is also correct, then this means that $300B-$350B in projected mortgage related losses are due to loans that are NOT subprime. This certainly supports the dirty little secret we uncovered earlier. If, on the other hand, one of the projections is wrong, then you have to question which one.

Let's take a look. Since the Fed made that forecast in July 2007, it has since lowered rates by 62% from 5.25% to 2.00%. This included the first interim (between Fed meetings) rate cut since the terrorist attacks. On January 22, 2008, the Fed cut rates in an emergency session by .75% and that was the largest single rate cut in twenty-five years. Many people saw this interim cut as pure desperation to stave off a national, and potentially global, recession. Two days later, Congress, under pressure from the President, agreed to a $150B economic stimulus package, which was later increased to $167B and ratified by the Senate. The Congressional package was followed up a week or so later with another .50% cut by the Fed, which only reinforced the market's perception of the Fed's desperation.

Yet, even more bad news kept rolling in, and the stock market continued its downward trend, often losing hundreds of points per day! Part and parcel with all this, the treasury department and the President brokered a voluntary deal with the lending industry to mitigate some of the projected damage. Just three months earlier, they were fully opposed to any such actions. You don't have to be too good at math to see that the market (Goldman-Sachs, in particular) had figured this thing out while the government was making the problem worse, saying it was contained, and pointing fingers at the lending industry. Well, now that all the denial is behind us, the only question being debated is whether we are headed towards a recession or whether we are already in one.

Let's dig into this one. **Economies become unstable when wages and earnings don't rise proportionately with prices. This is exactly what happened when aggressive and creative loan products coupled with artificially low rates and liberal underwriting standards fueled a nearly 300% increase in house prices nationally over the past ten years. Meanwhile, personal income increased only a small fraction of**

that amount. This created a deadly combination where people had significantly greater access to equity than they could afford to pay in the long run [meaning, low start rates].

This is the mechanism for a housing bubble which was unaffected by any efforts on the part of the Fed to avoid it. As a frame of reference, after the dot-com crash of 2000, Greenspan explained in 2004 that "instead of trying to contain a putative bubble by drastic actions with largely unpredictable consequences, we chose, as we noted in our mid-1999 Congressional testimony, to focus on policies to mitigate the fallout when it occurs and, hopefully, ease the transition to the next expansion."

As explained earlier, the next "expansion" was the housing market which was triggered by the extraordinarily low rates and availability of aggressive alternative loan products, both of which tied back to the Fed (extraordinarily low rates and Greenspan's encouragement for the market to create even more alternative loan products). As we all know, the housing market has since become another exploded bubble. Despite Greenspan's hopes, that "transition" was anything but eased; rather, it was turbo-charged by the Fed's policies.

We need to be aware of this recipe for bubbles. The government uses the same play from the bubble book time after time. As a case in point, and as the result of various financial circumstances, the S&L industry was in significant trouble back in the early 1980s. The government responded with decreased rates, reducing them from 19.04% in July 1981 to 8.63% by May 1983! They also responded by stimulating an increase in monetary supply - sort of. In that case, the increase in money supply was caused by the deregulation of the industry that allowed S&Ls to hold lower reserves and to invest deposits in virtually anything. However, the FDIC as a branch of the US government insured those deposits to the tune of $100,000 per account.

Since the S&Ls did not hold the ultimate risk for these deposits, they were able to dramatically increase the rates they paid on CDs and other investment certificates. This brought massive amounts of money into the S&Ls. In turn, they could invest that government insured money in high risk, high reward ventures. When they worked, the S&Ls profited wildly. When they failed, and they usually did, the FDIC picked up the tab.

Indirectly, this fueled the boom in the housing industry that quickly became a housing bubble. It was a classic case of inflation, with too many dollars chasing too few goods. That bubble popped in 1991, along with the collapse of the S&L industry.

Over the next several years, the availability of low priced capital fueled the next boom in the dot-com industry. This bubble burst in a prelude to terrorist attacks and corporate scandals. The reaction of the government was the same:

they decreased rates and increased money supply. This led to the next bubble in housing, which burst in 2007. The reaction, as we know, has been lower rates and increased money supply. The result appears to be revealing itself in the form of the next bubble in oil speculation, which is largely responsible for driving up the price at the pump. This recipe for deflating bubbles does nothing to prevent them from bursting and, worse, only serves to quickly inflate the next bubble. This is exactly why government efforts to date have done nothing to alleviate this crisis but have done everything to drive up the cost of gas and all oil related products.

What is that expression about insanity? Doesn't it say something like, insanity is doing the same thing over and over while expecting a different result? Why then, do we expect different results every time we respond to bubbles with the same strategies?

Another economic fundamental is that we are not isolated from the rest of the world. Between the market's close on Monday, January 14, 2008 and its close on Friday, January 18, 2008, the Dow Jones Industrial Average (DJIA) dropped 679 points, or 5.31%! Our market was closed for Martin Luther King Day on the following Monday, January 22, but other markets around the world were open for business. On that day, benchmarks dropped 5.5% in Great Britain, 6.8% in France, 7.2% in Germany, 7.4% in Asia, 4.8% in Canada, 3.9% in Japan, 5.1% in China, and 7.4% in India. The common thread was that these countries, and all other countries as well, concluded that our economy was in a downward spiral and that the President's proposed economic stimulus plan was too little and too late to avert a recession.

So, following an emergency session, the Fed lowered its funds rate by 75 basis points (.75%) on Tuesday, January 22, 2008. Our market immediately stabilized and went up 122 points that very day. This is not a simple walk down memory lane. Rather this illustrates an extremely important point. If our economy tails off, the world follows suit. They, in turn, become highly reluctant to invest in American financial instruments and enterprises. Of course, that is offset by the continued devaluation of the American dollar against foreign currencies. But that's another story.

Foreign countries understand that (due to our trade deficit with other countries) as American consumers spend less money, a disproportionate amount of that reduction will be on foreign made and imported products. Contrary to Greenspan's assertions that we are at the mercy of world markets, it appears that the U.S. is the dog that wags the tail. That's a lot of responsibility for people all around the world, and it is more than enough reason to make sure that we are doing everything possible to avoid a recession.

There is another economic facet worth explanation. We know that the advent of mortgage-backed (MBSs) and asset-backed (ABSs) securitization was the key event that allowed for the explosion of the conforming mortgage industry since the mid-1980s and for the non-traditional markets since 1992. We also know that other countries, institutional investors and pension funds ultimately invest in these securities. Even if no one is talking about it yet, pensions funds are at tremendous risk.

Because lenders Rep & Warrant (guarantee against) for fraud and misrepresentation, they have significant financial liability in the form of potential repurchase demands from investors. However, it is also true that if the lenders' arms are twisted too far, they will likely just shut down. In that case, the investors, which are often pension funds, have liability for subsequent losses. So, in the event that the investors rely too heavily on Reps & Warrants, lenders go out of business and the pension funds themselves suffer.

That may not create much sympathy from the general public until we realize that it is these very same pension funds with whom most of us have placed our retirement savings. Without question, that money, your money is at risk. I'm not being overly dramatic to tell you that the bursting of the housing bubble may likely trigger an enormous problem in pension funds and retirement benefits. In fact, the first shoe may have already fallen. While writing this book, Bear Stearns (to be addressed in the next chapter), which was the fifth largest investment bank in the country, tanked into a $2.00/share fire sale. Along with its fall from a $23B company to a $230M company, almost all of its value was wiped out. What do you suppose happens to all the private investors who thought they were safe having their pension funds and retirement accounts invested in Bear Stearns?

While the number of various subsets of the economy is virtually unlimited, there is one more that needs to be addressed. We discussed earlier how all ABSs and MBSs end up with bond insurance placed on them. These bond insurers guarantee the performance of the bonds in accordance with certain parameters or tolerances, which are established and paid for by the investors. Like all insurance companies, the bond insurers need to step up as required by the policies they underwrote.

This is no different from the insurance companies who insure cars, homes, property and life. The difference is that the bond insurers insure timely cash flow of payments on securities (in the case of ABSs and MBSs). That's all fine until the damage is so great that the insurance company itself runs the risk of not being able to honor their obligation. The same might be true for any homeowner insurance company who could become unable to pay up after a catastrophic earthquake simultaneously destroys thousands upon thousand of homes.

This is exactly the concern with the major bond insurers regarding the mortgage industry. Their own credit is in serious doubt, and they run the risk of being down graded by the rating agencies. As mentioned earlier, we know that Moody's has already downgraded the two biggest bond insurers, Ambac and MBIA. The domino affect is in full play on this one. These same bond insurers also insure virtually all municipal bonds, which nearly all cities and counties depend on for their growth and development, like roads, schools and key infrastructure.

Without solid bond insurance, investor appetite for muni-bonds dwindles and cities cut back on projects and lay off employees. Warren Buffet recently extended an offer to re-insure the bond insurers, thus bolstering their financial capacity. However, the bond insurers rejected the proposal based on the conclusion that Buffet's company, Berkshire Hathaway, would not re-insure the bonds that created the most risk to the bond insurance companies. In particular, he apparently would not have anything to do with bonds in any way related to subprime or other alternative loans. I suppose he had his fill of subprime exposure as the majority shareholder in H&R Block that was the parent of Option One Mortgage, which, at its peak, was funding about $4B/month in subprime loans.

Despite the impact on world markets and critical sub-sets of the American economy, like retirement, pension funds and municipal bonds, it's clear that the separate but related decisions, actions and inaction on the part of Congress, the Fed, the Treasury and the Regulatory Agencies served to trigger and magnify the mortgage and housing crisis. That, in turn, immediately permeated the rest of the economy and has put us in, or on the brink of, a serious recession.

Recessions occur when the growth rate of the GDP (Gross Domestic Product) is negative for two or more consecutive quarters. Gross Domestic Product (GDP) is commonly accepted as the total amount of all goods and services produced inside the United States. This includes consumer spending, such as food, retail goods, insurance and medical care. It also includes total investments like, machinery, housing and inventories. It includes all domestic government spending for things like government salaries, public schools and military equipment. GDP also includes the total amount of net exports, which represents the difference between spending on domestic goods by foreigners and spending on foreign goods by domestic residents.

Here's the asterisk. GDP only includes production of goods and services created inside the United States, regardless of who is doing the work. For example, the production from a Ford automobile plant in Mexico would not be part of our GDP. However, the production from a Toyota automobile plant in the U.S. would be included in the GDP. Therefore, industry growth outside of the United States does nothing to pull us out of a recession. It is only domestic growth that matters. This makes sense when you step back and think about it.

Now, back to the definition of a recession. What exactly does "negative growth" in GDP that must exist for two consecutive quarters really mean? This oxy-moronic measurement used by economists just means lower, reduced or declined. Therefore, a recession technically exists when the GDP goes down for two consecutive quarters. It's that simple, at least in theory.

In reality, however, two things disconnect this definition in practice. The first happens when the GDP goes up at a slower and slower pace in each subsequent quarter. This may feel very much like a recession because the economy is slowing down, but that doesn't mean it's getting smaller. It's just growing at a decreased rate.

The second and more significant conflict occurs when individual quarters of reduced GDP are interrupted by quarters of slight increases in GDP. For example, consider three consecutive quarters where the GDP declines by 1% per quarter. In this example, the GDP would decrease 3% over nine months, or three quarters, and would be considered a recession. Compare that with an individual quarter where the GDP declined by 5%, followed by a 1% increase followed by a 4% decrease. This second example would yield a combined reduction in GDP of 8% over three quarters, which is more than 2 ½ times greater impact than in the first example. Yet, it would *not* be considered a recession.

So, the numbers, the analytics and the definition can be misleading. But the feeling is not. The government, economists, analysts and politicians can get paralyzed in technical debates over the matter; meanwhile, we have to live with the very real affects of a recession. This is why there is strong debate about whether we are, or are not, actually in a recession. Technically speaking, we may not be. But it sure feels like we are.

The first thing that happens in a recession is that consumer spending declines. We typically start with the extras, like home improvements and furnishings, Starbucks (which explains why they are closing six hundred stores nationwide), eating out, vacations and entertainment, including movies and sporting events. Then we start digging in a little deeper and put off automobile repairs, clothes purchases, medical and dental procedures. The extent of these cutbacks in discretionary spending relies heavily on the availability of home equity. We can all say that in an ideal world everyone would live below their means, spend only what they made and never used debt to finance their lifestyles.

But in the real world, most households are supported by 2 incomes, the national savings rate is around 0% (sometimes less) and inflation outpaces increases to income, which effectively raises the net cost of living (think about gas, oil, medical insurance, college education, etc.) Add to that the "keeping up with the Joneses" phenomena, the allure of aggressive marketing on all products and services (including home equity loans) and the constant availability of cheap credit and "no interest" incentives that eventually come due and payable.

Given all these factors, is it any wonder that people rely on their home equity to subsidize their standard of living? Short of having access to sufficient home equity, entire populations turn to credit card and other unsecured debt. This is not hard to see; just look at how credit card debt and delinquencies have spiked to historic levels since the mortgage market was frozen in mid-2007. Contrary to popular belief in some circles, human behavior cannot be legislated. So when people became unable to subsidize their cost of living with home equity, (as fueled by product, price and secondary market demand), they turned to unsecured debt. The root cause(s) of borrower behavior and needs were never addressed, and so we ended up rearranging the deck chairs on the Titanic. Nothing more.

As a result of the reduction in consumer spending, companies and businesses make less money and unemployment goes up. Historically, the rise in unemployment associated with recessions has been fairly significant and has always made the recessions painfully obvious. This time around, however, there may be something of a mask over the face of unemployment. Because manufacturing jobs have been steadily off-shored over the past couple decades, the rise in unemployment may not be as high as it was in past recessions. Currently, manufacturing jobs account for about (only) 20% of all jobs domestically. So as manufacturers start to reduce output, comparatively fewer people inside the United States will lose their jobs as a result.

Nonetheless, it's easy to see how this cycle becomes self-sustaining. As home values go down, people have less equity in their homes. On March 5, 2008, it was announced that home equity on a national level has dropped to its lowest level since 1945! But even this is optimistically misleading. While the average homeowner has about 50% equity, the truth is that national homeowner equity is greatly bar-belled, with the vast majority of homeowners having either very high amounts of equity (90%-100%) or very low amounts of equity (<0%-10%).

Further, it serves to reason that the people with high amounts of equity have learned to live within their means and have paid down their mortgages over many years. These people typically don't rely on equity to subsidize their standards of living and they're not likely to start now. The people who do rely on their equity, no longer have it. This leads to greatly reduced discretionary spending which leads to greatly reduced output of products and services (the

GDP). Consider why Ford posted the largest quarterly loss in its history for the 2nd quarter of 2008, why Levitz is in bankruptcy and going out of business and why GM just posted a $37.8B loss for 2007, which is the largest annual loss in history for an automotive company.

These corporate losses, of course, obviously involve increased unemployment. For example, in responses to its losses for 2007, GM has offered buy-outs to all 74,000 of its unionized, hourly wage earners. Similarly, but to a lesser extent, Chrysler intends to cut the number of its models in half and to close as many as a third of their dealerships nationwide. Yahoo just announced it is going to lay off 1000 employees, which represents over 7% of its workforce.

But that's not anywhere close to the end of the story. Who else is going down with this ship (while the band keeps playing in order to help keep people calm)? Take a look at just the lending industry itself. According to Implode-O-Meter.com, 280 significant lenders or large lending divisions have already gone out of business since late 2006. This number is changing daily but, for sure, this does not include the countless little correspondent lenders who had small warehouse lines with other lenders. It certainly doesn't include the thousands upon thousand of brokers who have closed shop. No, it just includes the relatively big ones like IndyMac, New Century, Option One, Fremont, Argent, Saxon, First Franklin, Aurora, Washington Mutual Wholesale, e-Trade Mortgage and 270 other lenders. Because the number of companies on the list keeps growing, the average number of employees per company is hard to determine. Some of these companies had some fifty to a hundred employees. Some had thousands.

In addition, and this is big, there are the many thousands of employees who have lost their jobs even though the companies have not (yet) imploded. For example, Countrywide alone has already announced over eleven thousand lay offs. All in all, hundreds of thousands of people in the lending industry alone have lost their jobs. It's interesting that we don't hear much about this. What would we hear if 100,000 employees from the automobile industry lost their jobs? What if 100,000 people from the airline industry lost their jobs? Would there be silence?

Worse yet, some unfair discrimination may be happening. I know several people who feel as though former mortgage industry employees are being blackballed from other industries. In fact, they are sure of it. These stories are anecdotal at best, as there may be many other reasons they are not being picked up by other employers. But, just in case, let me say that holding mortgage industry employees accountable for the mortgage crisis is like holding soldiers accountable for war. I don't know when "mortgage" became a four-letter word, but the employees did not cause the problem. The vast majority of them are skilled, dedicated people who are passionate about customer service.

Having worked for several mortgage companies, both large and small, I can tell you that except for the very rare exceptions, the employees cared greatly and passionately about the customers and the borrowers. Make no mistake, these employees are also paying the price, and at a very personal level. Like other borrowers, many have already lost their homes, while many others are at risk of losing their homes. But in a classic, double-whammy fashion, they have also lost their jobs. This mess is not their fault.

While these are just a few examples, there is no avoiding the fact that increased unemployment, along with less home equity to protect, causes an increase in mortgage defaults and foreclosures. This leads to greater inventory on the market, which leads to lower prices and even lower availability of equity (if that's possible).

That's why, despite statements to the contrary from the Fed and the Treasury way back in early 2007, we have definitely not reached bottom. In fact, employers slashed sixty-three thousand jobs in February 2008, which is the most in any single month in the past five years. This was followed up by six consecutive months with more than sixty thousand job losses. These disturbing numbers and trends indicate that, unless we change course, we may be headed directly into the teeth of a financial collapse. This view is shared by Representative, and former presidential candidate Ron Paul (R-TX), who, on July 9, 2008, said"

> "There are reasons to believe this coming crisis is different and bigger than the world has ever experienced... Little doubt exists as to whether we'll get stagflation [sluggish economic growth coupled with high unemployment and a high rate of inflation]. The question that will soon be asked is: When will that stagflation become an inflationary depression?"

The way we are going, this doomsday type prediction is not outside the realm of possibility. Whether it gets that bad or not, we have a lot to fix. Increased unemployment, increasing defaults and foreclosures, declining equity, increased inventory of homes, lower home prices and greatly reduced discretionary and necessary spending all need to be turned around. Eventually, these cycles run their course, the same as a massive firestorm would ultimately burn itself out even if we did nothing about it. But, in the meantime, the costs and risks are far too high for us to just sit back and wait for that to happen. People do not want these cycles to run their course. They expect them to be acknowledged - not denied, addressed - not ignored and solved - not just discussed.

This brings us to the subject of politics and, in particular, the upcoming general election in November. We all know that political races are won and lost based on the economy. But the only other thing we know for sure is that our next President is currently a Senator. This has happened only thee times in history: JFK in 1960, Harding in 1920 and Garfield in 1880. It's fair and appropriate to question why this is such a rare event. Political pundits generally attribute it to the tendency for Senators not to have any direct economic experience. Typically, they have not run anything with a budget. This should be concerning to all of us given the scope of this problem and given the fact that politics and economics are inextricably linked together.

Perhaps, no one understood this better than Bill Clinton. While many economists do not give him credit for the economic recovery that happened under his watch, he clearly understood what people wanted. In 1992, he ran for the presidency based on a simple and memorable platform. "It's the economy, stupid" resonated across the country and across political aisles. By the end of Clinton's second term, we were headed into an economic recession just like we were at the end of Bush (41's) presidency eight years earlier and just like the one we are headed into at the end of Bush (43's) presidency eight years later. It's hard to tell for sure, but maybe there's a trend here.

We are now again in the midst of election season, and it's an understatement to say that there are significant differences between Democrats and Republicans regarding what issues are most important to them. However, there is no question that the economy has recently surged up the list for both parties.

Ironically, perhaps, both parties have selected a nominee with virtually no experience running an economy. This lack of experience is shown most clearly by their lack of a comprehensive understanding of this mortgage crisis. While the mortgage industry is the key driver of our economy, it has been relegated to the subject of occasional speeches and political sound-bites.

For instance, Hillary Clinton, who has since lost her bid for the nomination, referred to the subprime problem during her acceptance speech following the primaries held on Super Tuesday. She mentioned "the couple so determined to send their daughter to college that they're willing to mortgage their home with a subprime 2nd mortgage." This is what I call politicizing an issue. At the very least, let's just say that I'm skeptical. How did that conversation happen? Did this couple make it through the multiple lines of defense surrounding the Senator and blurt out that they had obtained a subprime 2nd mortgage?

Did she even consider the possibility that this hypothetical lender lost money making that loan? If the loan was real and was made during the past several years, I guarantee the lender lost money making it. Lenders make

2nd trust deed loans primarily as an accommodation or as a mechanism to supplement a first trust deed in order to finalize some transaction. On their own, second trust deeds lose money and they're risky for lenders.

But, for the sake of argument, let's say that the couple did leverage the equity in their home to pay for their daughter's college education. Does it concern the Senator that this couple no longer has the ability to make that type of decision? Maybe that couple was comfortable with their 2nd mortgage, was able to pay it on time, enjoyed the tax advantages of writing off the interest and, most importantly, was able to pay for their daughter's education. Contrary to Clinton's implication, these people may very well have been the beneficiaries of the product as opposed to the victim of it.

Frankly, I don't know if her issue was subprime lending or the cost of a college education. Either way, she implied that only people with perfect credit and completely verifiable income should be able to use their equity to finance their kids' education. Unfortunately, the point is moot. With the virtual elimination of these products, this couple, and everyone else like them, no longer has control over their own equity and their own financial options and decisions.

Less than a month later, Clinton suggested the government should require all institutions eligible for the Federal Reserve's credit to follow the same regulations required of commercial banks. She recommended Federal oversight of newer financial arrangements like "complex derivatives" and making rating agencies more independent in order to reduce potential conflicts of interest. Clinton said that the recently enacted $168 billion stimulus package "did next to nothing to help homeowners and communities struggling with foreclosure."

In perhaps her most interesting proposal, she seemed to pull a play from the Republican book when she said she would offer legislation "to provide mortgage companies with protection against the threat of such (investor) lawsuits." She went on to say that:

> "Many mortgage companies are reluctant to help families restructure their mortgages because they're afraid of being sued by the investment banks, the private equity firms and others who own the mortgage papers. This is the case even though writing down [reducing the payoff amount of] a mortgage is often more profitable than foreclosing."

There are some aspects of her statements that are just too enticing to pass over. First, she is correct with respect to lenders' fear of lawsuits keeping them from being more flexible and accommodating with borrowers. Further, she is actually talking about a mechanism that would help resolve the problem with the mortgage crisis of today and not just address ways to prevent another disaster in the future. But one has to wonder how she came upon her epiphany.

On February 10, 2008, just a day after she lost to Senator Obama in a clean sweep of Louisiana, Nebraska, Washington and the U.S. Virgin Islands, Clinton appointed Maggie Williams as her new campaign manager. Is it possible that the Senator's new-found wisdom is the direct result of appointing Williams? Maggie Williams, who was the former First Lady's Chief of Staff, is also on the Board of Directors of Delta Funding. Delta was one of the nations largest subprime lenders until it went bankrupt. Delta's history goes back several years before Williams entered the picture and, depending on whom you ask, had already established its reputation as the poster child of unscrupulous subprime lenders.

I'm not saying that Clinton's campaign manager contributed in any way to the performance and reputation of Delta Funding. I am suggesting, however, that Clinton's sudden awareness of some of the very real pressures on lenders (investor lawsuits) may have resulted from appointing a person who had some real insight into the lending industry. Yet, at the same time, she recommended an expert mortgage working group made up of Fed Chairmen, Treasury Secretaries, Regulatory leaders, and such while making no mention of including lending industry participants. **This type of arrogance is the same thing that fueled the problem in the first place, while Congressional committees were working with regulatory groups and the Fed to create the IAG while ignoring prophetic input from the industry itself.**

Further, while talking about the legal fears that handcuff lenders, Clinton said, "This [lack of flexibility to restructure loans] is the case, even though writing down the value of a mortgage is often more profitable than foreclosing." This may sound somewhat trivial to the casual listener, but it's quite significant because it shows her mindset regarding lenders (and therefore, her limited ability to work with them towards a solution). Neither write-downs nor foreclosures are "profitable" events for lenders. She was close on this issue to the extent that lenders do lose less money on write-downs that subsequently perform or payoff than they lose if they have to foreclose. But neither one is more "profitable" than the other. Both propositions are financial losses for lenders. It's as if she can't get herself to admit or see that lenders are anything but thieves.

As just mentioned, while still in the race, Senator Clinton called for the creation of an Emergency Mortgage Team (ostensibly made up of the people who largely created the problem). Obama's camp responded that there was nothing new in her suggestions since he had sent a letter to Federal Reserve Chairman Ben Bernanke and Treasury Secretary Henry Paulson "to convene a homeownership preservation summit" suggesting the same idea about a year earlier. This is a classic example of politicizing a crisis. While it's nice to know that Obama sent a letter some twelve months earlier, does that really matter? Did the meetings take place? Were the leaders brought together? Were solutions created? No, but apparently, a letter was written.

Senator Obama continued by saying:

> "The government must revive the economy by tightening regulations and reforming its own Agencies to adjust to the realities of modern finance... to renew our economy — and to ensure that we are not doomed to repeat a cycle of bubble and bust again and again — we need to address not only the immediate crisis in the housing market; we also need to create a 21st century regulatory framework, and pursue a bold opportunity agenda for the American people."

I have no clue what either of these statements means accept that they imply and involve more government bureaucracy and intervention.

While he mentioned the need to address the "immediate crisis," I didn't pick up on any clear, direct suggestions or ideas. It is clear, however, that both he and Clinton support a $30B stimulus package aimed specifically at troubled homeowners. Both use the logic that if we can support or bailout large investment banks with a $30B guarantee, then we can provide the same amount of money to homeowners.

It's not like he's an outsider; he's a Senator running for President! He certainly should have the clout to pull people together if he were really interested in solving the problem. While Representative Frank and Senator Dodd were, and still are, painfully and dangerously misguided in their efforts to solve this problem, they at least have been dedicated to the cause. They wrote letters, too, but they also gathered constituency and have kept momentum behind their cause. Frankly, Senator Obama sounds much more interested in being perceived as forward thinking and ahead of the curve than in getting the problem solved.

As we know, Senator Obama swept the Democratic side of the "Potomac Primaries" on February 12, 2008. On the very next day, he made a speech about the economy at a General Motors plant in Janesville, Wisconsin. The timing is significant because exit polls from both parties showed something very interesting. First, voters in both parties in both states most often picked the economy as the most important issue facing the country. Secondly, Democrats and Republicans had very different views about the condition of the national economy. Half of Virginia Republicans and four in ten Maryland Republicans said the economy was still in good shape, while nine in ten Democrats in both states said the economy was in bad shape.

With this information in hand, Obama seized the opportunity as if he were waiting for it to happen. He said:

> "We are not standing on the brink of recession due to forces beyond our control. The fallout from the housing crisis that's cost jobs and wiped out savings was not an inevitable part of the business cycle. It was a failure of leadership and imagination in Washington.
>
> It's in Washington where politicians like John McCain and Hillary Clinton voted for a war in Iraq that should've never been authorized and never been waged - a war that is costing us thousands of precious lives and billions of dollars a week that could be used on infrastructure, job training and health care."

We can all recognize the brilliance of connecting a newly crowned top issue (based on the exit polls) with his stance on the war. That's good strategy. Further, I certainly agree with Senator Obama that this crisis was not inevitable and with his implication that it is at the root of weakness in the economy. Likewise, I completely agree that this situation resulted from lack of leadership in Washington. But this is where we part ways.

His statement fails to even mention his own party's responsibility, which includes the actions of Barney Frank, Christopher Dodd and company in their committees that launched us onto the brink of recession. Of course, he's not running against them, so there's no value in making that statement. To the contrary, it would be political suicide.

Senator Obama's position had become clearer as we approached the general elections. By July 2008, he had joined ranks with the rest of the political world in his position on the causes of the crisis. He, like most of his counterparts in Washington, is firmly laying blame on the lending industry. More specifically, he blames the predatory, abusive and unscrupulous lenders that took advantage of at-risk borrowers. This is quite scary considering the fact that the Senator may become our next President.

Yet, we need to be aware of liberal thinking that says the government knows better for us than we do for ourselves. Specifically, until these products were taken away, people made the right decisions for themselves.

Then there is the Republican nominee for President, John McCain. He attributed the problem to rampant speculation, to complacent lenders who failed to use common sense and to sophisticated financial structures that made it difficult for lenders to negotiate solutions with borrowers. He called for a rational solution process and promised not to politicize the crisis by offering overly reactive measures just because it is an election year. He called for more transparency in lending and higher capital reserves for lenders.

McCain called on homeowners to provide "responsible" down payments for homes, saying government-backed companies, like Fannie Mae, should never back loans when the borrower "clearly does not have skin in the game." McCain said he opposed any government bailout of "those who act irresponsibly, whether they are big banks or small borrowers." Finally, he said, "any assistance must be temporary and must not reward people who were irresponsible at the expense of those who weren't."

Okay, so that all sounds good on paper, but it's a real disappointment. Talking about "responsible down payments" and "skin in the game" does nothing to address the millions of people who are at risk of losing their homes. These comments are analogous to the statements Bill Clinton made to the Russians when they were at the height of unemployment and people were freezing outside in the food lines. President Clinton acknowledged the importance of people getting back to work, but for the wrong reason. His emphasis was on the payroll taxes the government was not receiving due to extreme unemployment. Starving, freezing, unemployed people do not care about the taxes that their government is not receiving. Likewise, American homeowners who are losing their homes don't want to hear about future borrowers and future lending practices. They want, and need, solutions for their problem - today.

The fact is that the comments from all three Senators are nothing more than timely political sound-bites. They are not solutions and they do not reflect the seriousness and the urgency of the situation. Just as troubling is McCain's statement that he would turn to the advice and writings of Alan Greenspan for economic advice. I'm sure you know where I stand on that one.

As we head into the general elections, we should expect both parties to shift their campaign strategies. Both parties will need to court their bases, but they will very likely move towards the center in order to get the centrists, the "undecideds," the moderates, the independents or whatever you call the people who will, in fact, decide our next President. By then, the economic picture will be clearer, and we should know whether or not we took a major hit but avoided an all out recession. Given our current instability and all the economic indicators the experts look at, it has to be one or the other.

In the meantime, I would suggest that the real leader is the one of them who steps up NOW to help solve the problem and not just claim that they will do something once, and if, they become President. At the very least, the right candidate should be able to deliver a specific plan on how to address these challenges.

Clearly, I am saying the problem is bigger than the Fed and the Treasury will admit. It's mortgages and housing. It's pension funds and retirement benefits. It's national and international. It's private, and it's government. The good news is that neither President Bush nor the Democratic leadership on either side of the Hill can afford a recession.

A recession would virtually guarantee a victory for the Democrats in the Presidential election, and that would mean a premature end to the war in Iraq and in our immediate exit from the region. This would create great instability in the region and have immeasurable negative consequences for generations to come. For Bush, his legacy will be cemented in failure, and his vision will never be realized. He knows that. The last thing the Democrats want within two years of taking over the House and the Senate is responsibility for a recession.

One thing is for sure: Every American, every business, every employee, every politician and every voter has been, or will be, directly affected by this crisis. As a result, one other thing should be for sure. Everyone should be fully motivated to take drastic measures to stop the bleeding and reverse course.

Chapter 10:   Paper Tigers

"The government's view of the economy could be summed up in a few short phrases: If it moves, tax it. If it keeps moving, regulate it. And if it stops moving, subsidize it."
- Ronald Reagan

Any effective solutions to this growing crisis need to address three key strategic and philosophical questions. <u>First</u>, should the government be directly involved in solving this problem, or should we rely solely on the open market forces of capitalism? <u>Second</u>, should less-credit-worthy people have access to similarly priced and structured capital? <u>Third</u>, why haven't efforts to date worked to help people keep their homes and open up the capital markets and the mortgage market in particular?

Question # 1:   Should the government be directly involved in solving this crisis?

Passage of the Housing Rescue Bill 3922, the government-backed bailout of Bear Stearns, the continuous cuts to the Fed rate and the $168B economic stimulus package make moot the question of whether or not the government is going to be involved in this crisis. That ship has long since sailed. However, there is still a question as to whether or not they should have been involved and if they should be involved moving forward.

Market purists are not happy about this government intervention. They expect the government to stay out of the private sector and let the forces of capitalism work their magic. They would likely conclude that Bear Stearns, for example, should be allowed to fail as a result of faulty business practices and should not be bailed out at any price or with any government guarantees. After all, the government's deal allows JPM-Chase to pick up a company with some upside but no risk. This included the acquisition of the 47-story, midtown Manhattan Bear Stearns building that is worth about a billion dollars for $236M. This looks a lot like government favoritism as they step in to prevent the collapse of one company and simultaneously ensure the increased market position of another one. On the surface, this is hard to justify.

I can certainly understand, and in fact share, the frustration of market purists who recognize the dangerous precedent set when the government bails the private sector out of one jam after another. And, of course, this precedent does not just apply to companies, but to individual borrowers as well.

I was certainly not alone in obtaining a long-term fixed-rate loan several years ago. Just like me, millions of other borrowers decided to pay higher rates in exchange for long-term stability even though adjustable rate products were all the rage. As we know, most people wanted the low start rates associated with the 2-year ARM loans, the Neg Am (negative amortization) loans and the Option ARMs. Meanwhile, millions of us took the safe and conservative route.

Yet, all of us are personally at risk. We are at risk as values continue to decline, unemployment goes up, and availability of affordable and qualifying loan products deteriorates. Yet, none of us are helped in any way by most of the brokered government-industry rate agreements and programs. What is our reward for being financially responsible? We are on our own.

Not only are we not helped, but we also have to flip the bill for these government programs that will protect, to *some extent*, millions of people who knowingly took the lower rates in place of long-term stability. Nonetheless, the government *does need* to be involved, and they will need to increase their involvement even more. The reason has nothing to do with the severity of the crisis or the alternative costs if the government were not to intervene.

The justification for their involvement is a bit more basic; it's about responsibility. They need to repair the damage caused by the triple whammy they put on the mortgage industry. **First, extraordinarily low rates were coupled with an explosion of new products, as encouraged by the chairman of the Fed. Then, the rates were raised dramatically, quickly and continuously for an extended period of time. Finally, once borrowers became unable to pay these new rates, the Regulatory Agencies and their friends in Congress removed the refinance alternatives from the market.**

Furthermore, both sides of the Democratically controlled Congress continued to chase the proverbial horse from the already burned barn by creating legislation that would impose rules on a market after it had already begun to correct itself. By the time Congress had acted, Wall Street was already paying far less money for riskier loans and that was forcing lenders to tighten lending (credit and income) standards and to price appropriately for risk.

It's fair to question what would have happened had the Congressional committees not become involved in the first place. Were there loans on the books made to people who could not afford the re-sets? Would some people have lost their homes? Would some lenders have been squeezed out of business under the pressure of repurchase demands from the investment banks? Would other lenders have collapsed under the financial pressure of having to hold excess reserves for expected losses? Would some people have lost their jobs? Would property values have deteriorated across the country? The questions could go on and on, but the answer is always the same. Yes.

But let's ask some different questions. **Would that market, which was in the process of correcting itself due to normal market forces, have led to a collapse of the lending industry? No. Would property values have plummeted at historic rates? No. Would millions upon millions of people have lost their homes or fallen into foreclosure? No. Would the government have had to get involved brokering rate freezes with the private sector? No. Would the Fed have needed to drive its rate down so far and so fast, thus creating more economic instability? No. Would we be on the brink of a recession? No. Would the government have enacted a $168B economic stimulus plan or a $300B mortgage bailout bill? Absolutely not.**

These actions by the government catapulted people into foreclosure by the millions and prevented them from having a way to get out. More than anything else, this forced down the value of housing because financing quickly became available only for fully income-documented, conforming borrowers with strong credit. Then, the Treasury turned a blind eye to the brewing situation until it was boiling over. Finally, the Treasury, which oversees two of the five Agencies involved in the IAG, along with the other governmental Regulatory Agencies, acted to finalize those rules despite clear (and accurate) warnings from the private sector, particularly that from the Consumer Mortgage Coalition and the Mortgage Bankers Association.

Even the Bear Stearns debacle falls under the umbrella of the government's triple whammy on the mortgage industry. Bear Stearns certainly chose to invest aggressively in the arena of alternative loan products, and that's not the government's fault or responsibility. Without a doubt, Bear Stearns pushed the credit and pricing envelopes in their appetite to get more alternative loan product. They were strategically and intentionally more exposed than just about every other investment bank. However, it's important to understand that their strategy was logical and conscious. The problem is that it was based on the continuation of an open market. And there's the rub.

There's a specific reason the loans that Bear Stearns purchased and securitized didn't perform as expected and why they created fatal losses for the company. They are the exact same reasons that the borrowers became unable to pay. The loans in the securities were subject to increasing interest rates driven by the previous actions of the Fed, which triggered massive defaults. Meanwhile, all loan products that were previously available for borrowers to use as an exit strategy were no longer available. The borrowers had no way to keep up with the increases and had no way out. Even though rates were subsequently reduced, the loans were already in default and the borrowers could not get current. The borrowers were trapped in their loans, and Bear Stearns (like all investment banks) was trapped with the borrowers.

In hindsight, had the government's efforts been coordinated amongst themselves and openly with the private sector, and without prejudice against the industry, the lending standards would have stabilized due to normal market forces. Existing loans would eventually have bled out of the system instead of being locked into re-set traps. Then, and only then, should the Fed have started raising rates. This simple difference in sequence of actions would have prevented the vast majority of the consequences we're living with now. Strategies, including economic ones, need to be executed in the correct order in order to work. Fire, ready, aim rarely works. It certainly didn't in this case.

If this combination of out-of-synch government actions (legislated lending practices simultaneous with rising Fed rates) were not the root cause, then why has the government since taken the actions they've taken? They have placed a retroactive stop on rate increases for existing borrowers (which is irrelevant since the Fed has lowered rates to previous levels) and rolled back rates for new borrowers. Let me say that another way.

They effectively rolled back the clock in order to get legislative actions in synch sequentially with Fed rate increases that drove so many people into foreclosure. Unfortunately, this reversal does not get these people out of foreclosure or prevent them from losing their homes. Once borrowers get behind, they typically cannot get caught up on their payments. The primary reason for this is that most servicers and lenders will not accept partial payments (anything less than the full amount) because that makes the lengthy foreclosure process (which is their only remedy) start all over again from the very beginning.

I doubt that anyone in the government is going to recognize the government's role in this disaster, let alone to stand up and admit to it. To the contrary, I suspect they firmly believe that they came to the rescue of another industry meltdown as if they had been nothing but an innocent bystander. On February 27, 2008 our leaders once again demonstrated their collective disconnect. On that day, Finance Committee Chairman Barney Frank said to Fed Chairman Bernanke:

> "I don't want to appeal to you to use the word recession because I'm not going to be responsible for the nervous people at the stock market who overreact when you twitch your nose. But the problems we now have are different."

This is literally stunning. Now he doesn't want responsibility? Let me say it a different way. Now that the consequences of his personal actions have contributed to a train wreck in housing, mortgage and the economy in general, he doesn't want responsibility. He sure wanted it when he was playing the race card in his internal "Dear Colleague" letter that caused people to line up, lest they be judged as racist, and sign on to support the development of HR3915.

Not to be outdone, in that same meeting with Congress, Bernanke responded to a question about the housing market with this gem:

> "Later this year it will stop being such a big drag directly [on the economy] ... But home prices probably will decline into next year."

He then qualified that by saying:

> "It is very difficult to know, and we've been wrong before."

So, in their own words, some aspects of the government do not want responsibility for their own actions and don't know the depth or breadth of the problem (that they created). Most importantly, they know "they've been wrong before." Now we can agree on something. I guess it's true that the first step to recovery is admitting you have a problem.

To reiterate, the problem is not that the government intervened in an open market to help solve a crisis. They, in fact, needed to get involved in order to mitigate the predicted affect on the economy. Rather, the problem is that they got involved in the first place and largely created the mess. They pre-empted the market with bad Fed rate management, monetary policy changes and industry influence through both Houses of Congress.

Having put to bed any debate over whether or not the government should be involved in the solution, and in order to develop meaningful and effective solutions, some other very important questions need to be answered.

Question # 2:   Should less-credit-worthy borrowers have access to competitively priced capital?

This sounds like a simple question. Until the non-prime market was decimated, about three million subprime borrowers per year had access to competitively priced capital. Should these people be relegated to the status of perennial renters? What about the many millions of other people who make up the rest of the non-traditional mortgage market: should they be excluded from the market, too? Asked most simply, should the mortgage market consist only of conforming loans to employed borrowers (not self-employed) with strong credit and fully documented income?

From an ethical and moral perspective, the answers to all three questions should be "no." From an economic perspective, the answers are the same. Our economy depends on these people being able to participate in homeownership.

Imagine how flat the market will stay, and for how long, if demand for housing and loans is limited only to conforming borrowers. The only way to get supply back in balance with demand so that values stabilize is by increasing demand through availability of more loan products for more people. As of right now, we've come full circle back to the consumer finance days when borrowers had access to desperately little capital and always at a high price.

We might all agree on this issue in concept; yet, we're not going that direction in practice. Two words and three letters tell the whole story; "prepayment penalty" and IAG.

Ben Bernanke and the Fed have gone after prepayment penalties as a significant cause of this crisis. As of July 2008, lenders will no longer be able to charge prepayment penalties on loans to "high-risk" (undefined) borrowers if the rate can change in the first four years. They also will not be able to charge a penalty for pay offs within the first two years of longer-term, fixed late loans. Well, that's how the Fed looks at it. I look at it another way. The way I see it, borrowers will be denied the opportunity to make the choices they believe are right for them.

Commonly, borrowers might prefer to have a prepayment penalty provision on their loan in exchange for a lower rate than they would receive without the penalty. Or, they might prefer a higher rate with no penalty. This choice would be significant because loans without prepayment penalties are much less attractive to investment banks. Remember, it is their appetite for product that drives securitization and the availability of low rates for subprime and non-traditional borrowers. As a result, investors will reduce the price for the loans they purchase from lenders. In response, lenders will need to raise their rates. There is no free lunch.

Admittedly, this is relatively academic since there is no appetite on Wall Street for non-conforming mortgages right now. It's also academic because the prepayment rules are a done deal. At this point, a new law would have to be created at the federal level to override these rules. Nonetheless, it is important to discuss because it reveals a very clear and dangerous mindset that will keep us locked into this catastrophe. This is particularly true if "high–risk" is ultimately defined as anyone who is not conforming.

As an aside, it's almost incomprehensible how and why the Fed would be using its valuable resources to shoot another arrow into the heart of a long-since dead horse. We have a crisis to solve, and they are focused on lending guidelines in the future so it doesn't happen again. Can we interpret this as a white surrender flag over the current situation? This is borderline incompetence, as there are no high-risk loans being funded and there is no interest in funding them due to the IAG.

That brings us to the three-letter part of the reason we are not actually supporting this less-credit-worthy borrower base in practice. As we've covered several times, the IAG has removed about 65% of available products from the marketplace. The people hurt most are the economically and credit challenged borrowers who need the money. We know that conforming borrowers still have a place to go.

Question #3: Why haven't existing efforts worked to help people keep their homes and re-open the mortgage and housing markets?

We cannot create meaningful solutions unless we understand why previous efforts have not, and will not, be effective. In general, these efforts haven't worked for a couple reasons. First, the government is attacking the wrong problem. Second, the solutions are so watered down with caveats and limitations that they have little to no impact. As we've talked about before, more effort is being spent on prevention of the next crisis rather than on the resolution of this one.

The key issue, that existing and prospective borrowers have frighteningly little access to capital, has not even been addressed. **The mortgage industry, and therefore the housing industry and the economy, is in a chokehold because too many people cannot borrow money.**

No one should understand this better than Fed Chairman Bernanke. He is a recognized scholar and author on the causes and consequences of the Great Depression of 1929. He has often cited lack of availability of capital (monetary policy) as a key driver behind the existence, duration and intensity of the Great Depression. In fact, he noted how reducing interest rates to zero did nothing to stimulate the economy. The problem was not the cost of money; it was the availability of it.

This is an overly simplistic review of the causes of the Great Depression but serves to indicate Bernanke's assessment of monetary policy as a key driver. The reasons for reduced access to capital are different today than they were back then, but the bottom line is the same. People do not have access to enough money. Now, here we are with the same dilemma, and paradoxically, the government is implementing macroeconomic remedies while doing nothing to increase access to capital.

On January 4, 2008, Secretary Paulson publicly announced the pervasive opinion and perception that "…there is no single or simple solution…that will solve this mortgage crisis." This is exactly why the government has implemented a good number of different measures to help solve the crisis. They certainly get an "A" for effort.

Conforming loan amounts have been raised substantially, albeit temporarily, to allow financing over $417,000. Industry coalitions have been established to facilitate cooperation between the government, lenders and borrowers. Rates have been frozen for many borrowers, including those conforming quality borrowers who took out Alt-A loans and Option ARMs. Hundreds of billions of dollars have been auctioned to the market at extraordinarily low rates to increase investor liquidity.

Additionally, the Fed has decided to extend emergency loans to investment banks rather than just to commercial banks. An economic stimulus plan, which includes temporary tax breaks and rebate checks to tax payers, has been executed. The Fed has passed new lending rules to protect future borrowers against dubious lending practices and the Housing Rescue has become law.

We need to understand why each of these measures have not, and will not, get us out of this situation. We need to recognize that they are paper tigers.

Conforming Loan Limits:

This is a greatly misunderstood issue, as most people think the loan limits were increased to $729,000 across the board. That is what should have happened, but it did not. The new amounts are limited to a principal obligation of up to 125% of the median home price in high-cost areas, not to exceed $729,750, except in Alaska, Hawaii, Guam and the U.S. Virgin Islands where higher limits may apply. What?? No offense to these outlying areas, but what about the continental coasts and everything in between?

This is a big issue so let's dig in a bit. I'll use Riverside County, California as an example. The median home price in Riverside County is about $307,000. This would yield a new maximum conforming loan amount of $384,000 (125% of $307,000). Because this amount is less than the previous maximum of $417,000, the old limit would still be available and would support the purchase of a $521,000 house at 80% LTV. However, like most counties, Riverside County is an economically diverse area with a wide range of property values that stretch far beyond the average. The county has properties in the high $100,000s all the way up into the millions. Yet, the maximum loan amount for the county is still $417,000.

In other words, the new conforming loan limits have done nothing to help solve the problem in Riverside County, California. Effectively, it keeps the market topped out at about $521,000 because non-conforming loans are no longer available. Even that would require a buyer to come in with approximately $140,000 in down payment and closing costs. Keeping this limit in place prevents home prices anywhere except for the most affluent counties from going up over $521,000. These affluent areas are not prevalent enough to lift us out of this economic downturn.

I didn't pick Riverside County because I live there. That's just a coincidence. I picked it because it is arguably one of the hardest hit markets in the country as measured by defaults, foreclosures, reduction in property values and building permits. Shouldn't new conforming loan limits do something, anything, to help lift one of the hardest hit markets in the country? But they haven't, and therefore, people are stuck in houses they can't afford to sell. So, foreclosures continue to rise.

To make the new limits even less effective, Fannie Mae / Freddie Mac set a cut off date on the new loan limits to loans *approved* in 2008. That was later revised to loans *funded* in 2008, which made matters even worse. For sure, it suggested that Fannie Mae / Freddie Mac did not intend to extend the program beyond 2008. It later became clear that this change was caused by the expected passage of Senate Bill 3922, which has a new conforming loan limit of $625,000 under certain conditions. Regardless, the temporary nature of the formula-driven increases work against the objective to help stabilize the market.

People held off buying higher-value properties because they justifiably feared that limits would go back down after the end of the year and their home values would plummet with them. People were looking at scenarios where they would get a loan for $729,750 on a purchase of $912,000 and then see the conforming loan limits drop back down to $417,000 by the end of 2008. Literally, overnight, their properties would drop by about $391,000 down to $521,000 which is the typical value required to get a $417,000 loan!

Would you take that chance? I certainly would not. The situation is even worse for builders and buyers of new construction homes. These homes are typically in escrow for about six months while the properties are being built. This is a lifetime in an era of loan limit vulnerability. What would happen to people who entered escrow, put down their deposits, paid for their upgrades and then saw their loan approval disappear if, and when, the maximum loan amount dropped back down to $417,000? Most people are not willing to take this chance and, as a result, sales of new home construction sank to the bottom of the tank.

One of the strongest provisions of the housing rescue bill is to raise the conforming loan limit to 110% of the local median home price, not to exceed $625,000. This is a big improvement over the existing limit of $417,000. But without the availability of jumbo, non-traditional and subprime loans, it is still very restrictive.

Under any circumstance, the temporary time line of the current enhancements to loan limits serves no positive purpose from the perspective of homeowners and borrowers. Let's remember, and this is critical, much of the subprime and non-traditional industries were driven by the need for jumbo products. Since the IAG has taken those away from us, shouldn't the government and the GSEs (government sponsored enterprises) shore up the market since they have the money and (literally) make the rules?

Industry Coalitions:

While working with the HopeNow Alliance before the crisis hit, we struggled to get the right people to listen or pay attention to us as we were waving the caution flag. We made some progress and got as far as coming up with a help line (phone number and support system), agreeing to allow billing statement advisories and notifying borrowers as early as six months prior to any pending re-sets. We also agreed to encourage the loan-servicing sector to use loan modifications more liberally instead of immediately placing loans and properties in foreclosure. While these may seem like simple events, they were quite significant in their logistics and results.

A few short months after the crisis hit, the HopeNow program became front-page news when the Secretary of the Treasury and the President introduced it to the public. However, the program had not gained any more substance. This was no fault of the members of the alliance (from which I had since departed as a result of my lay off from Option One). These people had done everything imaginable to create proactive solutions, to organize and provide support resources, to seek attention and support from the Federal government.

At that time, HopeNow was still a phone number and a verbal agreement amongst industry participants. Our government made a really big deal about it because it was all they had. For sure, the HopeNow Alliance provides a critical service by connecting and coordinating negotiations between distressed borrowers and foreclosing servicers. They have generated more real results than any other program created by the government. They have great influence and cooperation, but they have no authority or power to structure such resolutions. This somewhat limits their potential.

Lenders and loan servicers would like to be far more flexible and accommodating in restructuring loans, modifying terms, accepting payoffs in amounts far less than the outstanding principal (short pays) and other possible remedies. Without question, lenders lose less money if they restructure loans than if they have to foreclose. This is particularly true in a down market. However, that objective is often outweighed by concerns of potential lawsuits from any number of parties who could claim that any such actions on the part of lenders would violate the terms of the security instruments.

The issue of security instrument flexibility gets very complex and convoluted, but suffice it to say that different participants have different levels of risk, ownership, seniority and exposure. Therefore, while some participants in the security instruments might be more than willing to restructure individual loans, other participants might be unwilling, as their position is fully protected. Further, there are so many participants on any given security that it would be completely impractical and nearly impossible to get all parties to agree to changes at the security instrument level and even more so at the individual loan level.

Despite the success of the HopeNow Alliance, the Democratically controlled Congress kept pushing on lender accountability by initiating a number of bills purported to have some feature that would make it easier for any and all involved parties to sue lenders. This is nothing more than another example of doing exactly the wrong thing at the wrong time. If lenders had, in fact, taken advantage of borrowers, legal remedies were already available. Pursuing these remedies did not require new laws or new bills to go through Congress. However, just accepting the available remedies did not provide Congress with a platform to fuel their preconceptions that the mortgage crisis was caused by unscrupulous lenders that needed to be punished and stopped. So, activists in Congress looked for other means to achieve their objective. As Newt Gingrich has said:

> "It shows that if you're a Congress dominated by trial lawyers, you know what the answer to everything is. It's a lawsuit. You just don't know what the topic is."

Rate Freezes:

Freezing rates on 2/28s, Option ARMs, Alt-A and other ARM loans with discounted start rates will not work for two reasons. First, rates are lower now than when these loans funded. Second, a freeze on rates doesn't have anything to do with the terms of the loans. They will need to re-set to eliminate the discount, any negative amortization (increase in loan balance) or to re-amortize the loan over the remaining period of the loan.

To that point, former Texas Representative Dick Armey, a Republican who now runs a conservative think tank, FreedomWorks, suggested that:

> "The media fell for Bush's media spin, describing it as an 'interest rate freeze' and an 'agreement' hammered out with lenders and investors. But, infact, the Bush plan involves no mandates or legislation, just a voluntary agreement by lenders that lacks the force of law. There is no requirement that would force banks or investors to share the pain or be part of the solution. It isn't even clear if investors in mortgage-backed securities will allow the lenders to re-set the rates. They may even file suit to halt the freeze."

Even people from the other end of the political spectrum questioned the value of the program. Consumer activists and Democrats pointed out that:

"... the plan excludes most subprime borrowers, including those who are in the deepest trouble and are delinquent on their mortgage payments and facing foreclosure. Of the perhaps 2 million adjustable-rate mortgages that are expected to reset through the end of 2009, only 240,000 of them -- 12 percent--would be covered by Bush's proposal, according to Barclays Capital, as reported in The New York Times. The Center for Responsible Lending, a nonprofit group, estimates that only 145,000 households will qualify for the rate freeze. Most borrowers will be on their own to negotiate with their lenders on a case-by-case basis. Many families who persuade banks to temporarily freeze their rates still won't be able to afford to make the payments and will face foreclosure."

As long as the Fed is not planning to increase rates again, the rate freeze is an imaginary warm fuzzy.

Money Auctions:

In December 2007, the Fed started auctioning money to cash-strapped investment banks. The intent of these short-term 28-day loans was to help banks become more willing to lend to each other. Any lack of this willingness generally translates into a reduced willingness for banks to make loans to individuals and businesses for large ticket items like homes and cars. This partially explains why mortgage rates have remained relatively stable even though the Fed has dramatically cut the short-term rates.

The auction program has been very successful to the point that the Fed had sold off more than $660B over the period of seven months and is now auctioning $75B every other week. Typically, about seventy-five bidders compete for the money and about 85% of it has ended up in New York.

In a similar manner, the Fed has implemented the largest extension of lending authority since the 1930s. They have agreed to temporarily let investment firms obtain emergency loans directly from them. Until this was declared, only commercial banks had access to this money.

Both the auction and the emergency loan programs are viable and necessary to help stimulate the economy or at least to help keep it stable. However, they do nothing to help with the mortgage and housing crisis because lenders still won't lend under the ambiguity of the IAG.

Economic Stimulus Program:

This was a $168B plan designed to jump-start the economy by putting a little cash in the hands of most taxpayers. It's not going to put a dent in the mortgage and housing situation because that's not the intent. The government wants people to put more money back into the economy. That might be useful if it were a strategic stopgap until real solutions to the mortgage disaster were created. But that's not the case. So, one has to question why the government didn't just send us gift cards to use at gas stations in order to temporarily subsidize the rising cost of gasoline.

Interestingly, Congress was already teeing up another economic stimulus plan by July 2008. After meeting with several economists, House Speaker Nancy Pelosi said, " We will be proceeding with another stimulus package." But President Bush responded in a press conference that lawmakers should not pass another economic stimulus package until we "wait for the [initial] stimulus package to fully kick in." News flash: it is not going to kick in. The economy is heading south faster than $168B can take it north. Most people have used their money, not to stimulate the economy through purchases, but to pay their bills. In effect, the government has bought us $168B in gasoline and food with the taxes we gave them.

Rate Cuts:

As we all know, in a series of aggressive moves, the Fed has dramatically reduced rates. Yet, most Americans have not realized the ability to access lower priced capital. People are asking why this is the case. The simple answer is that price and product are two different things. The government has reduced the cost of borrowing money and reduced the rates that mortgage banks would ordinarily need to charge to hit their profit margin targets. But this does nothing to create a secondary market appetite for the products once the loans fund.

In theory, rates could be at 0%. However, if loan products aren't available to support a much wider swath of borrowers, then the lowest possible rates are irrelevant. It's like saying, "our loans are free; but no one can get them." Furthermore, banks need to keep charging higher rates than the lower Fed Funds rate might suggest. They need to do this in part to make up for losses being realized in other business operations. This is the same reason they need to take advantage of the emergency loans and the auction money. It is all the same thing.

Ironically and paradoxically, our Fed Chairman with his scholarly background in the causes of the Great depression is trying to solve our crisis by lowering rates when that is neither the problem nor the solution. He either knows a lot more than the rest of us do or he is confused and in way over his head.

New Rules From the Federal Reserve:

Some new lending rules were ratified on Monday, July 14, 2008. The good news is that they cleared up some of the ambiguity in the IAG. "High-risk" borrowers, whatever those will be defined as, will be required to fully document their income. They will also be required to reserve sufficient money to pay their property taxes and insurance (T&I). I suspect that the T&I can also be "impounded" into the monthly loan payment and paid out by the loan servicer. If not, this is just another way to restrict these borrowers from the market. No matter how we define them, "high-risk" borrowers typically do not have six months of T&I reserves lying around in order to get a loan.

The details of the new rules are loaded with implications. In addition to those that involve prepayment penalties, the specific objective of these rules is to prevent similar crises in the future. Unfortunately, that does nothing to solve this one. If you are personally facing foreclosure, wouldn't you like to know that the head of our central bank and the primary person at the helm of our economy is working on your problem? Once again, this is not the time to be strategic and prevent the next problem. It is the time to fix this one.

Additionally, the emphasis is obviously on subprime, meaning the Fed still does not understand the risks associated with the rest of the industry, including conforming and non-traditional loans. This is true even though the industry is replete with facts to prove other market sectors pose a greater threat.

To be candid, Fed Chairman Bernanke is taking us straight from the frying pan into the fire. And most people are not even aware that it's happening. He is as misguided on these rule changes as he was wrong when he told Congress back in February that the housing market would stop being such a drag on the economy later in the year. Then, less than six months later, the government passed the biggest housing bailout subsidy in American history.

Housing Rescue Bill 3922:

This one is too new to rate. It appears to be a giant step in the right direction. But it is a mixed bag. The bill originally passed the Senate by a vote of 76-10 with 14 Senators not voting. On Wednesday, July 23, 2008, the President retracted his opposition to the bill and announced that he would not veto it. This coincides exactly with his challenge for Congress to pass legislation that would prop up the flailing mortgage giants Fannie Mae / Freddie Mac. Within a few hours it passed the House by a vote of 272 to 152. In a rare Saturday vote in the Senate, the bill passed by 72-13 with 15 not voting. The strong showing in both Houses seemed to indicate a bipartisan awareness that something significant had to be done. I'm just not sure that this is it.

Some of the provisions of the bill, according to the extremely influential Mortgage Bankers Association (MBA) are:

FHA Modernization: Authorizes an appropriation to improve technology, processes, program performance, eliminate fraud and provide appropriate staffing. Effective January1, 2009, it also increases the FHA loan limits to 110 percent of the local median home price (not to exceed $625,000), establishes a 12-month stay on FHA's proposal for risk-based premiums, sets the down payment requirement at 3.5 percent and prohibits seller-funded down payment assistance (both direct or through a third party).

GSE Oversight Reform: Creates a new regulator (five year term, appointed by the President, confirmed by the Senate) with oversight authority similar to the other bank regulators, establishes a new affordable housing fund and capital magnet fund to be funded by a 4.2 basis point fee on all new loans and raises the conforming loan limit to the local median home price, not to exceed $625,500 (effective January 1, 2009).

FHA Rescue: Creates a voluntary program for lenders to write down the loan balance in exchange for an FHA guaranteed loan not to exceed 90 percent of the newly appraised value of home. The lender would pay a 3 percent FHA loan origination fee. To qualify, the borrower must have a debt-to-income ratio above 31% percent on the original loan. Program capped at $300 billion.

Tax Incentives: Creates an $8,000 tax refund for first-time home buyers, expands the volume cap for the low income housing tax credit, allows for tax-exempt treatment of bonds guaranteed by the Federal Home Loan Banks. Also provides for the use of low-income housing tax credits against the Alternative Minimum Tax, which should expand the investor base for this key generator of affordable rental housing production.

TILA Reform: Requires TILA disclosures to be delivered seven days prior to loan origination, requires that disclosures include examples of how payments would change based on rate adjustments in addition to disclosing the maximum possible payment under the loan terms and mandates that the consumer receive the disclosures before paying anything more than a nominal fee that covers the cost of a credit report.

Empowering States: Raises the caps on tax-free bonds that state housing finance agencies may use to help at-risk homeowners by $11 billion and appropriates $4 billion for states to purchase and renovate abandoned and foreclosed properties.

Licensing: Encourages state officials to create a national licensing system for residential loan originators, allows HUD to create their own national licensing system if the states fail, establishes minimum qualifications for all loan originators and requires federal regulators to create a registry for banks and thrift employees who originate loans.

These provisions are written with the primary intent to help distressed borrowers, to stabilize the market and to improve lending systems into the future. These are all good objectives. While there is fierce objection from those who oppose the bill, the fact that it is strongly supported by the MBA speaks to its merit. Many of the provisions in this new bill obviously reflect progress around the issues that prevented the MBA from supporting House Bill 3915, as described earlier.

My objective at this time is not to conduct a point, counter-point on the new law, but to address shortfalls in key areas. The first has to do with the new loan limits. On its face, the loan limit is significantly higher. However, the condition that it is based on the median home price in the local area cuts it off at the knees. This takes us right back to the example used in Riverside County, California. This loan amount will be insufficient to serve truly affluent counties. Meanwhile, economically diverse counties will not have the median home price necessary to get the higher loan limit. This appears to be another example of finding some way to get back to the same place we started.

The second area of concern is the $300B bailout subsidy, which was written with the intent to help about 400,000 distressed homeowners. To put that in perspective, the HopeNow Alliance has already helped coordinate the resolution of loans for more than one million distressed homeowners! The Senate has since acknowledged that the $300B amount may be insufficient, as there are more foreclosures than expected. How can this continue to be a surprise? The numbers can be calculated. It's straightforward: there will be millions of foreclosures unless we come up with real solutions.

In addition to the nearly one million properties that have already been foreclosed upon since the crisis started, the following chart shows a clear upward trend in foreclosure filings for eight consecutive quarters (and counting). And then, we still have the next 13 million loans yet to experience their first rate re-set!

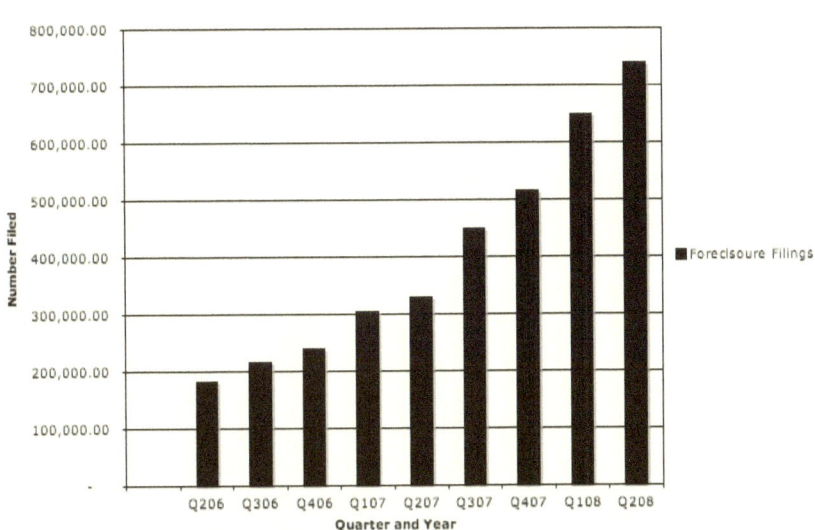

Even if the amount were sufficient, there is another reason this provision will not get us out of this situation. In order for the distressed borrowers to obtain conforming quality loans, the existing lender needs to write down the balance to 90% of the current market value. It is likely that the vast majority of these loans funded at the peak of the market when LTVs generally pushed 100%. Assuming property values have dropped 30% over the past two years, this means that lenders would have to write off 40% of the loan balance in order to participate in the program. They are highly unlikely to take that kind of hit.

To further complicate the situation, remember that most loans are not owned by lenders but by the trusts that invest in the securities. This means that the loans have been split into a large number of individual pieces with no one having full control over the whole loan. As explained earlier, different investors have different risk positions and different payment guarantees. They all have a different appetite for write-downs of principle balance. The only way to get the loans free from those shackles would be to have them paid off or to be foreclosed upon. Either way, at that point, the bailout would no longer be needed and the program would be moot.

Despite all this government involvement, the problem continues to get worse. Case in point, the government home price index just dropped by the largest amount in the seventeen-year history of the index from the fourth quarter of 2007 to the first quarter of 2008. Meanwhile, subprime delinquencies continued to increase! Specifically, subprime delinquencies went up 2%, 4% and 6% over the course of only one month from March of 2008 to April 2008 for loans originated in 2005, 2006 and 2007 respectively. This is a clear indication that these borrowers are completely trapped in their loans. Meanwhile, the stock market dropped into bear territory, falling below 11,000 for the first time in many years. The mortgage industry has continued to implode in on itself.

Best intentions aside, these government efforts and policies have not worked. That is simply because none of them address the core issue, which is availability of capital for consumers. The legislated guidance (IAG) prevents people from having access to money because neither borrowers nor lenders can meet the vague standards established for any and all non-traditional loans. This is THE issue that needs to be attacked.

What this really means is that we need to get away from well-intentioned solutions that target the wrong things and have too many workarounds. As a simplistic analogy, imagine being stranded on the side of the road in a vehicle that has run out of gas. Then someone comes along and replenishes the motor oil, the transmission fluid and puts more air in the tires. While all of these are necessary in order for a vehicle to run efficiently and safely, none of them will get the car back on the road.

Any real solutions to this crisis need to address two different objectives. **First, they need to stop the rising tide of foreclosures and allow most people to stay in their homes. Second, they need to reverse the declining value of homes so that equity stops pouring from them.** This way, people will have some equity to protect and some to access for discretionary spending. This is not to say, however, that we have two different problems. It's really one and the same, but with two required objectives.

There is only one way to achieve both of these objectives. We need to increase access to mortgages that support a much wider swath of potential borrowers.

Chapter 11:   Leave Us A Loan

"When the American people are aroused, they can, in fact, coerce the Congress."
  - Newt Gingrich

No reasonable solution is going to immediately re-open the markets. Even if they were to magically re-open, Wall Street will be busy licking their wounds for some time and would not likely have any significant appetite for non-traditional and subprime mortgages. At the same time, their wounds are being caused largely by the inability to rid themselves of non-paying borrowers. Keep in mind that these are borrowers who could, and probably would, be paying if they were in loans that were less than the value of their homes and had similar payments to what they were before their loans re-set.

While it may seem counter-intuitive when the market is so bad, what we need to do is *open* the markets. That is the master key to all doors - including housing, foreclosures, the economy, inflation and unemployment. But how do we do that, considering the fact that that is a far cry from all current efforts to further regulate and restrict the market? We need to tackle this on three related fronts involving **borrowers, lenders and government.**

Before we get into this, let me be clear that these are my ideas *alone.* To be sure, I have been part of several alliances, organizations and companies throughout my career. But I did not consult with any of them in regards to these suggestions. None of these should be interpreted as reflecting anyone's position other than my own. Further, no one has a corner on the idea market; and that includes Congress, the Fed and the Treasury. While I feel strongly about mine, I recognize that there are some other very good ideas being bantered about within the confines of one's own mind, in the hallways at work and at the kitchen table. I would like to hear about them.

Here, I am going to offer my most significant suggestions. They can also be found on my website at www.homecrisissolved.com. There you will also find a place to offer your own suggestions and ideas. I encourage you to submit them.

Borrowers:

Some borrowers have the ability to pay but choose not to because they owe more than their home or investment property is worth. I suspect that this applies to a comparatively small group of people; nonetheless, if this applies to you, I strongly encourage you to make your payments. This will reduce foreclosures and the new inventory of unsold homes. This will help stabilize the market, which will lead to stronger investor appetite for new origination.

In turn, this will help lift the entire market and get you back in an equity neutral or positive position. I know the temptation is strong to live without expense in these properties for a few months and then let them go in foreclosure. At a personal level, it would be very easy to rationalize that decision by riding the coattails of the market's crisis. However, I would suggest that we all have the responsibility to meet our obligations to the best of our ability, regardless how convenient it may be not to. All Americans are counting on us to pay the best that we can.

Within this small population may be a disproportionate number of investment properties. Our tenants depend on us to make the mortgage payments, regardless of how our investments are structured. If the tenants are making their rent payments, they would expect that the mortgage on the property is also being paid on time. If tenants get evicted because we willingly get foreclosed on, they are in a world of hurt. We should not let that happen to them.

On a closely related matter, some owners of non-owner occupied rental properties have become unable to pay their mortgage on time. This is about ability, not willingness. In this case, borrowers may want to evaluate whether they are charging current market rates. Rents have risen across the country as a result of the housing crash. If you are not charging current market rents, you may want to talk with your tenants and possibly revise the rental agreement. Think about it from their perspective. If you were they, would you rather stay in your home and pay current market rents or would you rather get evicted and then pay current market rents elsewhere?

If the tenants have even more capacity, you might want to sell them a share of ownership in the property in exchange for their increased financial responsibility. Maybe they have the capacity to make the entire payment. In this case you might be able to have them assume the loan and take ownership of the property outright. Most non-traditional and subprime loans are not assumable according to the note and deed. However, I guarantee that lenders will be very flexible on this one. Challenge yourself to be creative, open-minded and solution-oriented. But don't just walk away if you can at all avoid it.

Most of all, if you are in trouble with your mortgage, **CALL YOUR LOAN SERVICER**. It's amazing how many people don't even make that call. You should know by now that **YOUR LENDER DOES NOT WANT TO FORECLOSE ON YOUR HOME!** As selfish as it sounds, foreclosing on your home costs them too much money. They are eager to cooperate. At the same time, they are not going to just forget about you if you refuse contact. You might want to be invisible, but you are not. <u>Don't force their hand by breaking contact with them!</u>

When you do make contact with them, approach them like a partner. They want a viable solution about as much as you do. Don't attack them as if they caused your problem. The company that services your loan is very *unlikely* to be the same company that funded your loan. They are just servicing it. Even if they are one and the same, treat them like a partner. The information you have read in this book should provide you with a perspective that allows you to work with your servicer and not against them.

Lender/Servicers:

The market is flooded with talented AEs and loan officers who have become unemployed. This may provide a great opportunity for loan servicing companies. No offense meant to anyone, but most experienced loan servicers are not well honed in the art of loan workouts. Over the years, they have become better suited to call for money, do basic equity analysis and initiate the foreclosure process if borrowers didn't pay. Now, loan servicers need people with a different skill set. This does not contradict the advice offered above. I'm not saying that servicers want to foreclose. I am just saying that they tend to be more experienced and adept at that process than they are with loan workouts.

If I were running a loan servicing company, I would hire any number of the tens of thousands of wholesale AEs and retail loan officers who have lost their jobs in this crash. Many of them know how to structure deals of any kind. They are problem solvers. And they know how to work directly with customers without resorting to the hammer. Because sales people are motivated by income, I would pay them a healthy commission based on how much money they save the lender by avoiding foreclosure.

Portfolio lenders have quite a bit more flexibility than lenders who securitized their mortgages. As we know, mortgages in securities have been sliced and diced into pieces, and control is scattered across a wide array of investor participants. Portfolio lenders, on the other hand, own their loans.

Rather than foreclosing and selling the properties at a substantial loss, consider more creative solutions. For example, write the balance down to an amount the borrower can afford at their current rate structure. Carry the difference as a non-interest bearing second trust deed that gets paid back in five years (for example) or when the property sells, whichever is sooner. This might require the lender to write off the difference and take it as a loss on their balance sheet. However, the lender would not need to foreclose, and they would be able to post the money back as direct profits when the house sells in the future.

Another option may be to enter into a shared-equity agreement under similar terms. This creates a true partnership between the borrowers and the lender, which is a very good thing. The variables are numerous and the details of these ideas are beyond the scope of this book. However, if you are interested, you may want to connect with this author's consulting company at **www.homecrisissolved.com.**

The Government:

I have a 30-year fixed-rate loan at 5.25%. Nothing that I am going to suggest will help me personally.

I encourage our leaders to fully consider the information in this book and be open to different strategies. The ones our government is using are not working and will not work to the extent we need them to. Further, they will permanently deprive a large cross section of the population from enjoying the benefits of home ownership. I know that their intentions are good and that the legislature really wants to help people and protect them. But, people do not need to be protected from themselves. They just need to have access to the same knowledge that the rest of the industry has. The following bundle of proposed solutions is intended to provide people with that information and to restore their right to make their own decisions. These solutions will work within the context of fewer government regulations, less-stringent rules and more power in the hands of the people.

I know that will require a fundamental shift in ideology and will run counter to much of the legislative momentum going the other direction. This may require leaders to go against their instincts, and that will not happen without some serious prodding from the American people. *I encourage people to prod, prod and prod some more.*

Readers, our legislature is locked away from the people it represents. They are behind closed doors working towards various solutions that fit their assessment of this crisis. But they are not the ones trapped in their loans until their homes are foreclosed upon. We need to make ourselves heard.

To that point I want to tell people: do not fall into the trap of thinking that one single call, email or letter doesn't make a difference. It will! Representatives understand that most people will not call or write, so they always give great weight to one *single* contact. They typically assume that each contact represents about a thousand people. So ten phone calls is ten thousand people and a hundred phone calls is a hundred thousand people. You get the picture.

We need to speak up. Just call, write or email your Representative. The process could not be any easier. My website contains a link to a listing of all Representatives, with an interactive screen so that you can easily find your

Representative. All you have to do is use it! Think how hard you work to own your home. Is it not worth the time to make contact with your Representative? I certainly hope it is.

Tell them we need **Open Market Legislation** that includes several key components or provisions:

1.   UNWIND THE INTERAGENCY GUIDANCE (IAG). The ideas are well-intended, but the execution and ambiguity are an unmitigated disaster. This suggestion will not be considered lightly. Remember that the Regulatory Agencies and other government departments worked for over two years to get it where it is. But that is not a good reason to keep it. The only thing it achieved was the evaporation of virtually **all non-conforming loan products (about 65% of the market). We need these products back if we are going to get out of this mess.**

Many investment banks on Wall Street are too injured to just fling open the doors and tell lenders to bring in all their business. But *some* investment banks may have *some* refrained appetite that may help millions of homeowners get out of their traps. For these investment banks, this may be an opportunity to "buy low" when the market is soft. Under these conditions, these banks can be very critical about what they will and will not buy. They do not need to chase the market; they can *make* the market.

2.   Replace the IAG with (EXTREMELY) PLAIN LANGUAGE DISCLOSURES. This may seem redundant, as plain language disclosures are included in the IAG and in the new Housing Rescue law, SB3221. However, those are not clear enough. These disclosures need to be crystal clear. They need to show the different loan options that the lender approves and not just the one the borrowers receive. They need to show the lowest rate the borrower could have obtained and how much money the broker received in exchange for the higher rate. For example, it might say 8% at 2 points (YSP) to the broker, 7.50% at 1 YSP and 7% at 1 YSP (or "par") so on.

They need to show the value of the property and the Loan amount as a percentage of that value (LTV). They need to know their rate with, and without, a prepayment penalty. They need to include a simple, but comprehensive, chart of payment and rate re-sets. The list could, and should, go on. But the most important thing at stake is ideology. The government has taken away our ability to make what we believe to be are the right decisions for ourselves. We need to have that right returned to us. We have to believe that people, with the necessary information, are capable of making the right decisions.

3.   Unwind the recent Federal Reserve rule changes. The restrictions on stated loans, prepayment penalties, and the requirements for tax and insurance reserves on "high–risk" loans are not warranted. First, "high-risk" is not defined. Second, the vast majority of loans have paid as agreed, while only a relatively small percentage of loans with these characteristics have been a problem. Yet, the Fed has decided to throw them all away. Currently, these new rules are irrelevant because stated income doc loans, with or without tax reserves or prepayment penalties, are not being made. Nonetheless, these rule changes take us further in the direction of the IAG and prevent the expansion of the mortgage and housing markets.

4.   **Create national lending standards that preempt legislation at state and local levels.** There is a logical reason for this objective. Court trials normally cite precedence from other similar cases. In this manner, laws in one state get used in cases against lenders in other states. As mentioned earlier, several states have already used the IAG as a framework to adopt their own legislation. This needs to be reversed so that lenders can operate more freely and provide borrowers, across the country, with choices.

5.   **Revise the definition of "local median home price" for conforming loan limits.** The median home price is unlikely to accurately reflect the diverse needs of large counties. Property values are typically determined within neighborhoods, not counties. If you are buying a home, do you care what the median price of homes is in that county? Or, conversely, do you want to know that you are paying a competitive price in that neighborhood? Our regulators often get too hung up in negotiation and compromise that we end up with something that looks better but is not as good as it could be. The new loan limit restrictions are a perfect example of that dynamic.

6.   **Amend the design of the $300B bailout.** The new law requires participating lenders to write down the current loan balance to 90% of the current market value. That means they have to write off all foreclosure costs, including accrued interest, as well as much of the principle balance. I am skeptical that many lender servicers will participate under this structure.

Immediately following the passage of the bill by Congress, Chairman Barney Frank encouraged lenders to hold off foreclosing so that borrowers would have a chance to take advantage of the new program. If the program would work for lenders, they would already be motivated to wait, because they do not want to foreclose. They do not need more encouragement. On the other hand, if they continue to foreclose, it's because they determined that the program would not work for them.

Instead of requiring lenders to write down the balances on existing loans and then making new loans for the difference, allow the money to be used more efficiently. Use it to bring existing loans current and then let the borrowers qualify for loans available in an open market. No legislators would agree to this right now because they know the market is not open. Additionally, bringing these loans current would violate the terms of most security agreements. However, I'm confident that this is one area where total flexibility would be allowed and the payments would be accepted.

Admittedly, this would have limited initial impact because property values are low and people have minimal equity. Therefore, as another alternative, the money could be used to fund non-interest-bearing 2nd liens so that borrowers can get out of their existing loans. This could quadruple the number of people who can get helped with this money. The loans would be paid back when the properties are eventually sold. In effect, the government becomes a lender. Then they don't need to encourage lenders not to foreclose; instead, they *choose* not to foreclose.

7.   **Create a mortgage oversight** group made up of legislators, regulators, mortgage industry professionals and capital market leadership. Each group should have equal representation, equal authority and the meetings should be held on neutral grounds. This group should oversee the development and implementation of these suggested provisions. They should also develop meaningful and reasonable industry limitations, including:

> All (regulated and unregulated) lenders operate under the same rules and requirements.

> Statistical audits are conducted on every file. These rank the statistical probability that the files involve fraud on the part of the borrower, the property value (appraisal) and the broker (if there were one).

> Use government-approved appraisers (F/F) and provide periodic reports on their performance. Conduct field or desk reviews on every file.

> Sales people have NO loan authority.

> Operation personnel make no incentives for origination volume.

> Originate loans according to lending guidelines; we should not honor or allow loan exceptions to be made (over a third of non-prime loans are considered to be "exceptions".) This way, productivity can be tracked and measured specifically and adjustments can be made.

> Retail loan officers, loan brokers and broker-owned escrows should not be allowed to sign loan documents with borrowers. Third party signing services must be used

> Lenders should be limited to a maximum of 5% market share. Anything over that amount triggers irrational lending

behavior. This may seem like government interference in the open market. However, it's less restrictive than the effective limit we have today which is 0%.

In addition to the creation of Open Market Legislation, we need to vote for people who will help get us out, not bail us out, of this crisis. All Congressional Representatives come up for re-election every two years. They are *constantly* running for re-election, hence the tendency for them to overreact to apparently consumer-friendly issues like mortgage production and delinquencies. Fortunately for us, this two-year cycle can work against them, too. The last thing we need are opportunistic leaders creating overly enthusiastic and overly reactive legislation just so they can get re-elected.

Senators come up for re-election every six years, which means that every two years, a third of them are on the ballot. And, of course, every four years, we elect (or re-elect) a President. Take the time to find out where the candidates stand on these critical issues. Do they understand the problems? Are they willing to learn about them? Do they have preconceived notions that block their ability to create real solutions? In short, do your homework and vote for the candidates that you determine will best help us out of this crisis. By that, I do not mean the candidates most likely to approve more government subsidies, but, rather for real change in the mortgage industry and who will re-open the markets.

We need to vote for candidates who agree that most people:

- Want financial options and are able to make their own choices about them.
- Believe in less regulation and smaller (relatively speaking) government.
- Believe the markets should be open to all Americans, not just the ones who can verify every drop of their income, have great credit, almost no other debt and lots of money in the bank.
- Want demand for real estate, and the values that rise with it, driven by a dramatically larger pool of potential buyers and borrowers.

Most importantly, we need to vote out the politicians who created this disaster by opportunistically converting their prejudices about predatory, abusive and racially discriminatory lending practices into over-reactive legislation. I'm not trying to change your political party affiliation nor change your personal values. I *am* trying to get the overzealous Democratic Finance Committee Chairs out of their positions. Remember, whether you are a Democrat, Republican, Independent, Socialist, Libertarian, you may very well be voting with your house and your job. That's not a fear tactic; it's the truth.

We need to appoint new Finance Chairpersons in both Houses of Congress. It should not matter what party they come from. What matters is that we get people who truly understand lending, and borrowing, as the key drivers of our economy. Chairmen Frank and Dodd do not understand these things. Urge your legislators and Senators to vote against these incumbents. We need to get these people out of positions of extreme power.

Keep in mind that all the legislation as described throughout this book has been enacted since the Democrats took power in 2006. Their leaders' hearts may be in the right place, but intellectually and logically, they missed the mark. **Further, it is critical to understand that non-performing loans did not trigger the legislation. To the exact contrary, the legislation removed products from the market, which forced the ones already on the books to stop performing. This is exactly why foreclosures continue to rise even though rates are low again.**

Two other people need to go. While neither Fed Chair Bernanke nor Treasury Secretary Paulson created this problem, their inability to see it (including the real causes and the scope) is inexcusable. They made the problem infinitely worse by creating policies and making decisions that fueled the crisis.

Bernanke does not comes up for re-appointment until January 2010. That's a long way out but maybe Congressional pressure could get him to step down and out "voluntarily."

Paulson will probably be replaced when Bush leaves office. Our new President will likely nominate a new Secretary of The Treasury. We need to urge legislators to ratify that nominee only if he or she demonstrates command for this critical subject.

Real solutions are not easy solutions. But, at the risk of sounding like I'm on a soapbox, **we (you and I) really *can* make a difference.** Get this message out there to your friends, call your loan servicer, and call your Congressional Representative. Take action!

When I started writing this book, the mortgage and housing picture was clear, but wrong. As far as anyone knew, unscrupulous, subprime lenders had taken millions of victims for a ride. While the rest of us have come to understand that things can be clear and wrong at the same time, some key political leaders are still living in those dark ages and pointing the finger only at lenders.

There were certainly some bad lenders, but they were the exception. Yet, we have been led to believe that the entire industry was greedy, unscrupulous, irresponsible and corrupt. I certainly hope by now that your perspective has changed on this one. And let's give people credit. The subprime industry had been running almost continuously for seventeen years. While volume grew and fluctuated, it hovered around $500 billion per year for the last several years. Now ask yourself a question. Are there that many suckers out there? Or, was the industry serving a legitimate market need and along the way took down some innocent people due to the behavior of a few unscrupulous individual people and even fewer unscrupulous companies?

The more evolved political leaders have recently shown a willingness to explore responsibility on the part of the Fed and, in particular, with Alan Greenspan, who is canvassing the world trying to protect his formerly unquestionable legacy. Some of them are looking at investors, investment banks, bond insurers, loan servicers and everyone else in the zoo. But none of them seem willing to look in the mirror. Yet, the legislature, while acknowledging the need to be balanced and keep access to capital open, has gone the exact opposite direction and is continuing to drive us down deeper and deeper. We have to turn this around. We do not need, or want, a market the way we had it. For all the reasons discussed in this book, the market had become irrational from the origination end and to the investor (secondary) end, and all points in between.

Legislators and regulators are turning the screws because they fear that, if they don't, the market will end up where it was before the crash – irrational and overly-aggressive. But, this will not happen. In general, investors worldwide have significant fear of credit risk. Many of them are cash-strapped themselves. Bond insurers are not as strong as they once were. Borrowers have insufficient equity to get more cash out. The more notorious lenders are out of business and facing class action lawsuits and or FBI indictments. In other words, normal market forces will work to limit the market itself.

So, I am not talking about being reckless and irresponsible. Rather, think about all this within the context of a *market* (not just lenders or investors, etc.) that regulates itself through the incentives created by desire for profit *and avoidance of losses.*

If we want to get supply and demand back in balance so that home prices appreciate (or at least stop dropping), we need to open the markets back up. If we want to open the spigot to the economy, we need to re-open the housing market. If we want people to have options to get out of bad loans, we need to open the mortgage market back up. No matter what we do, the mortgage market is not going to be as free-wheeling and aggressive as it was before this crash. Investors will be licking their risk-avoidant wounds for years to come. But, money can be made available to millions of people who need it now so they can escape from their own HOUSE*trap*!

Afterward

A Final Thought

I once heard that the value of a pencil is not what you can buy or sell it for, but what you can create with it.

About a year before the crisis hit, a good friend of mine asked me what I saw happening in the mortgage industry and, specifically, what I thought he should do with an investment property he owned. While friends and money mix like oil and water, I had to tell him the truth. I cautiously but confidently advised him to sell his house as soon as he could. He did. Then the market crashed.

I knew the market was going to fall at the hands of the IAG, the new leaders in Congress and the double-whammy of increased rates and eliminated products that locked people into their loans. It was obvious that investors would be caught holding these delinquent loans and would need to push the burden downstream. Thus would begin the repurchase demands that would put lenders out of business, the fudged financials that hid the truth at major investment banks, the responsibility of the bond insurers to pony up on their policies and the pressure on the rating agencies, who rated the bonds.

I even knew my own company would not survive and that I would lose my job. That was no great stretch, as no subprime or non-prime lenders were expected to survive. Yet, despite all this knowledge, confidence and the advice I gave to my friend, I took a different path regarding my own home. Critical readers may wonder why I would have made this decision and might conclude that I kept my home because I didn't really see the problem coming. In turn, this might cast a doubt on how right I am about the problem moving forward.

The fact is that I kept my home because it was never intended to be an equity machine, something to supplement my annual income or an asset that tilted my balance sheet in one direction or another. It is a place to live and to help raise my family. My home was not worth more to me when the market said it would sell for more than a million. It is not worth less to me today even though the market would now pay only half of that amount. My house is just like the pencil. Its value is in its use. I didn't keep my house because I was wrong about the market. I kept it because its value is determined by me and not by what the market says it's worth.

I'm not preaching to you or offering financial advice. Maybe I did not make the best financial decision. I could have cashed out in a big way at the top of the market and moved into a van down by the river. But that is not what I wanted. That's why I didn't sell, and it is why I am telling you with 100% confidence, that unless we call to action, this situation will get much, much worse. Congress did not understand this when they took their most recent break. While they were away on vacation along with their 9% approval rating, more than 70,000 new foreclosure notices were filed across this great country. That's just wrong.

You can do a lot of things with this book right now. You can recommend it to friends and family. You can share your thoughts with others. You can become engaged in passionate debate on the subject. But most importantly, with the information and knowledge you have obtained, you can take action and help solve this crisis.

I sincerely hope that you do.

For more information updated regularly, and for copies of referenced documents, I invite you to visit our website at www. homecrisissolved.com

Dan R. Lee
Mortgage Crisis Solutions Group, LLC

1-800-807-4890

Addendum

RESOURCES:
Author's website: www.homecrisissolved.com;
visit for all referenced links, attachments, documents, letters and solutions.
HopeNow Alliance: 1-888-995-HOPE (4673); www.hopenow.com

CREDITS
Forward:
1.   Fed Chairman, Ben Bernanke, Testimony Before the Joint Economic Committee, U.S. Congress, March 28, 2007.

Chapter One:
1.   American Dialect Society, Annual Selection – Word of the Year, January 4, 2008.

2.   Warren Buffet, Speech at Annual, Berkshire Hathaway, Shareholder Meeting, May 4, 2008.

3.   Fed Chairman, Ben Bernanke, Testimony Before the Joint Economic Committee, U.S. Congress, March 28, 2007.

4.   Fed Chairman, Ben Bernanke, Dinner Speech at Columbia Business School, May 5, 2008.

5.   Fed Chairman, Ben Bernanke, Speech at Fed Conference, May 26, 2008.

6.   Michael Lewis, Liar's Poker, 1989.

7.   Michael Lewis, Liar's Poker, 1989.

8.   Michael Lewis, Liar's Poker, 1989.

Chapter Two:

No Sources Used.

Chapter Three:

No Sources Used.

Chapter Four:

1. Former Fed Chairman, Alan Greenspan, Speech to Credit Union National Conference, February 23, 2004.

2. Former Fed Chairman, Alan Greenspan, Speech to Credit Union National Conference, February 23, 2004.

3. Former Fed Chairman, Alan Greenspan, Article, Wall Street Journal-Asia, December 13, 2007.

Chapter Five:

1. Interagency Regulators, Interagency Guidance on Non-Traditional Mortgage Product Risks, October 4, 2006.

2. Interagency Regulators, Interagency Guidance on Non-Traditional Mortgage Product Risks, October 4, 2006.

3. Interagency Regulators, Interagency Guidance on Non-Traditional Mortgage Product Risks, October 4, 2006.

4. Interagency Regulators, Interagency Guidance on Non-Traditional Mortgage Product Risks, October 4, 2006.

5. Senators Dodd, Schumer, Sarbanes, Allard, Bunning and Reed, Letter to the Regulatory Agencies, December 7, 2006.

Chapter 6:

1. Senator Dodd, Opening Statement at Hearing on Predatory Lending, February 7, 2007.

2. Fed Chairman, Ben Bernanke, Testimony Before the Joint Economic Committee, U.S. Congress, March 28, 2007.

3.   Representative Barney Frank, Chairman of The House Financial Services Committee, Letter to his Colleagues, March 29, 2007.

4.   Interagency Regulators, Interagency Guidance - NTM, March 2, 2007.

5.   Kurt Pfotenhauer, Senior Vice President of Government Affairs and Public Policy for the Mortgage Bankers Association (MBA), Testimony Before the House Financial Service Committee, October 24, 2007.

6.   Senator Dodd, Senator Dodd's website, September 2007.

Chapter 7:

1.   Julie Hirschfeld Davis, Article in USA Today, June 17, 2008.

2.   Major Garrett, Article in Fox News, July 2, 2008.

3.   Karen Freifeld and David Scheer, Bloomberg, January 12, 2008.

4.   Unknown Journalist, CNN, January 29, 2008

5.   Unknown Journalist, Reuters, April 1, 2008.

6.   MBIA, Press Release, June 5, 2008.

Chapter 8:

1.   Charles Hugh Smith, data gathered from three sources as documented on his website at www.oftwominds.com, 2007. ©

2.   Inside Mortgage Finance, loan production data for 2001-2008 ©, Q1 2008.

3.   Credit Suisse, Re-Set Waves, 2007. ©

Chapter 9:

1. Treasury Secretary Henry Paulson, Interview with Jim Lehrer, May 17, 2007.

2. Former Fed Chairman, Alan Greenspan, Interview with Die Zeit, January 30, 2008.

3. Jan Hatziug, Goldman-Sachs Chief U.S. Economist, Internal Report, November 15, 2007.

4. Fed Chairman, Ben Bernanke, Testimony Before U.S. Congress, July 19, 2007.

5. Former Fed Chairman, Alan Greenspan, Speech to American Economic Society entitled "Risk and Uncertainty in Monetary Policy", January 3, 2004.

6. Colin Barr and Roddy Boyd, CNN Money – Fortune, February 13, 2008.

7. Hillary Rodham Clinton, Post-Primary speech, February 5, 2008.

8. Senator Hillary Rodham Clinton, Fox News, March 24, 2008.

9. Senator Barack Obama, Fox News, March 24, 2008.

10. Senator Barack Obama, Speech at General Motors Plant in Janesville, WI, February 13, 2008.

11. Senator John McCain, Speech to Nation, March 27, 2008.

Chapter 10:

1. Representative Barney Frank, Chairman of The House Financial Services Committee, Congressional Meeting with Fed Chairman Ben Bernanke, February 27, 2008.

2. Treasury Secretary Henry Paulson, Speech in New York, January 4, 2008.

3.   Former Speaker of the House Newt Gingrich, Speech on Oil Drilling and Energy Solutions, June 10, 2008.

4.   Speaker of the House Nancy Pelosi, The Hill, April 4, 2008.

5.   President George W. Bush, Meeting with Small Business Owners, April 8, 2008.

6.   Kieran Quinn, Press Release from the Mortgage Bankers Association, July 11, 2008.

Chapter 11:

1.   RealtyTrac, U.S. Foreclosure Report, July 25, 2008.

2.   Credit Suisse, Re-Set Waves, 2007. ©